Into the Silk . . .

The slipstream buffeting his face seemed to revive him and in the last seconds as he crouched half in half out of the cockpit his thoughts were clear and ordered. There was no fear, just cold objective reasoning that told him presently he must jump and that from that height it meant the end. The crippled bomber was beginning to behave sluggishly as it approached stalling point. He looked back and saw the others climbing out. As he did so the starboard wing began to drop so he stepped quickly out on to the wing root, seized his ripcord handle and pulled it as he dived off, praying the chute wouldn't foul the tail plane.

As he fell, Crews saw Evans dropping ahead of him and then a dark wall of green curved up to meet him. Instinctively he shut his eyes; about two seconds later he hit the trees. There was no noise – all he felt was a burning on his face as the pine needles scraped the skin, then a tremendous jolt, then silence. He opened his eyes.

Six feet from the ground he was hanging on his rigging lines held from the top branches of a pine tree by the half-opened canopy. Two yards away in the next tree was Evans, suspended in precisely the same way. For a moment they stared at each other, two shocked, bruised, dangling figures, neither yet grasping the full miracle of their deliverance. Evans was the first to find words. 'Christ,' he said awesomely, 'that will teach me to go flying without my lucky white elephant' . . .

Ian Mackersey

Into the Silk

Foreword by
Sir Douglas Bader, CBE, DSO, DFC

MAYFLOWER
GRANADA PUBLISHING
London Toronto Sydney New York

Revised edition published by
Granada Publishing Limited
in Mayflower Books 1978

ISBN 0 583 12793 2

First published in Great Britain by
Robert Hale Ltd 1956
Copyright © Ian Mackersey 1956, 1978
Foreword copyright © Mayflower Books Ltd 1978

Granada Publishing Limited
Frogmore, St Albans, Herts AL2 2NF
and
3 Upper James Street, London W1R 4BP
1221 Avenue of the Americas, New York, NY 10020, USA
117 York Street, Sydney, NSW 2000, Australia
100 Skyway Avenue, Toronto, Ontario, Canada M9W 3A6
Trio City, Coventry Street, Johannesburg 2001, South Africa
CMI Centre, Queen & Wyndham, Auckland 1, New Zealand

Made and printed in Great Britain by
Hazell Watson & Viney Ltd
Aylesbury, Bucks
Set in VIP Times Roman on the Pentamatic System

FOREWORD

I am delighted to write the foreword to this new edition of *Into the Silk* by Ian Mackersey. It is a fascinating book, especially to those of us who owe our lives to the parachute invented by the late Leslie Irvin.

It includes accounts of numerous and various bale-outs. It is always of interest to read of another's experience because no incident is ever quite the same.

I recall meeting a man not long after the end of World War II who had been blown out of a Lancaster bomber at about 12,000 feet. He came to in a snow-covered wood in Belgium. There was no parachute on him, nor was one found in the vicinity. He was, however, wearing his parachute harness. In these bombers some of the crew used to hang their parachutes in the aeroplane to make it easier to operate gun turrets, bomb sights and so on. They would wear only the parachute harness on their bodies. In an emergency, they would clip the chutes on before abandoning the aircraft. The man in question obviously did not do so. I have often wondered whether he applied for membership of the Caterpillar Club. Perhaps he became a half-member by virtue of using the harness but not the parachute!

In this new edition of the book, Ian Macersey has added new material to explain the sophisticated technical equipment used to save air crew from modern high-speed aircraft. In the far-off happy days, when something went wrong, the crew usually managed to scramble out somehow and 'take to the silk'. But when speeds advanced to the high subsonic and supersonic range in the years following World War II, it became virtually impossible to leave the aeroplane by manual effort alone. I am delighted to see the recognition the book gives to that great designer of ejection seats, Sir James Martin, who responded to the need for the pilot (and crew) to be ejected clear of the aeroplane and to be provided with oxygen during the subsequent descent. The Martin-Baker ejection seat does all this. A remarkable designer, Sir James – a forthright character if ever there was one – has saved many lives, as indeed did Leslie Irvin over the years since World War I.

The modern air forces of the world owe an enormous debt of gratitude to these two men.

I commend *Into the Silk*. It is well worth reading whether parachutes have come into your life or not.

Douglas Bader
May 1977

INTRODUCTION TO NEW EDITION

Although precise figures do not exist it is estimated that over 120,000 people have saved their lives in aircraft emergencies with parachutes designed by the late Leslie Irvin.

In the 1920s, Irvin formed two branches of a club to enrol the men and women who owed their lives to his internationally famous parachute. Both clubs are still celebrated institutions and although they gained their biggest influx of membership in the five years of the Second World War, they have never ceased to grow by several members every month.

Irvin called his club the Caterpillar Club. One branch, which serves North America, is at Irvin Industries Canada Ltd at Fort Erie in Ontario; the other, based at the parachute factory of Irvin Great Britain Ltd in Letchworth, Hertfordshire, serves the United Kingdom, Europe, and most other countries of the world outside North America.

At the beginning of 1977 the North American branch membership stood at around 11,300 and the Letchworth total was 31,505. But this figure of nearly 43,000 – which includes a dozen women – represents only a third of total successful emergency bale-outs. Many who have jumped to live another day have never heard of the Caterpillar Club; many have not bothered to join; many using Irvin-designed chutes manufactured under licence throughout the world by foreign factories would not have known, or probably cared, that a man called Irvin had invented the parachute that brought them safely back to earth; and in wartime many died before they could apply for membership.

The Caterpillar Club, whose members' stories are the substance of this book, is the Caterpillar Club of the Irvin parachute companies. It is not the only club which exists to enrol those whose lives have been saved by parachute; other chute manufacturers have their own clubs, some have also used the symbolism of the caterpillar, and at least one claims to be an older established institution than the Irvin

Club. A few of the parachute companies outside Britain and North America who make chutes of the Irvin patent established clubs on their own initiative and in Australia at least two annual re-union groups have been formed by enthusiastic local 'caterpillars'.

However, internationally, the Letchworth-run organization is easily the best known, has by far the biggest membership, and in Britain, certainly, is the only Caterpillar Club.

Most of the men – and one woman – who feature in my stories are members of the Letchworth branch. I should have liked to include the bale-out experiences of more North Americans, but their stories, filed at Fort Erie, were beyond my reach.

In the files of the Letchworth branch there are the names of many airmen who were wartime celebrities. But, with a few exceptions, their stories are not here. Most of the men you will read about have never been to Buckingham Palace to have a medal pinned on their chest, have never had their pictures in a newspaper, have never seen their escapes in print before.

Where possible, I have tried to group in chapters baleouts which had features in common. If some appear misplaced it is because they are many-faceted and remarkable for more than one reason.

Today most parachutes are made of nylon, so I should make it clear that 'the silk' in this book is sometimes literal, sometimes figurative. Some aircrew have saved their lives with canopies made from a cloth called Celanese Fortisan. But many 'caterpillars' could not tell you which fabric saved them.

It is 21 years since *Into the Silk* was first published in 1956. Although the Caterpillar Club's membership has not grown substantially since then the years between have seen dramatic advances in aviation and escape technology. The book has been revised and includes two new chapters. It describes these developments and records some of the classic – and routine – escapes of the last two decades.

IAN MACKERSEY
April, 1977

HOW TO JOIN THE CLUB

The Caterpillar Club will admit any person who has saved his or her life in an emergency with a parachute of Irvin design regardless of the company, in any part of the world, which manufactured it. This is the only qualification for membership.

Aircrew who make emergency ejections from ground level, or from the decks of aircraft carriers, are eligible.

Not eligible are paratroopers or sports parachutists who fly with the intention of jumping. Nor are those whose lives may have been saved in situations where the unopened parachute pack intercepts a bullet or shell fragment.

Applications should be sent to the Club Secretary, Irvin Great Britain Ltd, Icknield Way, Letchworth, Hertfordshire. In North America applicants should write to the Caterpillar Club, Irvin Industries Canada Ltd, Fort Erie, Ontario.

They must state the circumstances of the bale-out, the place, date and type of parachute, and must include a corroboratory statement from another person who can vouch for the facts – in the case of military aircrew, their commanding officer.

There is no entrance fee or subscription. Applicants are enrolled as soon as the Club is satisfied of the authenticity of the claim. Immediately on acceptance members are sent a membership card, followed soon afterwards by a gold caterpillar pin, engraved with the individual's name.

CHAPTER I

On the afternoon of October 20, 1922, a young United States Air Corps test pilot walked out to a small high-wing fighter which stood in front of the hangar at McCook Field, Dayton, Ohio. His name was Lieutenant Harold Harris, Chief of the Flight Test Section of the Engineering Division of the U.S. Army Air Service, and he was about to test this aircraft, a Loening monoplane, to which experimental balanced ailerons had been fitted the previous day.

Although he was only 27, Harris had already made a name for himself in the Air Corps. A few days before he had won the light aeroplane race at Detroit; and four years earlier while working with the Italian designer Caproni, he had led the first 'all American' flight over the Swiss Alps. The Italian Government had decorated him with the Order of the Crown of Italy.

Beside the Loening, Harris stopped to clip on his parachute. That morning he had had a new seat cushion fitted to it and now as he struggled to fasten the harness round his body he was annoyed to discover that the cushion had made the straps too tight. He called the timekeeper over and asked him to get another parachute. When it arrived he found that its harness was even smaller than his own.

For several minutes he fiddled impatiently with the straps of the second chute, trying without success to lengthen them. Finally in disgust he decided to break Air Corps orders and fly without one. Although these manual parachutes had been in service more than a year, nobody in the Air Corps had yet saved his life with one; and he knew there were many pilots who firmly believed that if they jumped in an emergency they would have insufficient control over their arms to pull the ripcord. Harris wasn't of this school. But nevertheless he had decided that if anything went wrong in the air he would do everything within his power to force land and would take to the silk only as a very last resort.

11

He was about to climb aboard when on an impulse he changed his mind. Better not tempt providence – not on a test flight: he would take his own chute, uncomfortable as it was. So he strapped it on, scrambled into the cockpit and started up.

Five minutes later he was levelling off in the blue sky 2,500 feet over Dayton. Presently he caught sight of another aircraft from McCook Field. It was a Thomas Morse MB-3, a squat, single-seat biplane fighter, and he knew that the pilot was his friend, Lieutenant Muir Fairchild, who had taken off ahead of him to test new elevators.

Both pilots had to make what was called a 'manoeuvrability' test. And the best manoeuvrability tests they knew were in practice combat. They turned towards each other – each with mock malevolence, determined to outfly and 'destroy' the other.

After a few minutes' diving and zooming and tight turning Harris was delighted to see Fairchild turn away, giving him the opportunity he wanted for his 'kill'. At full throttle, squinting through the ring and bead sights of his guns, he followed the other aircraft as it made a gentle left-hand turn towards the centre of Dayton.

And then it happened.

Suddenly Harris felt the stick snatched out of his hand and a tremendous vibration began to shake the aircraft. The stick slammed fiercely from side to side flailing and bruising the insides of his thighs. Every time he made a grab at it, it was torn from his grasp.

He knew immediately what was wrong. The new ailerons had been set with too big an area forward of their hinges and at the speed he was making, the pressure on the forward parts was overbalancing them. To regain control he pulled the throttle closed to lose speed. His nose dipped, the Loening went into a gentle dive but still the stick threshed about the cockpit. If anything it was whipping from side to side faster than before – so fast that his eyes couldn't keep up with the oscillations. And now as he glanced up he saw that the surface of the wing had begun to ripple and that pieces of the fabric were breaking away. Harris waited no longer.

Flinging off his safety belt he stood up in the cockpit. From then on the slipstream took control. He felt himself plucked out like a cork from a bottle and swept clear of the aircraft.

The next thing he knew he was somersaulting through the air and searching with his hand for the ripcord handle. He felt the cold of a metal ring and pulled. Three times he pulled. Nothing happened – he had been pulling the leg strap fitting.

Five hundred feet from the ground his hand found the handle, he jerked it hard, and his chute opened. He felt no particular relief. Instead he looked up 'admiring the beautiful silk of which the parachute was made and marvelling at how white and clean it was'. He realized, too, that as he had fallen he had had no difficulty controlling his arms in his fumblings for the ripcord; when he got down he'd be able to blow the frozen limbs theory sky high.

He was coming down in a residential area. Below he could see a school out of which a stream of children was pouring and every face was turned up to watch him. A few seconds later he dropped between two houses and landed heavily in the middle of a small grape arbour in the backyard of No. 337 Troy Street, Dayton. As he disentangled himself from the vines a man came running into the backyard to inquire if he was all right. 'I'm not hurt,' Harris reassured him, 'just excited.'

Harris had good reason to be excited. His was the first life ever to be saved in an emergency jump from an aeroplane with a manually-operated parachute. And when the news of his successful jump reached the Parachute Section half a mile away at McCook Field some other men were excited too.

One of them was a stocky young man in his mid-twenties with a wide cheerful face. He came from Los Angeles and his name was Leslie Irvin. Three years earlier he had jumped out of an aircraft over McCook Field to show the world that a manually operated parachute would work. That jump had marked a turning point in the science of parachuting, a science then more than 400 years old but one which for

13

the greater part of that time had been associated more with crowd-thrilling and exhibitionism than with the business of saving life.

Leslie Irvin had been obsessed with parachuting from childhood. As a schoolboy in Los Angeles his interest had been fired by parachutists who made exhibition jumps from hot air balloons in the city's amusement park. Fascinated, he had pleaded with the stunt men to be allowed to make a jump but they laughed at the 12-year-old boy who was so often hanging round their jumping site; they told him to come back when he was bigger. It was then that Irvin decided to make parachute experiments of his own.

He interested some school friends in the undertaking and together they made a paper hot air balloon and a parachute. Neither balloon nor parachute was of man-carrying proportions so for the maiden descent a small tabby cat was chosen to add a touch of realism. The unfortunate cat was strapped on to the end of the parachute which in turn was hooked to the balloon with an ingenious release mechanism of Irvin's engineering, designed to drop the cat and chute at a suitably spectacular height.

The balloon was duly released. It swung away with its cargo over the Los Angeles roof tops pursued jubilantly by the inventors. But the parachute did not disconnect. And after a long chase the boys were horrified to see balloon and cat drift out to sea finally to disappear as a forlorn speck over the Pacific. Guiltily the parachute team dispersed and there and then Leslie Irvin made a resolution. In future, he decided, he and he alone would be the subject of his experiments.

Soon after this Irvin took his first job. He was just 14. His parents wanted him to stay on at school but Leslie Irvin already had a strong will of his own. He went to work for a local inventor called Gil-Dosh, helping him to build an aeroplane. The machine flew – the first in Los Angeles – but it had no passenger space and Irvin acquired his second ambition – to fly.

Next he went to work for a stunt car driver – acting as

ballast as the car raced an aeroplane round a track. Then he got a job working on a small airship which took passengers joy riding over Los Angeles. After which he became a balloonist with the Universal Film Company. From films he drifted into circus work, became a high diver and gave exhibition plunges into a net from 70 feet. And then in 1911, when he was 16, he got his first chance to parachute; it was in the same amusement park where years before he had been an envious spectator. He took to parachuting immediately. The gentle floating thrill of it appealed to his sense of adventure. Soon he was a celebrity. He was billed as 'Ski-Hi Irvin' and found himself in demand at carnivals throughout California.

So far all Irvin's parachuting had been from balloons. But now the aeroplane had arrived to stay he was impatient to experiment with this new and infinitely more flexible and exciting jumping platform. First, however, despite the fact that a few jumps had already been made there was prejudice to overcome. No pilot was immediately willing to take up 'Ski-Hi Irvin' and his parachute; there was a deep-rooted belief that an aircraft's equilibrium would be upset and it would dive out of control the moment the parachutist left it. A sum of money offered to the pilot and parachutist who would make the experiment eventually broke down one pilot's reluctance. Irvin went up sitting on the axle between the wheels of his aircraft with a parachute stowed in a sack under the cockpit. He jumped. The parachute streamed out of the sack and opened. And the aircraft continued safely in straight and level flight. The parachute was keeping pace with aviation – almost.

For hundreds of years man had had no control over the opening of his parachute. The pyramid-shaped model which the Italian genius Leonardo da Vinci sketched in his notebook in the fifteenth century but which was never built was a rigid framework affair held permanently open. So were the chutes of the eighteenth century Frenchmen Lenormand, Blanchard and Garnerin, the first men to descend by parachute. And in the nineteenth century when the rigid umbrella style was dispensed with, chutes were packed in

15

containers fixed to the balloon and the line attached to the parachutist's body drew the canopy out. But now that the aeroplane offered the parachute a new role as a life-saver it was clear that the automatic chute was not enough. The very circumstances which would make a jump necessary could prevent it from opening; an aircraft diving out of control could fall as fast as or faster than a human body would fall and the crew might have difficulty in leaping far enough clear of it to draw their parachutes out of the container; in a spin they stood a fair chance of having their chutes wrapped round the aircraft. There was only one answer. If aircrew were to be guaranteed the means of escape in all attitudes of flight they needed a parachute that was attached to the body, had no link with the aircraft and could be opened when they chose. In short a 'free' type chute – manually operated.

Irvin was intrigued by the possibility of such a chute. Across the Atlantic a war was now raging and over the no-man's-land of the Western Front men were fighting and dying in aeroplanes, dying many of them, he knew, because when their machines were shot out of control they had to crash with them. This was because neither the British nor the Germans believed the container type parachute was then dependable enough for general issue. Until 1917, by which time American airmen, too, were dying in France for want of a satisfactory life-saving chute, it was an air war without parachutes – except for the occupants of observation balloons on both sides. British balloons were equipped with 'Guardian Angels', a chute carried in a container on the balloon and designed by E. R. Calthorp. His chute, which was later modified to be carried on the back and opened by a canvas strip attached to the balloon basket, saved the lives of hundreds of observers whose balloons were shot down. In 1917 German pilots were issued with container type chutes and used them fairly successfully for the remaining 12 months of the war. The British, French and Americans, however, maintained the 'no parachute' policy for their air forces until the bitter end. They insisted on a chute of 100 per cent reliability – or none.

16

During the war – he was now working for the Curtis Aeroplane Co. at Buffalo, New York – Irvin gave over most of his spare time to private research. He was determined to produce a workable free type parachute. And he intended to prove that the then widely held view that a man falling freely through the air would have no control over his limbs and would therefore be unable to operate his chute, was unfounded. From his high diving circus days he knew that it *was* possible to control himself as he fell. He had had to land in the net in a certain position and he had always managed to do so.

Slowly his parachute took shape. It was to have a silk canopy 32 feet in diameter, 24 silk rigging lines each 16 feet long connecting the canopy to the harness and a small 2½ ft pilot chute attached to the apex of the main canopy by eight short lines. The main canopy was to have a vent at the top to allow a certain amount of air to pass through to reduce oscillation, and the small pilot chute would be opened by a built-in wire spring. Both main chute, pilot chute, and rigging lines would be stowed in a pack held by elastic bands secured by two metal pins attached to a steel ripcord cable.

The idea was that a pull on the ripcord would withdraw the securing pins, the elastic bands would whip the pack open, allowing the pilot chute to spring out and draw the main canopy and rigging lines with it.

Irvin didn't fancy the formidable job of stitching his canopy together by hand so he persuaded the manager of a millinery shop in Main Street, Buffalo, to let him use one of the shop's sewing machines. When at last the chute was finished he built a dummy man. He put the chute on the dummy and fixed a rope to the ripcord. Then he took the dummy up in one of the Curtis Company's aeroplanes, fastened the end of the rope to the cockpit, and threw it out. Several yards clear of the plane the rope tightened, the ripcord came out, the chute opened and the dummy floated gently to earth. Again and again he took the dummy up. Every time the chute opened.

Only one test now remained. A live jump. And Irvin was ready to make it. But before he could do so events took a new turn. Early in 1919, a few months after he had patented his invention, he received a letter from Major E. L. Hoffman down south at McCook Field. Hoffman had been appointed by the Air Corps to build up a parachute research team. His orders were to develop a chute that permitted airmen to leave an aircraft in complete safety regardless of its position when disabled. So far all parachutes that depended for their operation on an attachment to the aircraft had failed to meet this requirement and experiments had the previous year turned more energetically towards the manually operated chute. Hoffman had heard of Irvin's chute. He wrote to invite him to join the team. Irvin needed no persuading.

When he arrived at McCook Field in the spring of 1919 he met another man who also had ideas about the free-type chute. In fact he too had designed such a parachute and although it hadn't been used in an emergency several test pilots were already flying with it. His name was Floyd Smith and like Irvin he also had come into aviation and Hoffman's team from carnival acrobating and ballooning.

Irvin and Smith went to work together. Between them they built another free-type chute which was labelled Model A. Although its canopy was four feet less in diameter than Irvin's this new 28 ft chute was fundamentally the same. The canopy was made up of 40 separate panels sewn together, the vent hole at the apex was made expandable with thick rubber bands and the whole chute was stowed in a back pack. On April 28, 1919, Irvin jumped with it.

Everyone at McCook Field turned out to watch. Some of them expected to see Irvin jump to his death, for the belief that a man falling freely would become unconscious still had wide currency. Even Major Hoffman and Irvin's design colleagues, although almost convinced that the manual chute was what they were looking for, had private misgivings that sunny spring morning.

Floyd Smith took him up in a de Havilland biplane – a DH.9. He wore two chutes of the same design – one on his chest and the other which he intended to pull first, on his back. At heart his faith in the chute was implicit; he had not the least doubt that it would work as it had done with the dummies. But at the same time he was acutely conscious of the morbid scepticism around him and as the DH.9 circled the field, gaining height, he was gripped with nervous excitement.

At 1,500 feet Floyd Smith levelled off and settled down for a straight and level run across the field at 100 m.p.h. Irvin stood up. The nervousness had gone now and he felt utterly detached from the spectators bunched together in little groups round the perimeter of the green field below. He chose his own moment, grinned and waved briefly to the man in front, then scrambled out of the cockpit and over the side. As he fell he planted his hand on the ripcord and gave it a smart pull. Yards of silk streamed out behind him and 1,000 feet above the ground he was swinging there under the wide white canopy – the first that a man, jumping from an aircraft, had opened in mid-air himself. Bursting with elation he drifted down and so excited was he with his success that he landed carelessly. As he rolled over on the grass he felt a stab of pain and cursed his luck – he had broken his ankle. But in that moment of triumph as people ran across the field to congratulate him it seemed to Irvin a very small price to pay.

Two weeks later as he lay in hospital at McCook Field, Irvin learnt that Floyd Smith had made the second jump and that there were any number of volunteers prepared to make the third. The parachute that he had designed, and which Floyd Smith had helped him to perfect, had proved itself. And the sceptics had been confounded. A man could fall freely through the air and operate his own parachute.

Irvin was still in hospital when the Air Corps put the seal of official approval on his chute with an order for 300. There was only one way he could fulfil that order; he would have to go into business.

He got in touch with his lawyer in Buffalo and instructed him to register the name of the Irvin Air Chute Company. A few days later when the articles of association were sent to him in hospital Irvin noticed that a 'g' had been inadvertently added to his name. He crossed it out and returned the papers with a note drawing attention to the small error.

It was too late. The company had already been registered as the Irving Air Chute Company and he was told it would cost money to alter it. Irvin had no money and Irving Air Chute it was to remain for many years.

The ankle mended and Irvin left hospital. He said good-bye to Major Hoffman and the Air Corps design team and went north to Buffalo. There in an old wooden dance hall he rented space and set up his first factory. It was to become the parent factory of many others which within a few years he was to open in 11 different countries and which before he was 30 were to make him a comparatively wealthy man.

In the months that followed the opening of his factory in Buffalo, Irvin made frequent visits to the Parachute Section at McCook Field which was to receive his first production order. At first he was disappointed to find that the Air Corps was still persisting in experiments with automatic chutes. As a life-saver he knew that type of chute could have no future – but the Air Corps had yet to be positively convinced.

In July 1919, it *was* convinced – by an accident which tragically showed up the very real limitations of the automatic system. Lieutenant Caldwell of the Royal Air Force came to McCook Field to demonstrate the latest model of the British 'Guardian Angel' – the chute that balloon observers had used during the war. While Major Hoffman's men watched, he jumped from an aircraft at 600 feet over the field – and plunged to his death. His parachute had fouled part of the aircraft as it streamed from its container, and broke. Once and for all the automatic chute was condemned as an emergency vehicle. In future, the Air Corps decided all chutes must be carried on the body.

Scores of live jumps had now been made with Irvin's chutes at McCook Field without a single failure. At the same time the Parachute Section was testing other manual prototypes which various inventors were submitting for official assessment. Ironically it was one of these rival inventions that on August 24, 1920, gave an Irvin chute the chance to save its first life.

The Jahn Aerial Life-Saving Apparatus Company sent

its parachutist, William O'Connor, to McCook Field to demonstrate the Jahn chute. The Parachute Section suggested that as a precaution O'Connor should carry an Irvin chute as a reserve. At first both Jahn, the inventor, who had accompanied O'Connor to McCook, and O'Connor himself refused. Their chute was as reliable as Irvin's and a reserve was unnecessary, they said. But the Air Corps men were firm and in the end it was agreed that O'Connor should take the reserve chute. He jumped from 2,000 ft over the field. The Jahn chute refused to open and 500 feet from the ground O'Connor pulled the ripcord of his reserve, which did. For Irvin, standing among the spectators, it was a moment of quiet satisfaction. All he wanted now was the supreme acknowledgment of a life saved with one of his chutes from an aircraft in a real emergency. For that he had to wait two years – two years during which a pilot who had left his chute behind was killed in a crash, as a result of which the Air Corps made the wearing of parachutes compulsory.

But for this order Lieutenant Harris might not have been wearing a parachute on October 20, 1922 – the day he became Caterpillar No 1.

A few days after Harris had jumped into the headlines two members of the McCook Field Parachute Section collected a number of souvenirs of the incident and decorated their laboratory wall with them. The trophies included parts of the aircraft and a set of photographs showing Harris standing by the wreckage, his parachute draped over the vines. The two parachute men, one of whom was Milton St Clair, were proud of their bale-out museum and soon it began to attract visitors. Inevitably two of the first were newspapermen from the *Dayton Herald* – Maurice Hutton, the paper's aviation correspondent, and Verne Timmerman, a photographer. Timmerman was specially intrigued by the mementoes. In time, he pointed out, as more and more lives were saved by parachute they would need a vast hall in which to display the relics. And then he made a suggestion. Why not start a bale-out club? They already had a foundation member; more were bound to come along, in time there might be hundreds, thousands even.

The parachute men thought that maybe Timmerman had something. They hadn't thought of a club. It had possibilities. Somebody asked what should it be called and the suggestion 'Sky Hookers' came up; someone else suggested 'Crawlers'. But somehow they didn't seem to fit. The sort of club they envisaged deserved a better name.

Several days later St Clair was browsing through some literature put out by the Caterpillar Tractor Company. It gave him an inspiration. The parachute canopy was silk. So was the tiny thread on which the silkworm safely lowered itself to earth from its leaf. What better symbol than the caterpillar?

Straight away he got in touch with Hutton and Timmerman. They liked the name immediately. The Caterpillar Club it was to be.

Major Hoffman, head of the Parachute Section, became an enthusiastic advocate of the Club. So did other members of his team – Leo Stevens, who had experimented with manually operated parachutes as far back as 1908, Floyd Smith, Glen Martin, Guy Ball, James M. Russell and Leslie Irvin. Especially Irvin. His Buffalo factory was already turning out parachutes and the idea of a roll of names of satisfied customers appealed to him. Some weeks later after Lieutenant Frank Tyndall, another Air Corps pilot, had baled out of an M.B.3A whose wings tore off near Seattle and became the second man to save his life with an Irvin chute, the Caterpillar Club came officially into existence and Irvin undertook to keep the records at his Buffalo factory. Harris and Tyndall were enrolled as the first two members and Irvin presented each with a small gold caterpillar tie pin. The pins were the brain-child of an unofficial design committee comprising Irvin, Tyndall, Floyd Smith and Guy Ball. They were made by a Buffalo jeweller, had tiny ruby eyes and the recipient's name and rank engraved on the under side. And Irvin made a promise, one he was never to break, that he would donate a caterpillar pin to every person, anywhere, who saved his or her life in an emergency with a parachute of his design.

It would be a club in name only, he decided. It would have no social premises, charge no entrance fee, no subscription. The only class of membership would be life, the only privilege, he declared, 'its continued enjoyment'. There would be no committee, no patron or president, just an honorary secretary – a post which Irvin himself decided to fill. In effect the only tangible evidence of the Club would be the filing cabinet in his factory office where members' applications would be kept.

For 17 months after the Club's formation Harris* and Tyndall remained the only members. Nobody baled out with an Irvin chute in 1923 and it was not until April 1924 that the third applicant, Wilfred Bottomfield, came along. Bottomfield was an exhibition parachutist. He jumped with six parachutes at an air circus at Kelley Field, Texas, intending to open five of them one after the other as he came down. The sixth was an Irvin chute which he had been persuaded to carry as a reserve and it was the sixth that saved him when all the others tangled and refused to open.

From then on the Caterpillar Club grew steadily. Almost every month brought a new member and by the end of 1925 it had a complement of 27 – all Americans. But not for much longer was it to remain an exclusively American club.

Already the Buffalo factory was supplying the Royal Air Force with parachutes and when the R.A.F. adopted Irvin's chute in 1925 the British Government told him that he must either license a British company or set one up in England himself. Irvin took the latter course. He came to England to look for a factory site. At Letchworth, in Hertfordshire, 35 miles north of London he found a tenement building. He rented the top floor, installed his equipment and recruited a staff of 30. Irvin Air Chute of Great Britain

---

* Thanks to Irvin's parachute, Lieutenant Harold Harris, Caterpillar No 1, went on to reach high rank. He became a Brigadier-General and Chief of Staff of the American Air Transport Command, retiring from military service in 1945.

Ltd was established and the European Branch of the Caterpillar Club was open for business.

CHAPTER II

When the Royal Air Force adopted Irvin's parachute in 1925 there was, among pilots at least, a certain amount of scepticism about the new appendage they were now required to strap on their backs. The truth was that the Service was not yet parachute-minded and although for the first few months of its use pilots accepted the chute good-naturedly enough they were inclined to treat it more as a welcome cushion on which to sit in their hard cockpits, than as a device that might in an emergency be the means of saving their lives. It was not until halfway through the following year that a young pupil pilot showed his colleagues dramatically that their chutes deserved to be taken seriously.

The morning of June 17, 1926 was warm, calm, and almost cloudless over Cheshire when Pilot Officer Eric Pentland took off alone from No 5 Flying Training School at Shotwick near Chester in an Avro 504 K biplane trainer. He was 22, had not been long in the R.A.F. and had flown only five or six hours solo but he was already badly bitten by the flying bug. On this flight he had been sent up to practise half rolls. His instructor had shown him how they were done earlier that morning and now he was going to try them for himself. He climbed away from the aerodrome to 2,500 feet over Heswall Golf Course. Peering over the cockpit side into the warm oily smelling slipstream he looked down at the smooth green course and the thought that if his engine should fail him he could probably force land there comforted him.

He tightened his straps, lowered the nose, picked up speed, eased the stick back then rolled to port. The horizon swung round, he steadied the aircraft on its back, hanging for a moment on his straps, then with a gentle pull on the stick he dived back to level flight. He opened the throttle and

24

climbed again to 2,500 feet. A bit ropey, but not too bad for a beginner, he thought. He did another half roll, then two more. On the fifth it happened. He was diving out of the roll when suddenly he found that he had no lateral control – he had lost all response from his ailerons. Next thing he knew he was inverted and the Avro was spinning giddily to starboard. For a few seconds he juggled with the rudder and stick but to no avail. By now he was down to 500 feet and decided to get out. He flung off his safety harness and remembering in that second a chance remark he had heard that the parachute could not be guaranteed to open from much below 1,000 feet he grabbed his ripcord and pulled it in the cockpit. Silk spilled out round his legs and as he saw it he thought 'Hell, it's going to foul the centre section struts.'

He caught a glimpse of the green countryside revolving below him and then he was thrown out of the cockpit. The green below stopped turning and rushed to meet him. Then he felt a jerk and he looked up – the big white canopy was open. Pentland thought he had never seen anything that looked so wonderful as that canopy. Ten seconds later he landed heavily but uninjured in a field, 100 yards from the wreckage of his aircraft. The first R.A.F. life had been saved by parachute and the European Branch of the Caterpillar Club had gained its first member.

The second member was not long in coming. He was Captain E. R. C. Scholefield, then Vickers Chief Test Pilot, and providentially the day he qualified was the first on which he had ever carried a parachute, the company's first stock having only just arrived from the new Irvin factory at Letchworth. He was testing a Wibault, an all-metal single-seater monoplane, near Brooklands aerodrome on July 1 when the aircraft went into a spin from which he could not recover. According to the Club records he 'jumped, pulled the ripcord and landed safely and uninjured, although he is a large man weighing 230 lb'.

Scholefield was the first British civil test pilot to bale out. But his story had a tragic sequel. Two years later he was testing a twin-engined Vickers aircraft when, over Shepperton, there was a structural failure of the tail unit. The aircraft dived into the ground and Scholefield and his mechanic were killed. Neither had been wearing parachutes.

European Branch Caterpillars Nos. 3 and 4 qualified within a few seconds of each other on July 20 when the Fairey Foxes they were flying collided near Andover in Hampshire. They were Sergeant Pilots H. C. Steanes and W. J. Frost – both of No. 12 Squadron, Royal Air Force. The Fox, a biplane bomber, was at the time the most advanced aircraft in R.A.F. service and Frost, newly arrived from flying training school and still proudly conscious of the wings he had so recently gained, felt specially honoured to have been posted to such a 'blue-eyed' squadron.

Although the Fox was a two-seater it did not have dual controls and new pilots were given a passenger trip to familiarize them with the aircraft's characteristics and then sent solo. After five hours' solo flying they were permitted to carry a passenger or another crew member. The day they became 'caterpillars', Steanes and Frost had been briefed to fly as a pair from Andover to the Isle of Wight and back to give them some flying time towards those five qualifying hours.

Steanes took off first and when he had climbed away, Frost followed. As he droned up into the blue summer sky, Frost could not see the other Fox. He levelled off at 1,000 feet, bending his head into the cockpit as he did so to check his instruments. When he looked up again his heart nearly stood still: another aircraft was heading straight for him. It was Steanes; he was so close that before either could take any avoiding action they had collided. Steanes' starboard tail plane clipped through Frost's starboard upper main plane, shearing it off halfway along. Frost felt his aircraft lurch and then pitch into a steep spiral dive. He tried to recover, but the aircraft was too badly damaged, so he unfastened his safety straps and tried to get out. But as he struggled to climb over the side the gravitational pull of the spiralling aircraft pressed him back. It was as if some big invisible hand was pinning him there. Straight ahead of him over the cowling he was aware of the whirling blur of the ground racing towards him. He was below 500 feet now; he gripped the cockpit side and tried again. It was no use. He knew then that only one thing could save him – his chute. He stood up, reached down for the pack hanging against the backs of his thighs, twisted round and pushed it out into the slipstream. In a last despairing effort he pulled the ripcord. He was just 300 feet from the ground. A mass of silk whipped out along the fuselage, his harness jerked tight and suddenly he was lifted from the cockpit. He felt himself hit the tail plane and then he was swinging in space. He looked up and saw with dismay that the canopy had been ripped in several places where it had dragged against the aircraft and that several rigging lines had snapped. In the same moment he heard his aircraft crash 100 feet below him and almost immediately he reached the ground near by. The damaged canopy had let him down fast but despite the heavy landing it gave him he was not badly hurt.

Meanwhile, Steanes, whose starboard tail plane had been ripped off, had found himself plunging down in a straight dive. He freed himself, stood up in the cockpit and was preparing to jump when he felt himself sucked out into the slipstream. He pulled his ripcord and drifted down to a gentle landing. Two pilots who, if they had collided a year earlier, would have had no parachutes and would have died in the wreckage of their aircraft, had lived to fly another day.

Another R.A.F. sergeant pilot who baled out when his control column jammed and a lieutenant in the Swedish Royal Air Force who failed to recover from a spin, brought the European Branch total to six for 1926. The following year it gained five more members – including its first Russian – and in 1928, a further 18, among them six Poles, three Swedes and a Yugoslav. By the end of 1929, during which 27 more names were added to the lists, the branch could boast a total membership of 56.

The most spectacular escape of 1929 was that of Flight Lieutenant S. L. G. Pope – probably the tallest man ever to bale out. Pope – 'Poppy' as he was better known – commanded the R.A.F.'s Fighter Experimental and Test Flight at Martlesham Heath in Suffolk. A good-looking young man of 30, he was 6 ft 6 in tall and wore on his chest the ribbons of an A.F.C. and a D.F.C. he had earned flying Nieuports in combat in France 11 years before.

Towards the end of 1928 a prototype single-seat fighter called the Pippit was delivered to Martlesham. It had been built by the Parnall Aircraft Company at Yate near Bristol, was powered by the new Rolls Royce Kestrel engine and had been entered into an Air Ministry competition among aircraft firms for a new fighter. The Pippit, a biplane exceptionally well streamlined for that time, looked to Pope like a fighter of some potential and from the moment it arrived he was impatient to give it a preliminary test flight. The first time he took it up, however, the tail plane fluttered so violently that he quickly came down again. He reported the flutter to the designer, and to Squadron Leader Noakes, the chief test pilot at Martlesham, and Noakes decided he would try the Pippit himself the following morning.

With some misgivings Pope stood on the tarmac with the designer to watch. They saw Noakes take off, make a wide circuit of the airfield and turn in towards them at about 800 feet. Pope turned to the designer and said, 'Now watch the tail.' They looked up and as they did so part of the aircraft's tail flew off and came fluttering down. Appalled, the two men watched waiting for Noakes to bale out; but he made no attempt. Instead he lowered his nose and tried to land. It looked as if he would make it until, just as he began to level out, the aircraft went out of control and plunged into the ground. The two men ran across to find Noakes badly injured beside the aircraft. He had been flung out but although his back was broken he survived.

Two months later, on February 24, 1929, a second Pippit, this one with a strengthened tail plane, was wheeled out of the Parnall factory at Yate. And Pope went down from Martlesham to give it its maiden flight. The memory of Noakes's crash was still acutely with him but if anything it added to his determination to take the Pippit up again.

It was a Sunday, a raw grey day with a blanket of cloud at about 4,000 feet. He examined the modified tail plane, decided it was an improvement, climbed in, started up, and took off. He hadn't been airborne long before he realized that something was wrong with the rudder. It wasn't responding properly so he decided to cut the test short and land. Gingerly he turned towards the aerodrome and began his descent. At 800 feet he felt the Pippit twitch. He glanced over his shoulder and was just in time to see the rudder and fin floating away in mid-air behind him.

This, Pope decided, was where he and the Pippit parted company. He jerked the throttle shut, pulled the nose up and reached down to undo the straps of his Sutton harness. For several long precious seconds he fumbled for the string attached to the pin, unable to bend his head because he was strapped in so tightly. At last his fingers grasped a length of string and he pulled hard. Nothing happened. Desperately he tugged again – fiercely this time. The aircraft had now rolled over on to its back and the nose was falling away for the final plunge. He could see the ground less than 500 feet below.

For the third time he yanked at the string – and this time it came away. But the straps of his harness did not. Only then did Pope notice that he had been pulling the wrong string. He had been pulling the string which held a pencil to the knee pad on which he scribbled his test data!

Frantically now as he hung upside down he groped for the pin that secured the four straps. His 15¼ stone sagged heavily in the harness and when he found the pin it was squeezed tight by his weight and wouldn't budge. He had to tear the straps off the pin one by one and as he did so he told himself that it was too late, that when he did get out there wouldn't be enough height left anyway.

At about 300 feet from the ground he flung the last strap aside and tried to climb out. It was a narrow cockpit and Pope was a big man. His shoulders jammed.

By now he had almost resigned himself to the inevitable. He strained upward through the cockpit opening and lunged with both feet. The next he knew he was falling free of the aircraft and his right hand was jabbing in search of the ripcord handle. He felt up and down the left side of his chest for it but the metal ring was not there. He had somersaulted and was falling feet-first; below him he could see a row of tall oaks coming up fast. In that same split second he saw the ripcord ring hanging by his leg – it had slipped out of its sheath. He reached down, gave it a despairing tug and his chute blossomed out above him with a bump. His first thought was that the aircraft had hit him but then he saw the ground swinging not rushing up at him. As he reached up to grasp the lift webs his feet slashed through the top branches of an oak and he burst through the brittle branches on to the ground.

'The people over at the aerodrome hadn't seen me get out,' Pope said. 'When they came running over they expected to find me in the wreckage. Instead I was running round the field like a madman, making sure that my back, which had received a severe jar, was in working order. The only visible injuries were two scratches on my ankle.'

Pope was the first R.A.F. test pilot to save his life by parachute. That evening he received a characteristic telegram from his colleagues at Martlesham. 'Congratulations,' it read, 'forwarding clean pair of pants.'

1930 brought the Club 40 more applicants. They included the first clergyman to bale out, the Reverend K. C. H. Warner, a Royal Air Force padre who with the pilot, Flight Lieutenant V. J. Somerset-Thomas, leapt from a DH.9A at 1,500 feet over the desert between Abu Sueir and Cairo when the crankshaft broke, and the first peer, Lord Malcolm Douglas-Hamilton. Lord Malcolm was serving in the R.A.F. as a Pilot Officer. He was flying a Bristol Bulldog, practising for the Hendon air display with two other Bulldogs when he was in collision with a Hawker Horsley bomber, 'We were diving on the bomber, which was flying at just over 1,000 feet, in turn, following close one after the other, and coming as near as possible to make it look spectacular,' he told the Club in a letter. 'I dived last of the three and possibly I got some of No. 2's slipstream; anyway, it all happened in a flash. I hit the Horsley at the bottom of my dive, on the tail and through the starboard planes. The Bulldog just broke up and dived for the earth with both wings folded back, luckily not over the cockpit. It was half upside down and I pulled the harness pin, the shoulder straps flew apart, and I fell clear. I pulled the ripcord and my parachute opened like a flash. My height from the ground was said by watchers to be between 150 and 300 feet when I left the machine.' The Horsley pilot and his passenger baled out, too, but the former got out too late. He hit the ground before his chute had opened and was killed.

Life insurance in the shape of Irvin's parachutes was catching on fast. Orders were now coming in from almost every country in the world and every week, somewhere, one of his silk canopies was saving a life. In 1931 the Club enrolled its first New Zealander, Mr G. W. E. Clancey who baled out near Ngaruawahia in the North Island. 'My home-made plane caught fire recently owing to a fractured petrol line,' he wrote 'After emptying the fire extinguisher without effect, I hopped out – still clutching the extinguisher!'

Applications for enrolment were reaching the Club in a host of foreign languages and some, like the application sent from Belgrade on behalf of Sergeant Pilot Dimitrije Ljumovich of the Yugoslavian Air Force, were in such quaint English that the tragedy of the circumstances was made to seem almost comical. Ljumovich baled out at 8,000 feet. Tersely the letter described the incident thus: 'By making loop he fell from aeroplane and in this moment the propeller cut his leg over his knee and he without his leg but with a cigarette in his mouth, fell on one foot and with your chute saved his life. This happened on August 17, 1931. He is still in the Flying Service but with one wooden leg.'

But still the R.A.F. – as indeed it was always to do – continued to supply the Club with most of its members. Month by month applications came in – from sergeant pilots, pilot officers, flying officers and flight lieutenants most of them – young men with stories of mid-air collisions, of structural failures, of propellers that flew off and crank-shafts that broke, of controls that jammed and of spins from which they could not recover, young men eternally grateful for the second stab at life that their silken 'brollies' had given them.

The Aeroplane and Armament Experimental Establishment at Martlesham Heath was inevitably a regular source of members. It had first given the Club 'Poppy' Pope four years earlier and now in 1933 it provided the European Branch with its 180th member – Flying Officer Arthur Pegg.

Although he was only 27, Pegg had spent nearly half his life in the Royal Air Force. He had joined as an aircraft apprentice back in 1921 when he was 15, had subsequently trained as a pilot and had been a test pilot at Martlesham for nearly three years when on March 21 he earned his gold caterpillar.

He had taken up an Avro Tutor, a new dual control biplane trainer which was about to enter R.A.F. service, for diving tests. His test pad was strapped to one knee and a sensitive altimeter to the other. The idea was that he should put the Tutor into a vertical dive and as he swept down with throttle wide open he would scribble on the pad altimeter, airspeed and engine revolution readings.

At 8,000 feet over Suffolk, Pegg began his dive. The engine screamed at full power and the struts whined in the slipstream. He bent his head into the cockpit and began writing. The altimeter on his knee began to unwind fast and the airspeed indicator swung past 200. At 3,000 feet the Tutor had reached 230 m.p.h. It didn't look as if it would go any faster and Pegg was about to make his final altimeter reading when there was a tremendous bang and he was thrown violently about the cockpit – the wings had broken off. For the moment Pegg was not sure just what had happened: but of one thing he was quite sure – it was time to climb out. He was, however, denied this privilege, for after he had fumbled the straps off, he was thrown out.

As he fell clear of the aircraft he was presented in the few seconds left to him with a trivial, but at the time, vital question. He was wearing a type of flying mitten which folded over all the fingers. They had already made it difficult for him to undo his safety harness and now he debated whether he should keep the mittens on and risk several attempts to get a grip on his ripcord or tear them off and grab the ring first time. He felt no panic in those moments as he fell at nearly 200 feet a second. Quite the opposite; his situation seemed to have sharpened his reactions and he found himself resolving the business of the mittens with almost studied calm. The mitten, he decided, must come off. He ripped it away, hauled on the ripcord and his parachute opened. He was still 1,000 feet above the ground; from wings off to chute opening had been just eight seconds.

Pegg landed in a field in which two sturdy farm labourers were working. He picked himself up, released his parachute, and began to walk towards them. More than anything else just then he wanted a smoke, but he had no matches. But with every step he took in their direction the two men, with deep suspicion in their faces, retreated. Pegg quickened his pace. So did the men. Before he could get near enough to speak to them, they turned round and fled. The parachute was still enough of a novelty in 1933 for the spectacle of a man – in Pegg's case with a bloodstained head – dropping down silently out of the sky to be greeted with mistrust in at least some corners of rural England.

Bale-outs were big news in the newspapers of the 'thirties and Pegg found next morning that his had been no exception. It was, in fact, the beginning of a great deal more publicity he was to receive throughout his career. For in 1936 he left the R.A.F. to join the Bristol Aeroplane Company. He became the company's Chief Test Pilot and pioneer pilot of what was, in its time, Britain's biggest landplane – the Bristol Brabazon.

Most 'caterpillars' qualified for their badges because for one reason or another their aircraft were no longer airworthy – but not all. Occasionally aviators were signed up who would have preferred not to have joined. Pupil Pilot K. T. Murray was one. He was flying solo, practising aerobatics at 2,000 feet near Southampton in September 1934, when he fell head-first out of his trainer. A Royal Australian Air Force instructor was another: in August 1937, he was teaching an R.A.A.F. cadet to fly a Wapiti bomber near Point Cook in New South Wales when he, too, fell out. He came down by parachute; the cadet landed the Wapiti. The instructor, one of the first R.A.A.F. 'caterpillars', did not want to accept the gold memento. It was not strictly an emergency, he said. But the Club persuaded him to join.

November, in the pre-war years, was often the Club's busiest month. November meant fog. And fog to an Air Force that had yet to be introduced to the sophistication of radar, instrument and automatic landing systems, all too often sealed pilots off from the ground until they ran out of fuel and the only safe way home was on the end of a parachute. Sometimes when unexpected fog crept swiftly in to blanket the whole of eastern England at night a lot of aircraft would be caught in this way and it was not uncommon for the Club to gain a dozen members within the space of three or four hours.

Fog brought Tom Newbould into the Club in November 1937. And it nearly cost him his life – three times in the space of 15 minutes.

Newbould was a tall, slim Flight Sergeant flying instructor at No. 11 Flying Training School, Wittering. He was 30 and the R.A.F. had been his home since he was 17. His two big interests in life were sport and flying: he was good at both and the afternoon of the day the fog nearly cut short his engagement he had played hockey for Northampton against Cambridge.

It was a cold, clear starlit night when Newbould and his pupil, Pilot Officer Farnes, took off in the Hawker Hart – an ideal night, he thought, for Farne's first night instruction. He took the Hart up to 1,000 feet, levelled off and turned to orientate himself on the flare path. But when he looked down there were no flickering goosenecks, no lights at all. They were above a dark grey carpet of fog. Newbould cursed. It seemed incredible that fog could roll in so quickly.

For several minutes he circled, scanning the greyness below him, without much hope, for a break through which he could dart back and land. But there was none and presently the clustered lights of several nearby towns which had been winking in the distance a few minutes earlier went under the advancing veil and showed now only as a suffused glow.

With no radio to consult Wittering about the extent of the fog or to be advised of alternate fog-free aerodromes, Newbould decided that the best he could do was to fly off and look for himself. Time for the moment at least was on his side. He had fuel for three and a half hours' flying. It had been nine o'clock when they took off. So they had until 12.30 to find a way down – somewhere in England.

Wittering were now firing white Vereys up through the fog to show them the aerodrome but although he flew down towards the curving flares, he found he dropped back into fog at 200 feet and he couldn't see through it. 'No future in sticking around here,' he told Farnes through the speaking tube. 'Let's go and look down south.'

For 20 or 30 miles they flew south passing the pale glow of several big towns. Soon, when their southward cruise had shown them just how extensive the fog was, they turned and headed back north. By 10.30 they were over Wittering again and Newbould was dismayed to see that far from dispersing in their absence the fog had deepened. It was now more than 800 feet thick and Wittering's Vereys could no longer reach through it. They had been replaced by signal mortars which burst at intervals in the black sky around them in brilliant white explosions.

This time they flew north into Lincolnshire. Past the lights of Spalding and Grantham until they could see the big warm glow of Lincoln itself. They circled R.A.F. Cranwell, identifiable only by the mortar flashes that bounced up, but still in every direction the fog lay in an obstinate endless sea.

At 11.30 they flew back over Wittering and Newbould saw that the fog was now up to 1,000 feet. It looked hopeless. At the most they had an hour's fuel left. And then he noticed a glow in the sky some miles away. It was a fiercer, redder glow than the towns and he recognized it as the Corby steel works.

There was just a chance, he thought, that the heat from the furnaces might have dispersed at least enough of the fog overhead to give him the opening he needed. They flew

35

to Corby. The glowing carpet of fog was certainly thinner there. But it wasn't thin enough.

Guided by the signal mortars that were still coming up Newbould returned to Wittering. 'Straps tight?' he asked. He felt the aircraft tremble slightly as Farnes checked his harness. 'Yes,' came the reply. 'Good,' said Newbould. 'I'm going to line up on the next mortar and have a go at landing.'

A flare cascaded light a few yards away. Newbould closed the throttle and trimmed the Hart into a glide. The stars disappeared and cold earthy-smelling fog engulfed them. The only sound as they descended through the black void was the putter putter of the idling engine and the sigh of the slipstream. Newbould was flying on instruments now. Like many of his colleagues of the pre-war heyday he had no love of nor faith in instrument flying. He belonged to the school who had been taught to fly by the seat of the proverbial pants and had an innate distrust of the artificial indications of his position in space which his instruments offered him. Now, as he slid deep into the fog he felt grateful to those who had insisted he become proficient on instruments.

His eyes rolled over all his instruments now, but most of all they watched the altimeter. He saw the hand drop back to 800, 700, 600 feet. It was sliding past 500 when suddenly there was a flash beside him and for a second the aircraft was bathed in a blinding light. A signal mortar had burst in the fog almost on the wingtip. Startled and momentarily blinded, Newbould looked up. Before his eyes could pick out the instruments again the nose had come up, a wing had dropped and they were spinning. Oh God, he thought, this was it. Four or five turns and they'd be into the ground.

With eyes that were still only half seeing he saw from the turn needle that it was a righthand spin. He stabbed on full opposite rudder. The whine of the slipstream grew louder. The turn needle swung like a pendulum gone mad. But they stopped rotating. He hauled with fierce hands on the stick and jerked the throttle wide open. The engine spluttered, faltered, picked up. They were climbing. Climbing back to the clear starlit sky above. As they broke out into the clear Newbound found he was trembling uncontrollably.

A spin – at night – in fog – less than 500 feet from the ground – no pilot could want a more unnerving experience than that, and as he struggled to get a grip on himself he began slowly to appreciate the full miracle of their blind spin recovery. For Farne's sake he forced himself to sound unruffled. 'We don't want any more of that to-night,' he said quietly, 'we're baling out.'

'Okay,' Farnes said and then, after a pause he asked: 'Look, Flight, do these parachutes ever fail to open?'

Newbould, who thought that even a chute that didn't open was preferable to another fog spin, said, 'Sure they're safe. I've never heard of one that didn't work yet.'

Then he told Farnes that he would try and put him out over a spot that as best he could calculate above the fog would be clear of high tension cables. The area was criss-crossed with power lines but he knew that Duddington Wood about two miles south-west of Wittering was free of them; he had often picknicked there in the summer. He climbed to 4,000 feet and gently circled what he hoped was the vicinity of the wood. 'Out you go and good luck,' he said. 'And don't forget to count three.'

He throttled back and saw Farnes undo his harness, stand up, clamber out of the cockpit and dive over the side. A few moments later he looked over and saw the white circle of Farne's parachute gliding down towards the fog. He looked at his watch. 12.25. Less than five minutes' fuel left. He turned back to where he believed the wood was, undid his straps, closed the throttle, stood up, climbed out of the cockpit and jumped head first.

The cold blast of the slipstream slapped his face and he saw the grey cloud of the fog below. Instinctively he began counting but then he realized he was not falling at all; he was hanging upside down and the heel of his left flying boot was jammed between his seat and the cockpit coaming. Somehow he climbed back into the cockpit, released his boot and jumped again. Presently he was swinging gently on the end of his chute, marvelling at the silence after the noise of the aircraft. He pulled the ripcord out of its housing and stuffed it into the pocket of his Sidcot flying suit. That anyway was half-a-crown he'd saved. It was an unofficial custom that aircrew who baled out and lost their ripcords were fined 2s 6d by their parachute section.

After the anxieties of the night Newbould's spirits began to revive with the exhilaration of the descent. Away in the distance he could see the Hart's starboard navigation light, a tiny green speck in the dark. He watched it for several seconds until the speck turned red and he knew the Hart was turning. It was making a wide descending left-hand turn and a moment later the dull burble of its engine came to him and he cursed his forgetfulness for not switching off. He looked down at the fog but he didn't seem to have got any nearer to it; in fact there was no sensation of descent at all. When he looked up again he saw to his concern that the Hart was now not only much closer but was heading straight for him. It seemed incredible that in the vast space of the night sky their paths should meet, but incredible or not, Newbould saw that if he took no avoiding action he was very soon going to be cut to pieces by the propeller.

The Hart was 50 yards away when he reached up and hauled on his rigging lines to spill some air out of the canopy and change direction. But when he did this he found to his horror that he was merely slipping further into the aircraft's gently turning path. For the second time that night he thought, 'This is it'.

Twenty yards away he saw the black shape of the Hart gliding in towards him and he shut his eyes tight waiting for the inevitable. He heard the whine of the slipstream in the flying wires and the sharp note of the engine and he braced himself taut. But the Hart didn't hit him. Not quite. The port wing tip swished past a few inches away – so close that he felt the rush of air and he opened his eyes to see his whole body bathed for a second in the red glow of the navigation light as it passed. Then the aircraft was gone, curving down and quickly disappearing into the fog. Newbould was still above the fog when the sound of the crash came up to him. And then he, too, dropped into damp blackness and reached up to grasp the lift webs ready for the landing shock.

The fog was deeper than he had realized and he seemed to have been falling through it for a very long time when a stout wooden pole suddenly rose up beside him. At the same moment something touched his back: there was a tremendous flash and a great shower of blue sparks poured down on him. It was a high tension line and he was on it.

For the third time in less than a quarter of an hour Newbould thought it was the end. He was doomed, it seemed, to die by some means that night and this was how it was to be – electrocution. After the elaborate precautions he had taken to position them over Duddington Wood it was the final irony.

But death didn't come to Newbould. Nor, despite the sparks which continued to crackle round his head, did he receive any shock. The next thing he was aware of was hanging by his parachute from the cables with his toes just touching the ground. He reached down, punched his release box and fell forward into a turnip field. As he dropped out of his harness his charred parachute, free of his weight, was snatched upwards by the cable holding it. It was a five cable grid and his chute had pulled all the cables together, snapping four of them and throwing a large area of Northamptonshire – including R.A.F. Wittering – into darkness.

In the fog and dark Newbould knew none of these details. He wanted only to get quickly away. He groped his way across the field and presently heard someone shouting. He called back and two men appeared out of the fog. The Hart had crashed near their homes and they were looking for the pilot. He was two miles from Duddington Wood, they said.

The two men took Newbould to the village policeman's house. The constable came to the door holding a candle. Behind him in the shadows was another man who said, 'Hello, Flight, it's me – Farnes.' Farnes had landed in the constabulary gardens. There in the doorway in the candlelight they shook hands and Newbould thought that life was indeed very sweet.

From time to time there came to the Club stories which

were dramatic testimony to the parachute's ability to bring a man safely down despite serious damage to the canopy. The case of Lieutenant Zivota Boskovic in October 1938, was a good example.

Boskovic was a pilot in the Yugoslav Air Force. He was giving a demonstration of aerobatics at 4,000 feet over Pancevo aerodrome, watched from the ground by a critical group of brother officers. Halfway through the display Boskovic's aircraft broke up. At about 2,000 feet he jumped out and a few seconds later those on the ground saw his chute open amid a falling shower of debris. But almost immediately the fuselage, minus wings and tail, spun down on to the parachute, the canopy collapsed and the silk wrapped itself round the fuselage. For a thousand feet Boskovic's colleagues watched in horror, as, dangling on his shroud lines, he was rotated helplessly like a plumb ball on a string round and round the falling fuselage. And then, just under a thousand feet from the ground, the canopy silk tore from top to bottom, the chute fell away from the fuselage, opened out again and Boskovic floated down to arrive, as his application put it, 'unhurtedly on very hard ground'. When Boskovic examined his parachute he found that it had been ripped from the apex to the skirt in two places – almost tearing his canopy in half. As a result 'of this dreadful event', the application concluded, 'the confidence to the Irvin parachute increased still'.

April 11, 1939, brought the Club two more test pilots. They were John Cunningham and Geoffrey de Havilland of the de Havilland Aircraft Company. Cunningham, who was to become the company's Chief Test Pilot, was then, at 21, its youngest. He and Geoffrey de Havilland (killed while testing the DH.108 over the Thames Estuary in 1946) went up together in a Moth Minor for spinning tests. The Moth refused to come out of one spin and over Wheathampstead in Hertfordshire both men baled out. Cunningham was the first to go and as he floated down the aircraft overtook him and spun past with de Havilland still in the process of leaving the cockpit. It occurred to Cunningham that here was a picture, and he tried to get his camera out of his pocket.

But the parachute harness prevented him. Shortly after he saw de Havilland's chute open below him and the aircraft crash into a field. A few minutes later the two newly qualified 'caterpillars' were celebrating their deliverance over a glass of beer in the nearby Bull Inn. It was midday. That afternoon both were flying again.

The Club signed up its first schoolboy in July 1939. Like so many enrolments it was born of tragic circumstances. Denis Nahum, a 16-year-old Oundle boy, was being flown as a passenger from Wittering in a Royal Air Force Blenheim under the public schools air liaison scheme. The Blenheim was one of a formation of three. Near Wansford, between Peterborough and Wittering, Nahum's Blenheim collided with one of the other aircraft and part of its tail was broken off. The Blenheim went out of control. Nahum's pilot, 25-year-old Sergeant J. A. Bullard, quickly reached down, pulled open the escape hatch in the floor and told the boy to jump. Seeing that Nahum was diffident about leaping through the narrow hole into space, he helped him from his seat, made sure he knew where his ripcord was and guided him feet-first out through the hatch. The Blenheim was now very low. Nahum had just enough altitude to save himself but a few seconds later when Bullard followed him through the hatch there wasn't enough height left. He hit the ground before his chute had opened and was killed.

When war came in September 1939, the grand total of American and European branch caterpillars stood at 4,000 – nearly three-quarters of them American. The Letchworth factory, which in 1934 had moved into modern new premises in Icknield Way, had until now been receiving applications at the rate of about two a week. They had been dealt with by Irvin's secretary (Irvin had now made his home in Letchworth) who ordered the gold caterpillars from Mappin and Webb, Ltd, the London jewellers, and sent each new member a personal letter of welcome and a membership card which Irvin signed. The Caterpillar Club was in truth a very minor fragment of the company's business. But it wasn't to remain that way.

As the phoney war grew hot and the R.A.F. went into action against the Luftwaffe, Mary Lofts, a tall, attractive Letchworth girl who had become Irvin's secretary in 1938, found that the Club's business was very quickly becoming a full-time job. Letters of application from grateful R.A.F. aircrew began to arrive daily; soon there were dozens in every post. The little fraternity, which had started as a novelty 18 years before, was on its way to becoming a substantial organization in its own right.

CHAPTER III

In 1922, when Leslie Irvin made his pledge to donate a gold pin to every person whose life one of his chutes had saved, he was not to know how formidable the fulfilment of that promise was one day to become. The war made it so.

The war made parachute manufacturing a front-line industry. It brought huge orders to his factories; at Letchworth it compelled a staff increase from 80 to more than 400 and a stepping up in production from the pre-war output of 75 to 100 parachutes a week, to close on 1,500 a week. The First World War had been a war without parachutes; the Second was a war in which few men flew without one. No longer was there any question of the parachute's ability to open in an emergency. Provided it had been packed correctly, kept dry and undamaged, it would open every time.

The men and women who worked on the long tables shaping, cutting, sewing and packing the seat, back, and chest type parachutes for the Allied Air Forces rarely met any of the men whose lives their craftsmanship had saved. But they knew just the same how many of their chutes had been put to the supreme test. At one end of the packing hall in which many of them worked was a big honours board on which was inscribed the name of every European who had saved his life with an Irvin chute up to the outbreak of the war. The war brought thousands more names than the board could hold, so a numeral indicator was attached and week by week the grand total of 'caterpillars' was brought up to date. If any incentive was really necessary then the growing strength of the Caterpillar Club provided it.

By the end of 1943 the Club had gained 6,000 wartime members. The total rose to 10,000 by July 1944 and to nearly 17,000 by February 1945. In all the war brought the European branch 23,000 members, raising its grand total to 27,000.

In 1939 Mary Lofts had handled the Club's correspondence in her spare time; the records filled only a couple of drawers in the office filing system. By 1944 she was often working until 10 o'clock in the evening to keep pace with the deluge of applications; two more girls had been engaged to help her, and the Club's filing cabinets occupied a room of their own.

In the hectic days of the war when Irvin was preoccupied with more vital matters of production and design improvements, Mary Lofts was the Club's mainspring. She personally wrote and typed thousands of letters which went out acknowledging the applications. Nor were they stereotyped acknowledgements; each was a personal letter welcoming the individual and sending congratulations related to the circumstances of his escape.

No club can have admitted so many members as expeditiously as the Caterpillar Club did between 1941 and 1945. A typical day would bring anything from 100 to 150 applications – and scores more letters inquiring about the conditions of membership or asking for replacements for lost caterpillar pins. For a time the Board of Trade banned the production of pins altogether – as a war economy. But Irvin persuaded them to revoke the order, pointing out the value of the insignia as a morale builder. Pins were issued again – but for the remainder of the war they were made of gilt instead of gold.

More than 8,000 of the war-time applications came from prisoners-of-war. Their requests arrived in cryptic pencilled sentences scribbled on p.o.w. cards – 'Dear Sir, will you please enrol me as a member of the Caterpillar Club. I baled out over Holland on August 15 from a blazing kite and made a wizard landing . . .' 'Dear Sir, shot down over France, July 20. Ship was ablaze and baled out. Request membership in the Caterpillar Club . . .' 'Dears Sirs, I beg the honour of my admittance to your Club. I have been shot down over Dusseldorf in November 2, 1944 . . .'

From aircrew who baled out over friendly territory came longer letters. Some described their experiences in lengthy detail: others wrote to praise the reliability of their chutes. A few, overcome with gratitude, began their letters to Irvin 'Dear Leslie,' one such applicant, an Australian sergeant pilot, going on to say: 'I'd like to thank you for the sweetest moments in all my life, when my parachute opened and I realized I was not going to die. Your chutes are so good I am going to name my son (when I have one) Irvin as it was due to one in particular that I am alive enough to woo, marry, and get me a son.' And a Canadian mid-upper gunner whose Lancaster was hit by flak over Germany and blew up, wrote: 'When I woke up I was falling through space. I pulled the ripcord and, miraculously, despite the explosion that had blown me out, my chute opened. When I landed I thanked God that I had had my parachute clipped on. I knelt in the dark and said the Lord's Prayer.'

Because they were in short supply, pins were not sent to prisoners-of-war. They were reserved for members still on active service. The p.o.w.s got theirs when they returned at the end of the war.

Despite the wartime inrush, the Club continued to guard jealously the right of admission. Except for Pow applicants, whose stories obviously could not be checked, it insisted on written confirmation from witnesses, commanding officers or adjutants that the jumps were genuine emergency bale-outs.

On one occasion when the crew of an American bomber baled out within sight of the Letchworth factory, Irvin himself was their witness. Waiting only to see where they were going to land he quickly got into his car and drove out to meet them. He found two of the men just as they reached the ground; five minutes later they were in his office back at the factory toasting their parachutes with the inventor's whisky, and being signed up by the Club – the swiftest enrolments ever.

Although Irvin insisted that jumps must have been made with a parachute of his design, this did not necessarily mean that only those made at his factories qualified the user for Club membership. Several other English companies were turning out parachutes but with one exception all their life-saving chutes were based on Irvin's design. The exception was the 'parasuit' designed and produced by the G.Q. Parachute Company of Woking. This ingenious piece of safety equipment was a flying suit with a built-in parachute. Those who wore them – chiefly rear gunners - never had to worry about clipping on a pack, either before take-off or in an emergency; their chute was always with them.

Occasionally, applicants whose interpretations of the conditions for admission were broader than the Club's, were refused admission. The group captain who claimed that his parachute had saved his life by keeping him afloat after he had ditched in the Mediterranean was told he was ineligible. So was the rear gunner who wanted a caterpillar because his parachute release box had stopped a bullet. And, too, the R.A.F. sergeant who, in 1944, was in a bomb-damaged hangar in Greece when part of the roof collapsed. An old piece of shrapnel came down with the debris and embedded itself in his parachute pack with which, lying down, he had protected his head. The sergeant's life had undoubtedly been saved by his parachute – but, as the Club reminded him, not in an emergency in the air.

Also refused was the application of a civilian passenger who baled out of an R.A.F. aircraft which went out of control over Somerset in 1941. His ripcord handle caught on part of the aircraft and his parachute opened too soon. The canopy wrapped itself round the tail unit and he was dragged along behind, dangling helplessly on the end of his shroud lines. Seeing his predicament the pilot decided to stay with the aircraft and try to force land it. He was unsuccessful.

The aircraft crashed and blew up; yet neither man was killed. The pilot was thrown clear; his passenger who had been dragged down by his parachute kept his head, waited until he was a few feet from the ground, then punched his release box. He fell out of his harness and dropped on to the ground a few seconds before the aircraft. He escaped with only a broken leg and minor head injuries.

The Club congratulated him on his escape. But as, after he had been hooked up, his parachute had in no way checked his fall, he could not, it held, be made a member.

Nor were applications accepted from aircrew who had baled out as the result of a misunderstanding; on the other hand if a man had been ordered to bale out because the aircraft was in danger yet was subsequently landed safely, he was admitted.

A flight sergeant whose Lancaster was returning to base from an exercise was making his way from one crew position to another when he felt the aircraft swing suddenly to port. The two port engines had failed and the pilot had feathered them. Quickly plugging in to the nearest intercom point he was just in time to hear the pilot's voice saying 'Jump! Jump!' – the executive command to bale out. Being a well-disciplined crew member the flight sergeant briskly acknowledged the order, unplugged, clipped on his parachute and baled out through the rear turret. Some hours later when he got to his station he was surprised to see his Lancaster safely in the dispersals. Mystified, he went to look for the pilot. The pilot greeted him acidly: 'Where the devil did you get to this afternoon?'

'You called "Jump, Jump". I baled out,' said the flight sergeant.

The pilot said: 'It was a pity you didn't hear it all. I said: "If we have to feather any more engines it'll be a case of Jump, Jump!"'

The flight sergeant didn't get a caterpillar. 'I am sorry that you should have had your jump for nothing,' wrote Mary Lofts.

There were no caterpillars, either, for the wireless operator and the two navigators of an Anson which was return-

46

ing to base from a training flight on one engine. Letting down through cloud the aircraft struck some turbulence and the pilot gave the precautionary order: 'Put on parachutes.' The chutes were duly clipped on while the second navigator jettisoned the main door and stood beside it. The aircraft was down to 2,000 feet and he wanted to get out quickly when the order came. A few minutes later he heard what sounded like the word 'Go'. He had not the least doubt that it was the bale-out command: he jumped. The first navigator and the wireless operator, meanwhile having disconnected themselves from the intercom, assumed that their colleague had received a positive order from the pilot, and swiftly followed him through the door. The three parachutists landed unhurt in a field. And when the pilot returned to base and made an uneventful single-engine landing he was perplexed to find that he had returned alone. He was specially upset – because he had given no order to bale out.

Although most wartime members earned their caterpillars for baling out of powered aircraft, not all did. A Blackburn Aircraft Company test pilot, Mr J. C. Neilan and his observer, Mr R. F. Stedman, joined the Club in July, 1942, after they had hurriedly abandoned a Hengist glider which began to break up during tests at Dishforth. A number of paratroopers – not normally eligible – were admitted when they had to jump from gliders that had been shot up en route to the dropping zone. And at least one parachute training instructor, Sergeant Albert Barnes, gained a caterpillar for an emergency jump from a balloon.

Barnes was an instructor at the Parachute Training School at Ringway. One afternoon in March, 1944, he had despatched his pupils from the captive balloon and was being hauled back to earth when the cable snapped. Barnes was thrown violently into a corner of the cage and stunned. When he got to his feet he saw that the balloon was making a rapid free ascent and, in his own words, 'not wishing to visit the moon, and having a date that evening, I decided to bale out'. Barnes landed safely to become the first parachute instructor 'caterpillar'; the balloon landed near Coventry – more than 100 miles away.

Of the 23,000 caterpillar pins awarded by the European branch during the war only one went to a woman. Corporal Felice Poser was a member of the W.A.A.F. serving with an R.A.F. meteorological unit at Heliopolis near Cairo. July 28, 1945, was the last day of leave she had been spending in Palestine and that morning she reported to the R.A.F. Station at Aqir, a few miles south of Lydda, in the hope that an aircraft might be flying to Egypt in which she could hitch a ride, thus avoiding an uncomfortable train journey.

She was in luck. There was an aircraft – an Anson bound for Shallufa in the Canal Zone – and she was given per-mission to go in it, along with two other passengers, an R.A.F. sergeant and another W.A.A.F. On the way out to the aircraft Felice asked the pilot, Warrant Officer Joseph Turvey, a New Zealander, how her parachute worked, and whether she should count ten before pulling the ripcord. Turvey told her it was very unlikely she would have to use it, but that if she did, not to count ten but to wait only until she was clear of the aircraft. An hour and a half later that advice was to save her life.

The first 80 minutes of the flight south-west across the Palestine frontier and into Egypt were uneventful. The Anson cruised peacefully along in a blue sky at 2,000 feet and Felice, watching the fawn sand of the Sinai Desert slide by below, began to peer through the windows looking for a glimpse of the green ribbon of the Suez Canal.

The canal was still several miles away over the horizon when suddenly the starboard engine spluttered and lost power – a valve had fractured. Turvey throttled back on the useless engine and opened up on the other; but the Anson began to lose height. There was still no sign of the canal so he ordered parachutes on.

Five minutes later Turvey was relieved to see the outline of the canal about nine miles ahead and he immediately altered course for Deversoir, the nearest airfield in the Canal Zone. He called Deversoir tower on the R/T, but got no reply. He called again saying he would fire a red Verey – but this message was not acknowledged either. Meanwhile back in the cabin, the wireless operator was helping the two women to clip on the chest parachutes and showing them again the ripcord handles. All the fun had gone out of the flight for the W.A.A.F.s now and the wireless operator seeing the fear in their faces reassured them: 'There's nothing to worry about. It's only a precaution.'

They were down to 800 feet when they crossed the canal and flew in towards Deversoir; the Anson was still losing height. Turvey, having tried again to raise the tower without success, now fired a red Verey. But the flare did not leave the aircraft; it exploded in the cockpit setting fire to the woodwork and filling the Anson with choking smoke.

Thinking that the aircraft was badly on fire, the wireless operator called Turvey on the intercom and asked what had happened. In the stress of the moment he thought he heard Turvey order him to bale the girls out – but Turvey had given no such order. Believing that they had been ordered to abandon the aircraft the wireless operator jettisoned the cabin door, led the girls to the entrance, put their hands on their ripcord handles and told them to jump.

The smoke was now clearing and Turvey, glancing round was horrified to see one of the W.A.A.F.s disappearing through the door. He was already down to 500 feet for his emergency landing and 500 feet, he knew, was a far from safe height for baling out. Realizing that it was too late to stop the bale-outs he quickly opened up on his good engine in an effort to gain height. But the aircraft would not climb and a moment later when the sergeant sitting beside him told him that all the others had jumped, he closed the throttle again and went in to make a belly landing at Deversoir.

When Felice had stepped out and seen the ground so close she remembered that she must not count ten as she had always believed was necessary; she must pull the ripcord immediately. She did so and her chute snapped open. After the initial relief she felt at having opened her chute in time she spent the remaining few seconds of the descent worrying about a new pair of shoes and a camera she had

49

left in the aircraft. Moments later she was safely on the ground beside the officers' mess, having narrowly missed the barbed wire entanglement which surrounded the camp. She saw the wireless operator come down nearby and then she looked around for the other W.A.A.F. But of her there was no sign. It was not until some time later that she learnt she was dead. Although the wireless operator had placed her hand on her ripcord she had, probably through fear, failed to pull it. She crashed through the roof of the station guardroom.

Into the wartime files went the names of many celebrated R.A.F. personalities, names, some of them, already well known to the Irvin Company from the newspapers. They included the New Zealander, Flying Officer E. J. 'Cobber' Kain, the legless pilot, Group Captain, now Sir Douglas Bader, the Pathfinder pioneer, Air Vice-Marshal D. C. T. Bennett, Flight Lieutenant K. W. 'Bluey' Truscott, and two men who were saved by their parachutes to become recipients of the highest award for bravery of all – Flight Lieutenant James Nicholson, V.C., and Warrant Officer Norman Jackson, V.C.

Nicholson, the only pilot of Fighter Command to be awarded the V.C., earned it in August 1940, when with his aircraft blazing and himself wounded he refused to bale out until he had destroyed his adversary – a Messerschmitt 110.

Jackson, a flight engineer, wrote to the Club in October 1945. 'I used one of your chutes on the night of April 26/27, 1944 after being shot down by a German night fighter,' he said. What he did not say was that that night he had crawled out on to the starboard wing of his Lancaster at 20,000 feet over Germany with a fire extinguisher stuffed inside his Mae West in a gallant attempt to put out a fire near a petrol tank between the fuselage and the inboard engine. As he was climbing out through the escape hatch above the pilot's head his parachute had opened and the canopy and rigging lines had spilled into the cockpit. Undeterred and despite injuries received earlier during the fighter attack which had started the fire, Jackson had pressed on while other members of the crew gathered his parachute together and held on to the rigging lines, paying them out as he went. He had succeeded in getting a grip on an air intake on the leading edge of the wing but in the process the extinguisher had been blown away and his hands and face had been badly hurt. Unable to hang on he had been swept away, dragging his burning parachute behind him; realizing that the fire could not be controlled the pilot ordered the other members of the crew to abandon the aircraft. Fortunately for Jackson his canopy had filled out but the fire had damaged it and he had made a rapid descent, breaking an ankle on landing. He had spent ten months in hospital in Germany and had been repatriated to England after the war, his burnt hands still not fully usable. Several months later he learnt that his action had earned him a Victoria Cross.

But of all the celebrities – and the thousands whose names never reached the newspapers – the Caterpillar Club remembers with most affection Warrant Officer 'Dicky' Richardson. One of the most pitifully wounded of all the wartime 'caterpillars' he was the only member it ever formally 'adopted'.

Richardson was a wireless operator/air gunner in No. 50 Squadron. On a night raid in May 1944 his Lancaster was hit by flak over France and caught fire. Severely burned on the hands and face, Richardson baled out. He was taken prisoner but despite his terrible burns was given only cursory medical treatment. Soon after D-Day the town in which he was in hospital in Northern France was heavily bombed. The Germans evacuated the town and several days later when Allied troops arrived they found Richardson lying in a cellar blind, and with a gangrenous right hand. The hand was amputated and he was brought back to England to the Queen Victoria Hospital plastic surgery centre at East Grinstead where the long slow process of his recuperation began. Plastic surgeons gave him a new nose, chin, ears, eyelids and upper lip; his sight they could not restore.

Having qualified for membership of the hospital's Guinea Pig Club, Richardson remembered that he was also eligible to join the Caterpillar Club. So the hospital's welfare secretary sent off a letter of application for him in which he said of Richardson: 'In this hospital of many grievous injuries his are by way of being the worst and yet his cheerfulness and spirit are as proportionately great as are his injuries.'

Mary Lofts showed the letter to Irvin. This was the first letter they had ever received from a blind man and they were both touched by it. They felt that somehow Richardson deserved more than a membership card and a gold caterpillar; they decided to 'adopt' him.

Richardson's 'adoption' was quickly translated into practical generosity. The staff were told about him, a collection was taken round the factory and Richardson got a cheque for £23. It was the first of many cheques and gifts which included parcels of cigarettes, chocolate, eggs and a radio set.

For the first year of his association with the Club Richardson received a cheque every month. And every birthday and every Christmas for the five long years he spent at the Guinea Pig hospital and at St Dunstan's, where he learnt Braille and to type and how to run a shop, the people who had made the parachute that saved his life sent him a gift. Only when Richardson, equipped with a new face and an artificial hand, went out to face the world again in 1950 did the Club consider his 'adoption' had ended. He acquired a tobacco and confectionary shop in Ronkswood, Worcester which his wife, Eileen, helped him to run. The wedding had been planned for August 1944. But in August 1944, Richardson was on the lists of the missing. When next Eileen saw him he was blind and disfigured almost beyond recognition. But to her her fiancé's tragedy was not half good enough reason for cancelling the wedding. And when it did take place there was a far grander reception than had been planned in 1944. It was held in Worcester's ancient Guildhall, loaned by the mayor as a civic gesture to Dicky Richardson's courage.

It is impossible to say with any certainty which member of the Caterpillar Club has baled out the most number of times. The Club does not award 'bars' to its caterpillar pins nor does it issue certificates for further bale-outs after the first qualifying leap. Some members who have saved their lives a second time write and tell the Club about it; many do not bother. The Club, therefore, has no accurate record of multiple jumps. It knows that several hundred members have baled out twice and a few dozen three times. A Polish airman once wrote to claim six bale-outs; he was sent a caterpillar pin and membership card. Several years later it was discovered that his claim was spurious. In fact he had not jumped even once.

Until 1940, as far as was known, the bale-out record was held by Colonel Charles A. Lindbergh, who had saved his life four times with an Irvin parachute – all in the space of two years. He baled out first in March 1925 when as a pilot in the U.S. Air Corps Reserve he was involved in a mid-air collision. Three months later he had to jump again – this time when his aircraft failed to recover from a spin. In September 1926 he was flying the St Louis–Chicago night air mail; he ran out of fuel over fog and abandoned his aircraft. Seven weeks later on the same night schedule he was caught in a snowstorm and baled out a fourth time. Lindbergh was enrolled by the Club's American office. It was not until the Battle of Britain when R.A.F. and German fighter pilots began to glide down out of the vapour trail-patterned summer sky over Southern England in increasing numbers that the European branch gained a member who had equalled Lindbergh's four jumps.*

He was Pilot Officer Tony Woods-Scawen, a 22-year-old fighter pilot of No. 43 Squadron. Short, slightly built and quietly spoken, Woods-Scawen was for a long time remembered in the R.A.F. for his bravery and determination, as the pilot who was shot down seven times in the space of three months and kept coming back for more, as the pilot who brought his parachute back from France.

In the two brief years of his flying career Woods-Scawen faced 12 emergencies in the air. He had to force land twice at his flying training school, twice more soon after he joined

---

* Pre-war runner-up to Lindbergh was Lieut.-General J. H. Doolittle. He saved his life by parachute three times between 1928 and 1931. The last time he sent Irvin a telegram: 'Aeroplane failed; chute worked'.

the squadron and when he took his Hurricane into the Battle of Britain he was shot down and crash landed three times; saved his life with his chute four times. He joined the Caterpillar Club in June 1940 when he abandoned his burning aircraft after a dogfight near Dieppe. He was posted missing and the soft strumming of his guitar with which, in the weeks before, he had soothed his fellow pilots waiting, tensed, in the dispersals at Tangmere for the alert, was not heard for eight days. In those eight days Woods-Scawen was making his way home.

Landing behind the German lines he had spent the first night hiding in a ditch. Then with his parachute bundled under his arm he had set out on a 20-mile walk to Bacqueville where he fell in with a retreating British column. Evacuated from Cherbourg he got back to England arrived at Tangmere driving an elderly bull-nosed Morris.

Squadron Leader George Lott, 43 Squadron's commander, was having a lunch-time drink in the mess with one of his pilots when Woods-Scawen walked in wearing an Army shirt and a tin hat and still clutching his parachute. 'I'm sorry I'm late, sir,' he said. Lott called for a drink and asked, 'Why on earth did you lug your chute all that way, Tony?' And Woods-Scawen said, 'Well, sir, I know now that this one works and I thought I might have to use it again.'

He did have to use it again – four times more. But the last time, near Ashford, Kent, on September 2, 1940, three days after he had been awarded a D.F.C., he abandoned his Hurricane too low. His chute streamed, but before it could open fully Woods-Scawen hit the ground and was killed.

His had not been a one-sided campaign. When the historians came to add up his combat successes, they credited him with seven enemy aircraft confirmed destroyed – one for each time he had been shot down and survived – plus three probables and one damaged.

In the files of the Caterpillar Club there are two folders for the name Woods-Scawen.* One is for Tony, the other

* During the war several published reports claimed that Tony Woods-Scawen had *baled out* seven times, but this was not true. His parachute

54

for his elder brother Patrick. Patrick was in 85 Squadron, earned a D.F.C. and was credited with the destruction of nine-and-a-half enemy aircraft and two probables. Tony died not knowing that his brother had been shot down and killed near Caterham the day before.

CHAPTER IV

When they exchange their crippled aircraft for the silk the moments of excitement and danger which make the jump necessary for most aircrew end with the snap of the opening canopy and the blissful peacefulness of descent. For some, however, it is a case of leaving the frying pan for the fire. For Squadron Leader John Hill in France, in May 1940, it certainly was.

During that disastrous month as the German armoured divisions rumbled towards the Channel and the British Expeditionary Force battled its way back to Dunkirk, the hopelessly outnumbered Hurricane squadrons of the British Air Force clashed with the Luftwaffe in the skies over Northern France. In the green countryside below, where spring blossoms still hung on the trees, the French farmers and the inhabitants of the little villages watched the air battles and waited. They waited with shotguns, sporting rifles and pitchforks, waited for any Luftwaffe pilot unfortunate enough to drop their way, waited too for the fifth columnists they had been warned would arrive by parachute in British or French uniform. From the Pas de Calais across the plains below the French-Belgian frontier to the foothills of the Ardennes the reception committees were ready. They were ready on Sunday, May 19, for Hill.

saved his life four times; on his fifth bale-out he was killed. The only other record the European Branch has had of four bale-outs was the application in 1943 of Flight Lieutenant F. C. Bradley, who wrote from R.A.F. Skinburness Towers in Cumberland. Bradley said he had baled out twice from Gladiators while flying for the Finns in the Finnish/Russian war, once from a Fox Moth at Carlisle, and once from a Battle in Canada.

Hill had just taken command of No. 504 Squadron based at Lille Marque on the outskirts of Lille. Short, brisk of speech and good-natured, he had been training for war for eight years, having joined the R.A.F. in 1932, and was eager for the real fighting that had at last come his way.

For the first two days of his new command urgent matters of organization kept him on the ground but on the third day he decided to fly. As he had only done a few hours on Hurricanes he told the senior flight commander, Flight Lieutenant Tony Rook, to lead the squadron, appointing himself 'tail-end Charlie', a position from which he hoped to see how the attacks were led.

It was a cool, clear morning when the 12 Hurricanes took off to patrol Lille at 20,000 feet and the Luftwaffe did not keep them waiting. As 50 Me 110s came down out of the sun Hill heard a warning call crackle over the R/T: 'Look out Johnny, look out Johnny'. It didn't at first occur to him that the message was intended for him. (In fact it came from a squadron leader friend of his – himself shot down later that day – who was also operating from Lille Marque and happened to be in the vicinity at the time.) When it did it was too late; the 110 was on his tail and the cannon shells were already hammering into his engine.

The dogfight lasted less than a minute. Hill quickly found that he had been jumped by a highly experienced pilot – one he assumed had fought through the Polish campaign – and as metal rattled against his armour plating and large pieces of his cowling began to fly off he knew that he wouldn't be much longer in the air. The end came when his opponent caught him in a steep turn. With his tail shot off, his engine stopped and a slight wound in his knee from which blood was oozing, he decided it was time to swop his Hurricane for the silk.

He opened the hood and jumped out. It was a 20 minute journey down from 18,000 feet and as he drifted down the gentle quiet of his descent seemed to contrast strangely with the scream of engines and the clatter of guns from the mêlée of Hurricanes and 110s which he could see above him.

Hanging there on the end of his parachute he felt terribly

naked and vulnerable and he fervently hoped that the 110 pilots would be kept too busy to come and shoot at him. He wished now that he had remembered to obey his own orders to the squadron and had not opened his parachute so quickly. Away to the west was Lille cloaked in industrial haze and he saw that a strong wind was drifting him further and further east.

He began to wonder whether he would land in Allied or enemy-held territory and looked down anxiously for any signs that might tell him. But the flat fields and the white ribbons of the roads below seemed deserted.

Presently, as he neared the ground he saw that he was going to land in a stubbled field from which the hay had recently been cut.

He was only a few hundred feet above the field and was reaching up for the lift webs preparing to land when the stillness of the morning was broken by a fusillade of shotgun fire; at the same moment he felt a number of sharp pricks in his legs. Looking down he saw a number of French peasants crouched behind a hedge on the edge of the field. Three of them were armed with 12-bore shotguns and they were firing at him.

The last 100 feet seemed the longest of his whole descent. The farmers had him in close range now and as he swung there, a perfect target, he felt so utterly helpless and stunned by the unexpectedness of his reception that he could find no words to shout down at the protectors of France behind the hedge.

More shots banged from the hedge, more pellets zipped stingingly into his legs and then he was down, tumbling among the folds of his canopy in the sharp stubble. He was about to stand up to talk the matter over when several more shots banged at him and a shower of lead rushed over his head. Quickly he lay down and crawled under the silk, thankful that the white overalls he was wearing helped to camouflage him. Pushing up a corner of the canopy and hoping that the Frenchmen would think he was lying there, he slithered on his stomach to the other end of the chute

57

and lay motionless with thumping heart waiting for the next move.

His ruse worked. For several minutes the silk fold he had pushed up was peppered with gunfire. Then the firing stopped, he heard a whispered consultation from the hedge and assumed that at last they had exhausted their ammunition. When he lifted a corner of the canopy and peeped out he saw the reception committee advancing slowly across the field towards him, the three armed men pointing their guns menacingly.

Hill flung the folds of the parachute aside and leapt up, pulling the top of his flying overall down to reveal his blue R.A.F. uniform. He had picked up some French during the nine months he had been in France and he was grateful for it now. 'Je suis Anglais,' he called. 'Je suis aviateur et alors maintenant je suis blessé.'

Immediately the cold suspicion in the six faces vanished, the men lowered their guns and presently one of the peasants, a short, sharp-featured man with the black beginnings of a beard on his chin, spoke in rapid French. Hill understood enough of it to know that they had mistaken him for a German fifth-columnist. And so to establish his position once and for all he fished out his green identity card. The peasants passed it from one to the other and as they saw that the photograph tallied they began to joke and apologize with Gallic profuseness. They were extremely sorry, they said, but these things happened in war.

Seeing that he was wounded they picked Hill up with great tenderness and carried him across the field to a road. There they laid him down, fussing around him while one of them went off to telephone the French Air Force authorities. It wasn't long before a French Air Force corporal arrived in a car and Hill was lifted on to the front seat beside the driver. About 20 French – men and women – had now arrived and they crowded round the car to shout *au revoir* and to wave as he moved off. He lay back in the seat waving and smiling, impatient now to get back to the squadron he had yet served so briefly.

The car moved about 20 yards down the road and stopped.

When he looked around to see why, Hill was delighted to find that a British Army jeep had pulled up ahead of them and that a major, a sergeant and five privates had alighted and were walking towards him. This was an excellent bit of good fortune; he was back in British hands already. He wound the window down and was about to shout a cheery greeting when the major called to him crisply: 'Put your hands up – you're fifth column!'

Fifth column be damned, thought Hill. What sort of Army humour was this? He poked his head out of the window and retorted: 'Look, Major, I'm an R.A.F. squadron leader. Don't be bloody silly.'

The major said harshly: 'You heard me. Put your hands up.' Incredulously, still fully not grasping the deadly seriousness of the major's suspicion, he stared at the seven men of his own country's Army who stood there in their steel helmets blocking the road. Almost unbelievingly he saw that the major had now unsheathed his revolver and that the sergeant and the five privates were all levelling rifles at the car. He looked hard at the major and because he saw in his face that this was no game he slowly raised his arms. The major, he noticed, was a man of about 55; white hair showed from under his helmet, and his face, which Hill noticed was also very white, showed agitated indecision.

'Listen, I don't know what you're playing at but I can easily prove who I am,' Hill tried again. He saw that all the fingers were on the triggers and, nervous and less sure of himself now, he kept his hands well up near the roof inside the car.

'You're a fifth columnist,' the major insisted. 'Keep your hands up and don't move.'

'All right,' Hill shouted angrily. 'If you don't believe me come over and look at my identity card – and my uniform.

But the major made no move. Nor did he send any of his men towards the car. The seven of them stood there, a hostile armed squad, 20 feet away, waiting for Hill knew not what.

Several long seconds dragged by. The peasants he had just left were now walking curiously towards the car, obviously wondering if they hadn't been duped by a fifth columnist after all. He could hear their mutterings and, his impatience nearly exhausted, he tried once more to end this comic opera farce.

'I'm not armed, Major,' he said. 'For Christ's sake will you please stop this nonsense and send one of your men to identify me. Search me if you like.'

The major did not reply. Exasperatedly Hill dropped one of his hands to feel in his breast pocket for his identity card. And in that instant one of the rifles fired, the windscreen exploded in a shower of glass and the driver slumped in his seat screaming and blaspheming. Oh God, the fools, thought Hill. He ducked below the windscreen and as he did so all the rifles fired. The major and his men had fanned out and were systematically riddling the car.

Crouching on the floor, Hill heard the bullets smacking against the metal around him. If he stayed there he knew that sooner or later he must collect one. So he reached up, opened the door and rolled out into the ditch.

It was not a very deep ditch but fortunately for Hill it was choked with hay which passing waggons had shed. He crawled under it and heard bullet after bullet slap into the dry clay near his head. What a hell of a way for a pilot to die this was. Shot by his own Army in a ditch like a dog.

The bullets were getting closer now. The hay couldn't be covering him properly. So to confuse the firing squad he began throwing handfuls of hay into the air, squirming along the ditch as he did so. And every time a bundle went up they fired at it. But still he wasn't hit.

Presently the firing became spasmodic. Then it stopped. For a whole minute Hill lay trembling, waiting. He could smell the cordite even through the hay. At last he concluded the Army had run out of ammunition; he poked his head up. The major and his men were still standing 20 feet away, and seven barrels still pointed at him, threateningly.

'Now are you satisfied?' he called to the major. At heart Hill was a gentle man – not easily made angry or bitter; but he was angry now. He had come to France to fight the Germans, not to be slain by his own side. He sat up on the edge of the ditch and gave vent to his feelings, shouting every curse he knew at the major. But the major did not answer him. For a fifth-columnist who had been dropped in France the man in the ditch, it must have occurred to him, had a startlingly genuine line in basic Anglo-Saxon.

'Of all the bloody fools – why don't you find out who you're shooting at before you loose off with those firearms? Now will you give me a chance to prove who I am?' The major started to speak but Hill was never to hear what he had to say.

The peasants had seen enough to convince them that Hill must certainly be the fifth-columnist they had at first taken him for. Spurred on by the groans of the corporal whose shoulder the British had shattered, they gathered round Hill, hauled him roughly from the ditch and began to beat him up.

Almost uncomprehendingly Hill fought back with bare fists. The law of the jungle, it seemed, was determined to have him killed by some means that sunny morning. Half a dozen bare-armed peasants bored in, flailing him from head to waist and others less gallant laid about him with pitchfork handles while their womenfolk stood off and smashed eggs and tomatoes into his face. A few yards away the major, the sergeant and the five privates stood watching; they did not intervene, still believing, apparently, that the man whose face was being pulped in front of them was a German.

The peasants had him on the ground now. His face and hair were streaked with egg yolk and tomato, both eyes were closing and he was groggy from the torrent of blows. As he lay there covering his head with his arms the women moved in and began to kick. They wore big wooden clogs and they kicked mercilessly, screaming, 'Sale Boche. Sale Boche'. Too weak and dispirited to fight back any more Hill writhed on the dusty road. A few more head kicks and he knew they would certainly kill him. He saw the clogs coming again, felt a paralysing blow on the forehead, and then he knew no more.

When Hill opened his eyes he was still lying on the road

but his head was in the lap of a French Air Force Commandant. The major and his men had gone and the peasants who had beaten him up were standing contritely around him talking in hushed whispers. He looked up, recognized the Commandant's face and was puzzled. Then he remembered who he was: he had known him when he had been based near Rouen during the months of the phoney war.

'Hello, Jean,' he said. 'Where do you come in?'

'This is your lucky day, Johnny,' Jean said. 'I am driving past the end of this road. I see a lot of people kicking an object on the ground. I stop my car and come to see what it is all about. And what do I find? The object is an old friend – it is you.'

The commandant told the peasants: 'I know this man; he is Squadron Leader Hill of the Royal Air Force.' Then Hill produced his identity card and they saw that was indeed the name on it. Twice within an hour they had been sure this man was a German, twice it had been proved he was not. How confusing were the issues of war.

Now, however, there were amends to be made. From nearby houses they produced bottles of wine, bunches of flowers, eggs, pots of honey and jam which they pressed upon Hill, apologizing again for their mistake.

For his own protection the commandant had placed Hill under arrest, which was fortunate, for just as he was about to take him back to Lille the British Army made another attempt to claim him. A youthful subaltern arrived in a truck. His colonel, he said, had seen the parachute come down and had ordered the capture of the man on the end of it. The subaltern didn't get his parachutist: loudly cheered by the peasants, Hill drove off in the commandant's car, back to rejoin the R.A.F.

An experience of a very different kind terminated the descent of an Australian bomber pilot, 22-year-old Pilot Officer Lionel Rackley. Captain of a 630 Squadron Lancaster, he took off from East Kirkby in Lincolnshire on the night of June 21, 1944, along with 129 other Lancasters of 5 Group, Bomber Command, to attack an industrial target at Wesseling on the Rhine, just south of Cologne. Thirty-seven of the bombers did not return. And Rackley's was nearly one of them.

Over the target the aircraft was shot up by a German night fighter and its control surfaces badly damaged. 'We set off for home', says Rackley, 'and as we went three things became very clear. First, with luck we would reach England – our engines were still intact. Second, there could be no question of controlling the aircraft for a landing – we would have to bale out. Third, the rear gunner's parachute pack had been hit by a shell and was useless. And there was no spare chute for him.'

Back over England decisions had to be taken fast. The Lancaster had now become uncontrollable and Rackley gave the order to bale out. The bomb aimer, Doug Morgan, offered to attempt a jump taking the rear gunner with him. While the two men stood face to face the crew roped them together. The gunner clung to Morgan with arms and legs and together they dropped out of the forward hatch.

But, as on so many wartime double jumps, this one failed. The moment the chute snapped open the sudden deceleration broke the ropes, the two men lost their grip on each other and the gunner fell away. Subsequently Morgan was awarded the British Empire Medal for his brave attempt.

Meanwhile the other crew members jumped and Rackley followed them out into the night. From 10,000 feet he could see a layer of cloud far below. 'For some time I didn't seem to be getting any nearer the cloud. The illusion was so strong I convinced myself I was being carried upwards not downwards.'

The cloud layer was shallow. When he reached it Rackley dropped through in seconds. And landed on a moving train. Of the moments that followed he has only a brief memory for he was soon knocked unconscious.

What he didn't know was that his parachute was entangled on one of the carriages of a passenger train travelling at some speed from Luton to London.

'All I knew was that I was being dragged along at a terrific rate and rattling beside my ears was the distinctive sound of train wheels. I was being bumped about violently, but

63

for some odd reason it didn't seem to hurt; nor was I aware of any fear.'

Then Rackley blacked out. How far he was dragged he will never know. But at some point he was saved by the quick-release box on his parachute harness. It was smashed, allowing the parachute to be ripped off his body.

'The next I recall was wandering along a railway line. It was still dark. I hadn't the least idea where I was. I had lost my flying boots, my parachute had disappeared, my head was bleeding, and I couldn't move my right arm.'

It was another train that rescued Rackley. A slow moving goods train. He waved it down and a suspicious train crew, not wholly convinced he was not an enemy airman, put him in the guard's van and took him to a signal box from where an ambulance collected him.

Of the parachute? 'I later heard that it had travelled all the way to London. It caused quite a commotion on arrival at the terminal? They sent a search party back up the line. But the owner was by then in bed in the Luton and Dunstable hospital.'

Today, back in Queensland, Lionel Rackley, DFC, over 30 years after the event, is still a very active 'caterpillar'. He is a member of the locally formed 'Brisbane Group' of the Club. Its 30 members meet once a year for a re-union dinner. And 90 miles away in Toowoomba there's another such group. The Queensland 'caterpillars' often wonder if among the widely dispersed brotherhood of the Club there are other groups. They know of none.

CHAPTER V

When aircrew first began to carry parachutes the question was often asked: What is the lowest safe height for jumping?

There is no rule of thumb method for deciding whether or not a certain height is safe or unsafe for jumping. It depends on many factors. Men have been killed who did not get their chutes open during a fall from 1,000 feet; a few have landed uninjured after bale-outs from below 100 feet. The aircraft's speed, its flight attitude, the height of the ground above sea level, the air temperature, the weight of the man, the delay in pulling the ripcord, and the way the man leaves the aircraft – all these things may influence the distance he falls before his parachute is fully open and supporting him; all these things may add or subtract the fractions of a second which at low level can mean the difference between life and death.

Before opening his parachute, a man falls at about 175 feet a second – 120 miles an hour – when he has reached terminal velocity (once his parachute has checked his fall he descends at a sedate 19-21 feet a second – about 11 miles an hour). At that speed the cushioning effect of the air created by his passage through it balances the pull of gravity and no matter how far he drops he falls no faster. If he somersaults as he falls his body offers greater resistance to the air and his terminal speed might be only 160 feet a second. (If his body is in a flat spin, it can be as low as 100 feet a second; in a vertical dive, as high as 300 feet a second). Baling out in the tropics where the air is warmer and less dense he would fall faster than 175 feet a second; so would he, too, if he jumped at high altitude where, again, the air is less dense, although as he fell towards lower levels his rate of fall would slow down to about 175 feet a second.

A parachute that is dry and has been freshly repacked will open fully in from one to two seconds of pulling the ripcord. Theoretically then, a chute pulled at the moment of leaving the aircraft and allowing for the time taken to pull the ripcord, should be open in less than 100 feet. But such a swift opening carries with it the risk of the chute fouling part of the aircraft; so that allowing a second or two to clear the tail assembly the lowest safe height for exit from an aircraft in straight and level flight could be put at around 300 or 400 feet.

The faster the aircraft is travelling the quicker the chute will open. Because a man leaves an aircraft at its speed, in the seconds while the momentum is still carrying him forward and before he is falling vertically under the effect of gravity alone, the force of the air from this forward speed will inflate the canopy much more swiftly and more violently than it would if he were merely falling free at 120 miles an hour. If, however, the aircraft is diving towards the ground then the intitial speed it will impart to him will almost certainly exceed 120 miles an hour and the margin of time left for getting the chute open may be greatly reduced; even 1,000 feet might be too low in these circumstances.

But in moments of crisis in the air, aircrew, although they are fully aware of these margins, often prefer to take a chance on an exceedingly low jump than face the certainty of death in a burning or uncontrollable aircraft. And so it was that during the war there came to the Caterpillar Club from time to time reports of bale-outs from heights so low that in some cases, but for the word of witnesses, they might not have been believed.

Such was the jump of Flight Lieutenant Dudley Davis, a Hampden pilot of No. 61 Squadron. In the early hours of July 21, 1940, a few seconds after he had dropped a mine under the German battleship *Tirpitz* in Wilhelmshaven harbour, an Irvin chute brought him down from his burning aeroplane – from 50 feet.

A serious lean-faced young man with a big bushy black moustache, Davis looked a good deal older than his 27 years. He had joined the R.A.F. as a sergeant pilot in 1935 and by June 1940 was one of the few original pilots left in 61 Squadron which had been formed three years earlier.

On the night of July 20, he and two other pilots were detailed to attack the *Tirpitz*. The mines they carried were timed to explode an hour after release and to make sure they went under the ship they were briefed to drop them from 50 feet above the water.

The three Hampdens took off separately from Hemswell in Lincolnshire around 10 o'clock. It was a bright moonlit night and apart from some isolated flak, the journey to the target, where they were due to arrive at eight-minute intervals, was uneventful. They went into Germany near the Ems estuary and from Emden flew the remaining 50 miles to Wilhelmshaven at low level to avoid detection by enemy radar. They knew that the *Tirpitz* was heavily protected and that the surrounding docks and harbour bristled with flak guns but they were relying on a high-level diversionary bombing attack, timed to begin a few minutes before their arrival, to distract the defending fire.

Unfortunately unexpected winds upset the timing between the two attacks: when the three Hampdens came in towards Wilhelmshaven from the north during the half hour after midnight, the diversionary raid was over and the guns were able to give them undivided attention.

As he swept in low over the rooftops of the town Davis, who was the last to arrive, saw streams of flak pouring towards him in glowing red lines; no amount of weaving could avoid them. Again and again the Hampden was hit and long before the docks came in sight the aircraft was on fire.

At last he was clear of the town and only a few yards of dark oily water separated him from the square inland dock in which he could see the huge grey bulk of the *Tirpitz*. The Hampden's fuel tanks were blazing now and Davis was aware of an uncomfortable heat underneath him. But still he kept the aircraft's nose heading for the target and because the mine was liable to break up or bounce if dropped too fast he closed the throttles, glided down to within a few feet of the water, losing speed as he ran in under a spray of tracer.

About 100 yards from the *Tirpitz* he pressed the release button and the mine splashed into the water close beside it. The ship's superstructure was above him now and he pushed the throttles wide open, hauled back on the control column and climbed over it. His one desire was to get down low near the water on the other side and away through the outer harbour. But the Hampden was done for. The controls had become sloppy and the fire was spreading; flames were spurting up through the cockpit floor and a long fiery trail streamed away in the moonlight behind them.

Out of the corner of his eye he could see roofs and spires and cranes above him close by on the shore to starboard. The mast of a small craft rushed towards him and he winced as it slid by inches only below the wing. And then all 'feel' went from the control column. He closed the throttles. There seemed nothing helpful to say to the others behind; it was too low to order them to jump, tracer was still slamming into them, and they were almost in the sea.

Of the next half-minute Davis has only vague and disconnected memories. He remembers noticing that the control column had gone limp – in fact the whole tail had been almost shot off – and had flopped forward and to one side. As a last hopeless gesture he reached down to try and exert some control with the trim wheel but the heat that welled up from the floor drove his hand back. From every direction searing heat seemed to envelop him and there was so much smoke in the cockpit he could not see.

Suddenly a great flower of flame rose up round him. The cabin behind him was an inferno and he knew there was nothing he could do for the others in there. He could stand the heat no longer. Quickly he slid the hood open and the next thing he recalls was crouching on the starboard wing hanging on to the cockpit edge savouring the cool, strong wash of the airflow and shouting abuse at the Germans. He was surprised to see that the Hampden was still airborne but from the feel of the aircraft he knew that it was close to the stall and couldn't be in the air much longer.

His thoughts fuddled by the heat he had endured and by the merciless fire which the flak batteries continued to pump into his dying aeroplane, he was suddenly obsessed with the idea that if he could stretch inside the cockpit and reach the flap lever he might be able to lessen the impact of ditching. But as quickly as the thought came to him he realized the utter futility of it. Then the aircraft began to roll to starboard and he knew the end had come.

He pulled the ripcord. He cannot remember clearly why, because he knew the Hampden was no more than 50 feet above the water; knew, too, that the intercom wires from his helmet and the oxygen tube from his mask were still connected to the cockpit. But just the same, he pulled it. And as he did so the wildly improbable thought came to him that if he clung to the cockpit wall as it opened, the drag of the chute might stall the Hampden on to a German ship and set fire to it. (Looking back on that inspiration later, Davis said: 'You must forgive this apparent lack of understanding of aerodynamics, but it was extremely hot and my personal war effort was running at high boost at that moment!')

The parachute streamed back in the slipstream, the canopy filled, and he was snatched backwards off the wing. His back struck part of the aircraft and a second later he hit something hard and found he was lying on his side on a stone mole which projected out into the sea. His 'descent' had been but a brief pendulum-like swing, down off the wing, under his canopy and on to the ground.

For a moment or two he lay there not fully comprehending that he was alive. And then he stood up. Incredibly, apart from a few bruises and a minor face burn which had destroyed most of his moustache, he was unhurt. A few yards off the end of the mole the Hampden was ablaze in the water and he watched it with twisted emotions thinking sadly of the others of his crew who were dead and of the miracle that had brought him down alive. Behind him he heard the ring of boots on the cobbles and he turned round to face the German soldiers who were to lead him away to five years' captivity.

But before he left the dock area he had the satisfaction of hearing a deep explosion from the harbour; his mine hadn't failed him. Later, in prison camp, he learnt that both the other Hampdens had also been shot down and that some of the crew of each had survived.

It was not until 1945 when Davis had returned to England that he wrote to the Caterpillar Club to apply for, as he put it, 'half a caterpillar, or perhaps one with one foot on the ground!' And Irvin, writing to congratulate him, said: 'I can only say that you must consider yourself extremely lucky that the chute operated as fast as it did . . . I would not suggest that you repeat your performance except in dire necessity!'

The only other men the Club knows of who have survived bale-outs from below 100 feet, without ejection seats, owe only partial thanks to their parachutes. For their chutes did not have time to open fully and their falls were providentially checked by other means. Which introduces the story of Flight Lieutenant C. A. R. Crews and Leading Aircraftman T. Evans.

Crews was a flight commander in No. 218 Squadron and Evans was his wireless operator/air gunner. In the spring of 1940 the squadron, then equipped with Fairey Battles, was based at Auberive, near Rheims. The German armies were streaming into Belgium and Holland when, on May 11, Crews was ordered to lead a low-level bombing attack on a vital bridge on the invasion route, two miles north of St. Vith on the German-Belgian frontier. He took off at 10 a.m. with Evans and a sergeant navigator, in formation with one other Battle.

The flight north-east across the flat plain of Champagne and over the wooded folds of the Ardennes was uneventful at first but about 30 miles from the target where their track began to cross the German convoy routes, the two aircraft came under heavy fire from enemy light and medium anti-aircraft guns. The slow obsolescent Battles made an all too splendid target for the German gunners and presently Crews had his instrument panel smashed by a long burst from machine-gun fire. But they pressed on and after a lot more peppering by accurate ack-ack were soon within sight of the bridge they had come to destroy.

Crews signalled to his No. 2 to turn for the run-in to the target. As he did so another burst of anti-aircraft fire hit him. Flames and glycol poured from a big hole behind the engine and burning petrol streamed back along the cockpit floor under his seat. A great stifling wave of heat swamped him and his throat and lungs felt as if they were being seared with a hot knife. They were over rolling wooded country and he knew that to put down, on fire, on the tree tops would be suicidal. Better, despite the pitifully little height they had, to jump for it.

With both hands he pulled back on the control column, shouting through the intercom: 'Bale out – bale out!'

Holding the stick hard back with his knees, Crews reached

70

up and slid the hood back. Out of the corner of his eye he could see a long wooded slope whose summit was above them and it was then that he realized that the engine had lost power and they were gaining almost no height at all. With the hood open the flames gushed up, burning his legs and face. To escape them he stood up on his seat with his body half out in the slipstream, still pressing the stick back with his left hand, in a last despairing effort to wheedle some precious height out of his aircraft. But when he glanced down he was appalled to see that they were still no more than 200 or 300 feet above the trees and he knew then that they would go no higher.

The slipstream buffeting his face seemed to revive him and in the last seconds as he crouched half in half out of the cockpit his thoughts were clear and ordered. There was no fear, just cold objective reasoning that told him presently he must jump and that from that height it meant the end. The Battle was beginning to behave sluggishly as it approached stalling point. He looked back and saw the others climbing out. As he did so the starboard wing began to drop so he stepped quickly out on to the wing root, seized his ripcord handle and pulled it as he dived off, praying that the chute wouldn't foul the tail plane.

As he fell, Crews saw Evans dropping ahead of him and then a dark wall of green curved up to meet him. Instinctively he shut his eyes; about two seconds later he hit the trees. There was no noise – all he felt was a burning on his face as pine needles scraped the skin, then a tremendous jolt, then silence. He opened his eyes.

Six feet from the ground he was hanging on his rigging lines held from the top branches of a pine tree by the half-opened canopy. Two yards away in the next tree was Evans suspended in precisely the same way.

For a moment they stared at each other, two shocked, bruised, dangling figures neither yet grasping the full miracle of their deliverance. Evans was the first to find words. 'Christ,' he said awesomely, 'that will teach me to go flying without my white elephant.' (The elephant was a tiny lucky

71

charm he never normally flew without; on this trip he had forgotten it.)

It was then that they saw the navigator. He lay on open ground between them and the burning pyre of the aircraft which was only 30 feet away, and he was dead. Crews and Evans released themselves from their harness and dropped out of the trees.

Apart from minor cuts and bruises neither was injured. They walked over to the navigator. He had been killed instantly. His parachute had streamed but hadn't had time to open. As they stood looking down at his body they realized for the first time how generously luck had served them. For the three of them had left the aircraft together. They had all been too low for their chutes to open enough to break their fall. The trees had saved two of them. But where the navigator had plummeted down less then 15 feet away there was no tree. Such were the margins between life and death.

Crews and Evans tried to get back through German-held territory to the Allied lines. They didn't make it and spent the rest of the war prisoners.

In the small hours of August 8, 1944, an R.A.F. Wellington of No. 70 Squadron having deposited a 4,000 lb. bomb on Zombathely airfield, 150 miles west of Budapest, was hurrying away south-westwards across the Hungarian plain on the long journey back across Yugoslavia to its base at Foggia in Southern Italy. It was a bright moonlit night and the pilot, Flying Officer H. W. James, all too aware of the target the slow bulk of the Wellington presented to the defending night fighters, had dived away from the airfield to get clear of the area as quickly as possible; as the last aircraft in the main bomber stream he felt particularly vulnerable.

But the Wellington's luck was out that night. A few miles from the target the fighters caught it and although the rear gunner, 37-year-old Sergeant Henry Whittaker, who had been a policeman in Birmingham before joining up, shot one down after a long duel, another fighter came up from underneath and poured a stream of cannon shells into them. Fire which they could not control broke out on the under side of the fuselage and James gave the order: 'Prepare to abandon ship.'

Whittaker climbed out of his turret, crawled back into the fuselage to collect his parachute from its stowage, clipped his chute on and wriggled back into the turret ready to bale out through it as soon as he heard the executive command. He sat there for perhaps half a minute feeling the heat of the fire behind him, his turret filling with bitter-smelling smoke, watching the ground, very near, flashing by in all too close detail in the moonlight below. If he didn't jump soon, he thought, it would be pointless baling out at all for as best he could judge they were below 200 feet. At first he decided not to bother the pilot, but then as his anxiety grew he flicked on his microphone switch and called, 'Rear gunner calling skipper—' Immediately James's voice snapped back – 'Haven't you gone, Harry? Get out, get out!' Whittaker asked, 'Have the others gone?' and James said, 'Yes – get out!' Whittaker knew then that he must have missed the order when he had taken his helmet off to collect his chute.

He swung the turret round. Through the smoke he saw trees zipping by almost it seemed as high as the aircraft. For a second he hesitated. He was convinced it was suicide to jump. Then a wave of terrible heat hit him and he hesitated no longer.

Backwards, he fell clear of the turret. And as he somersaulted both hands went to the parachute on his chest: with his right he pulled the ripcord and as the silk burst out he seized a handful with his left and flung it over his shoulders in a desperate attempt to speed the process of opening.

But the chute had only begun to stream when he hit the trees. His journey down from the aircraft had been like a dive from the top spring board at a swimming bath – certainly it had taken no longer. As he crashed through the branches he had only one thought: that at all costs he must keep his legs together. He waited for the terrible bump of the ground – but it did not come. Instead there was a powerful jerk and he felt as if his shoulders had snapped: he had stopped falling and was swinging on the end of his half-opened parachute high up in a tall pine tree. A moment later he heard the explosion of the crashed Wellington – 15 seconds at the most after he had left it.

Whittaker undid his harness and tried to pull the parachute down from the branch on which it had hooked. He wanted to hide it and leave no trace of his arrival in Hungary. But the chute was too firmly caught up and in the end he had to climb down to the ground without it.

He stood there in the pine wood for a few minutes collecting his wits. His right arm seemed to have lost all its strength but otherwise he was unhurt. 'I had a feeling of elation not unmixed with awe that I had come through so miraculously,' he says. 'Although I knew I was in the heart of enemy territory, at least 200 miles from Marshal Tito's forces in Yugoslavia, I was not afraid because I felt so strongly that the Power that had brought me down against a million-to-one chance would not desert me now.' Unfortunately for Whittaker it did.

He made his way out of the pine wood to a road from where he could see the flames from the burning Wellington, leaping above the pines about half a mile away. He looked at it for a moment, knowing that James could not have survived, then walked off along the road in the direction which he judged must lead to Yugoslavia. Presently he came to a village. 'It looked so beautiful and enchanting in the moonlight,' he says, 'that hungry and tired as I was, I felt for one brief moment like going down there and giving myself up, as I reasoned that people living in such a beautiful place could not fail to be kind and decent.' But the temptation did not last and he took to the woods again to bypass the village. He had travelled several miles through the pines and it was daylight when he heard sounds of rustling and tugging in the trees ahead of him. He stopped and listened. It sounded, he thought, as if someone was pulling a parachute down; probably another R.A.F. man. He crept nearer. A Hungarian policeman stepped from behind a tree and prodded him with a bayoneted rifle. It *was* a parachute the police were hauling down; it belonged to a British airman they had already captured. And Whittaker went to join him in custody.

Of the other four members of his crew that night two, who baled out at 500 feet, came down safely. Flying Officer James stayed with the aircraft to give the others a chance; he was killed in the crash. The bomb aimer got out with more height to spare than Whittaker but was not so lucky. He fell into the same pinewood but no tree hooked his streaming parachute and he was killed.

It was from a Hampden of No. 61 Squadron at Wilhelmshaven that Flight Lieutenant Davis made probably the lowest of all wartime bale-outs and it was from a Hampden of the same squadron that nine months later Warrant Officer Ken Downing made an equally spectacular escape.

Davis had saved his life from 50 feet because his chute had all but fully developed in the slipstream before he was plucked off the wing; it was a 'pull off' and although he didn't appreciate it at the time, it was the only way he could have been saved from that height. Downing came down from what many witnesses agreed was no more than 130 feet – with a straight jump.

A wireless operator/air gunner, he was acting as rear gunner in a 61 Squadron Hampden which took part in a daylight shipping attack in Cherbourg Harbour on April 18, 1941. The German naval base at Cherbourg was heavily defended – not a healthy spot in daylight. But on the day of this operation the attacking force had the protection of a cloud blanket with its base down to 900 feet over the French coast.

The Hampdens flew from Watton in Norfolk. The first one airborne was detailed to attack an airfield near the naval base to interfere with defending fighter operations and this as it happened was the aircraft in which Downing was flying.

They broke cloud close to the Cherbourg Peninsula, found the airfield, and went in at 850 feet bombing the fighters where they sat like sitting ducks in the dispersals. The Germans may not have been expecting them but they were none the less ready and as the lone Hampden swept across the airfield dropping its bombs intense anti-aircraft fire opened up at it. When the last bomb had gone the pilot called up the navigator for a course home and pulled up to escape into the cloud. He had almost made it when a shell thudded into the port engine which immediately began to stream fire. The remotely controlled fire extinguisher in the engine failed to check it and Downing heard the pilot call, over the intercom: 'I'm going to have a crack at landing her – anyone who wants to can bale out.'

Immediately Downing said he was going. He knew that a belly landing in a Hampden was a risky proposition at the best of times for the rear gunner; he knew that it sometimes tore the bomb bays and rear gunner's position right off. So he clipped on his parachute and pulled the jettison wire on the main door.

He had known the doors jettison in flight when the wires had been given the merest accidental touch. Now that he wanted to get out of that door quicker than ever before no amount of pulling on the wire would release it. He stopped pulling, sat down on the floor with his back braced against the opposite side of the fuselage and kicked. Still the door would not open. And he knew that all the time they were losing height and his chances were growing slimmer and slimmer. Fiercely he kicked again. With a whoosh the door disappeared. Downing slid quickly out, pulling his ripcord as he went.

His head just missed the tail plane and although his chute was already streaming, it cleared the aircraft. He did not see the ground for he was facing upwards, but he knew it was dangerously close. He had scarcely cleared the aircraft when he felt a jolt and his harness tightened. For a second or two he blacked out.

When he opened his eyes he was sitting on the ground. He was alive. Less than ten yards away on the other side of a hedge was the burning wreck of the Hampden. His parachute, which could only have opened a fraction of a second before he hit the ground, was lying through a gap in the hedge and was so close to the Hampden that the top of the canopy was already on fire.

76

Downing looked round to see if any other parachutes lay near him. There was none and he knew that he alone had survived – with, he presently discovered, a broken right thigh and leg. It was he reckoned, in the circumstances, a small price.

He lay, he saw, in deep soft mud among tiny pools of water where the rain had filled up the impressions left by the cattle. It was the only patch of mud for as far as he could see and looking at the hard ground around him he realized that the mud had saved his life.

As he crawled away from the Hampden's exploding ammunition, a party of German Air Force men came running across the field. They picked him up and he was taken to the naval hospital at Cherbourg there to begin four years behind barbed wire. Next morning the German commander of the Cherbourg air group came to visit him. He had heard from those who had seen him come down that he had baled out at 40 metres and he wanted to congratulate the British airman on this prodigious feat.

CHAPTER VI

While a certain aura of providence inevitably surrounded the survival of men who jumped from below 150 feet there were many equally narrow escapes from low but slightly less hazardous levels. In this category came the abrupt journey to earth of Lieut. Commander P. E. I. Bailey.

In June 1944, when the invasion armies were streaming ashore on to the Normandy beaches, Bailey, a Fleet Air Arm pilot, commanded a squadron of Seafires at Lee-on-Solent. The squadron's D-Day role was bombardment spotting for the naval ships whose guns were supporting the ground forces in their drive inland, a task the squadron quickly found to be not without a certain amount of hazard – not so much from enemy fighters for they were little in evidence, but from the gunfire of the ships with whom the Seafires were co-operating. The first day of the invasion several Seafires had been mistaken for enemy fighters and had narrowly avoided the galling experience of being shot down by their own side.

On the second day, D plus one, when Bailey flew across the Channel from Lee-on-Solent in company with another Seafire, it was, therefore, with some apprehension that he approached the ships he was to spot for off the coast near Le Hamel between Boulogne and Dieppe. And his misgivings were well justified for no sooner were they within range of the first ships than they were vigorously fired upon. Quickly they turned round and flew out to sea again.

Although Bailey was not to know it the fleet had been strafed a few minutes earlier by Focke-Wulf 190s and the gunnery officers were understandably sensitive at that moment to approaching aircraft.

Curtly Bailey called up on his R/T and asked the ships to hold their fire. He couldn't name the ship that had shot at them but one of the headquarters ships promised to pass his message. Again the Seafires flew in. Again the same ships fired at them and once more they retreated seawards. A trifle more abruptly this time Bailey spoke to the headquarters ship; he was told to wait ten minutes before trying again.

When the ten minutes were up they made their third run in, flying at 900 feet just below the grey lid of cloud which lay over the Channel. Confident now that they were safe, they flew in straight and level, passing over a heavily armed anti-aircraft cruiser. The cruiser waited until they were directly overhead; then it let go with everything it had.

The guns couldn't miss. Bailey's Seafire was sprayed with metal. Shell after shell tore through it, banging against the armour plating, puncturing his fuselage and wings, carving his tail off and setting fire to the belly drop tank.

As the tail broke off his nose went down and he began to dive, out of control, towards the beach. He grabbed the small round ball which operated the hood jettison but the hood was damaged and wouldn't fly off. He began to tug at it with his hands. Almost grudgingly it opened about nine inches and then jammed. He glanced at the altimeter

– 400 feet. The dive was steepening; he was going down almost vertically now. He thrust his head out of the narrow gap he had opened, thinking that perhaps he could force his shoulder through. But he could not.

And so he sat there with his head out in the slipstream waiting to die. In those seconds as the ground came up towards him he noticed that the sun had broken through the cloud and was shining on the beach. There was none of the equipment of invasion on that part of it and with the fatalistic calm that had come over him he thought how serenely beautiful it looked.

At about 250 feet, pointless as the gesture seemed, he pulled his ripcord. He knew it couldn't save him but just the same he pulled it; as he did so there was a tremendous bang. He felt his harness jerk tight, heard his chute crack open and realized he was lying on the beach, half in half out of the water. The drop tank which had all but emptied on the flight across from England and which was by then filled mainly with vapour, had exploded; the aircraft had disintegrated and he had been blown out. But Baily reconstructed all that later. All he remembered at the time was in swift succession the bang, the jolt as his chute opened, and the bump as he hit the beach.

Before he could meditate on the mechanics of his salvation, the wind filled his canopy and he was hauled off along the beach, dragged on his back over the sand. And as he went he heard several sharp, vicious cracks and realized to his dismay that he was in a minefield. They were small anti-personnel mines attached to stakes near the water's edge but fortunately the canopy exploded them before he reached them.

At last he managed to collapse the canopy and stop his runaway chute. He undid his harness and stood up, surprised to find that he had emerged uninjured. A group of British beach commandos armed with tommy-guns came running down the beach towards him. Deeply distrustful now of Allied firearms Bailey raised his arms high above his head until they reached him. They regarded him suspiciously but he wasn't aware of that at first. The reaction was setting in and he was seething with bitter resentment at what his own Navy had done to him. He could see the cruiser that had shot him down lying offshore and he badly wanted to get out there and meet its gunnery officer face to face. That was impossible, but then he noticed that one of the commandos was a signaller. He called him over and ordered him to make a signal to the ship from the commanding officer of 886 Squadron congratulating the gunnery officer on his easy kill and adding: 'It is no fault of yours I am still alive.' The signaller began to click out the message on his Aldis lamp and Bailey felt better.

By now more troops had arrived and for the first time Bailey became aware of the atmosphere of distrust in the little group which surrounded him. When he demanded to be taken to the nearest naval authority a private truculently countered with, 'Who are you anyway?' He said, 'I am Lieutenant Commander Bailey of the Fleet Air Arm.' There were sniggers at this and one of the men said, 'That's very funny – you Germans haven't got an Air Arm.' And then Bailey realized that the black flying overalls he was wearing and the fact that he had been shot down by a British ship must certainly have made it appear that he was a German.

Angrily he shouted, 'Don't be bloody stupid – go and find somebody responsible,' but the men only retreated a few paces and pointed their tommy-guns threateningly at him. Then one them said, 'If you're not a German identify yourself then'. He had no answer to that because he hadn't been wearing an identity disc that morning and such pieces of British equipment as his pistol and maps he had lost when the aircraft broke up. He thought of the Seafire, but it had exploded into so many small pieces there was no sign of it.

Incensed by this second indignity he had suffered within the space of ten minutes and protesting volubly, Bailey was marched up the beach, then a short distance inland to a temporary wire cage. Inside sat about 150 disgruntled-looking German prisoners, some of them shell-shocked and wounded. Bailey was put among them.

For some time he stood by the wire complaining loudly

about the injustice of being shot down and locked up by one's own side but he was ignored. Then a German officer in the cage came over to him, commiserated with him in faultless English and called to the guards that Bailey was indeed not a German. The guards just laughed and went on patrolling the wire.

Bailey spent two hours in the cage. It was not until he caught the attention of the first British officer he had seen that morning that he was taken out of the cage and marched into the presence of a brigadier. The brigadier did some telephoning and presently having satisfied himself that Bailey was the man he purported to be, he ordered his release. Next day Bailey returned to England in an L.S.T.

Saved by an explosion at low-level but in a different way was Sergeant Roger Peacock. He was the mid-upper gunner in an R.A.F. Blenheim which was returning to base from a night raid on Jever, near Wilhelmshaven, in July 1940. Near Oldenburg the aircraft was badly shot up by flak, both engines stopped, the pilot gave the order to bale out and, assuming that Peacock had gone, he and the observer jumped.

That was at 6,500 feet. At about 4,000 feet, Peacock who had not heard the order and who was sitting uneasily in his turret as the Blenheim went down in a slow spiral dive, began to wonder if the pilot was going to recover in time. He called up on the intercom, 'Ready to go. Shall I bale out now?' There was no reply, so he repeated the question. Still no answer.

Assuming that the two men in front were too busy for conversation, he decided not to bother them for a while. He sat there for what seemed a very long time, listening to the whirr of the windmilling propellers, patiently waiting for a voice to speak in his helmet phones.

At about 1,000 feet he could contain himself no longer. *'Shall I bale out now?'* he demanded. This time he was worried by the silence. Perhaps they needed help up front. He took off his parachute, laid it on the floor, and went forward to the cockpit to investigate. The two seats were empty. Only then did he realize that he was alone in the aircraft.

81

Through the windscreen he saw the ground, very close, revolving below. He scrambled back for his parachute, clipped it on, and knelt down beside the small escape hatch in the floor. The altimeter beside him showed 450 feet. He could see the shapes of the trees, even in the darkness, now.

Stay and be killed instantly: jump and be terribly injured? For a second or two he was undecided. Then on an impulse, he jumped.

As he fell away he saw the black carpet of the ground so close he knew he had jumped too late. But then a fantastic thing happened. As his parachute began to stream and the ground rushed up, the Blenheim crashed under him and exploded.

A blinding orange flash lit up the ground for hundreds of yards around and Peacock felt a great upsurge of hot air. A few feet from the ground the blast snapped his canopy fully open and blew him *upwards* and sideways away from the blazing aircraft. When he landed safely a few moments later he was some distance from the wreckage, in another field.

Although he had been the last to bale out, Peacock was the first down. In the spiralling aircraft he had overtaken the pilot and observer. The former, who must have left the aircraft at the same point on the spiral as he had done, but 6,000 feet higher up, landed close to him about five minutes later. The observer, who had gone out at another point on the spiral, landed in a ditch several miles away.

Sometimes the topography of the ground over which they baled out saved 'caterpillars' who jumped at unsafe heights. In December 1942, Sergeant F. W. R. Cumpsty, a New Zealander, was in an R.A.F. Wellington on a training flight from No. 11 Operational Training Unit, Westcott. The aircraft crashed in the Welsh mountains near Fishguard. Just before it hit, Cumpsty baled out – 50 feet above a mountain top. A gale-force wind was blowing and he was carried clear of the high ground into a valley. His chute opened and he landed safely 200 feet below the peak.

Flying Officer Alan Law, a South African serving with the R.A.F., also owes his life to a valley. In November 1941, he was giving dual instruction to a pupil in a Hind at Waterkloof, a South African Air Force station near Pretoria. Eight hundred feet above the airfield as they were approaching to land, another aircraft, an Audax, collided with them and the two aircraft, locked together, began to spin down. The two occupants of the Audax and Law's pupil were killed instantly. Law, unhurt, struggled out past the wings which had folded back over the cockpit, and jumped clear. He was then 400 feet above the airfield.

People on the airfield saw him fall, but as his parachute didn't open immediately they thought he hadn't a chance. He was about 50 feet from the ground when the first white puff of silk appeared behind him, and then he disappeared from sight. They ran across expecting to find him dead. But Law hadn't landed on the airfield. The edge of the field was on the crest of a hill and he had dropped into the adjoining valley, missing the crest by a few yards. They found him alive and unhurt 50 feet down on the floor of the valley side. His chute which had only begun to stream when he disappeared from view, had just had time to open in the extra 50 feet which fate had given him.

Of the thousands of bomber crews who were shot down over Europe by flak, few ever had the doubtful privilege of meeting the man whose gun had ended their active participation in the war. One man who did was Sergeant Joseph Cashmore, a flight engineer in No. 90 Squadron who baled out from below 300 feet.

Cashmore was in a Stirling which, on the moonlit night of March 4, 1944, was bound for a dropping zone in the Upper Savoy district of France with a load of sabotage equipment for the Maquis. Halfway across France, between Bourges and Nevers, the Stirling, which was flying at 300 feet to avoid radar detection, was caught by searchlights and came under heavy anti-aircraft fire. Part of the rudder was shot away, both starboard engines were hit and put out of action, and the outboard fuel tank in the port wing was set ablaze.

The pilot, unable to take any effective evasive action at that height, gave the order 'Abandon aircraft', but almost immediately, remembering how low they were, he cancelled the command with 'No, no – wait.' He tried to pull the Stirling up a few hundred feet but the aircraft wouldn't climb and a moment later he shouted over the intercom 'Bale! bale!'In quick succession each member of the crew briskly acknowledged the order and prepared to leave.

Cashmore clipped on his parachute and went back to the rear floor escape hatch. There he found the mid-upper gunner, Flight Sergeant James Buchanan, an Australian, wrestling with the hatch, unable to open it. In desperation, Cashmore pulled him away, kicking the locking handles until they broke off, and presently he and Buchanan stood facing each other over the square opening through which they could see the snow-covered ground rushing by in the moonlight. But then, although both knew that the aircraft was losing height and that every second they remained reduced their chances of survival, they indulged in the time-honoured courtesy of insisting that the other go first.

'After you,' said Buchanan who felt that having forced the hatch open Cashmore was entitled to be first out.

'No, after you,' Cashmore shouted back.

'After you,' Buchanan persisted.

'Come on, after *you*,' Cashmore yelled again, with an impatient gesture towards the hole, and Buchanan jumped.

Cashmore was about to follow him but then he changed his mind. Something about the way the aircraft was now flying suggested to him that perhaps it wasn't going to crash after all. Thinking that he might be able to help the pilot he went forward and climbed into the mid-upper turret to see if the fire was still burning on the port wing. What he saw sent him hurrying back to the hatch; the entire port wing was one fiercely burning mass; it was ablaze from the tip of the fuselage and flames were pouring back beyond the tail. Before he could reach the hole in the floor he felt the Stirling's nose pitch down and he knew it was in its last dive from 300 feet. The negative *g* swung his feet off the floor and he had to claw his way back gripping the ammunition feeder belts on the top of the fuselage for support. When at last he reached the hatch and sat on the edge looking down, the ground looked so close he couldn't decide for a moment whether to jump or stay with the aircraft and hope that the pilot would make a satisfactory crash landing.

Fortunately for Cashmore he jumped. He pulled the rip-cord and looking up, saw the rigging lines paying out, so slowly he thought it didn't seem possible that the canopy could develop in time. Then he felt a sharp jerk as the harness tightened between his thighs and a thud, after which he knew no more.

When he revived and found that he was unhurt he saw that he owed his life to the fact that he had landed in a depression which contained the only patch of deep snow in the whole field. The Stirling had crashed half a mile away; he could see it burning and hear the crackle of its exploding ammunition. Not until later did Cashmore learn that the pilot, the only man in the crew who did not save his life by jumping, had been killed in the crash.

Cashmore linked up with the French Underground but was captured, escaping, near the Swiss frontier. In 1946 after his return to England, he was appointed Warrant Officer-in-charge of an enemy prisoner-of-war camp at Melbourne in Yorkshire. One day he got into conversation with one of the prisoners, Unteroffizier Heinz Ulrich. When Ulrich learnt that he had flown in Stirlings he told Cashmore with some pride that he had been awarded an Iron Cross for shooting a Stirling down in 1944. He had been N.C.O.-in-charge of an anti-aircraft gun in France, he said. When Cashmore heard that it was March 4, the night of his bale-out, he was so curious he fetched a map and asked Ulrich to show him where he had made his kill. Without hesitation the Unteroffizier pointed to a spot between Bourges and Nevers – precisely on the track the Stirling had been flying that night – and then he pointed to the village of St Hilaire de Sondilly, six miles south-east of his gun position where, he said, the Stirling had crashed; he remembered the incident clearly. This particular Stirling was a lone aircraft and it was flying at about 300 feet. Cashmore asked him what time it was. Ulrich told him. It was almost exactly the time that his aircraft would have been at that point – flying south-east alone at 300 feet. Cashmore knew then that there was little doubt that Heinz Ulrich was the man who had abruptly terminated his flight to the Upper Savoy two years earlier. They became friends and for several years after the war, when Ulrich had gone to live in Berlin, they corresponded regularly.

The loneliest man in the wartime bomber was the rear gunner. Not for him the companionship of the cockpit or the sight of colleagues sharing the routine of flight. His small turret was an outpost in isolation, his only link with the others the intercom through which he could hear the conversations of the men he could not see. Even in an emergency when the aircraft had to be abandoned and those up forward were following each other out through a hatch, his was a lone departure, a backward tumble out of his turret into the night. If a man got stuck or was wounded and needed assistance to make his exit up front there was usually someone to help him out: if the rear gunner was stuck and he had disconnected himself from the intercom he often had to resolve his own salvation. As Flight Sergeant Eric Sanderson did on the night of March 22, 1944.

Rear Gunner of 'R' for Robert, a Halifax of No. 578 Squadron, Sanderson and his crew were on the last operation of their tour. The target was Frankfurt and because it was their last trip, Group Captain N. W. D. Marwood-Elton, D.F.C., their station commander, flew with them as second pilot. Soon after passing Hanover where they turned south for the run down to Frankfurt the bomber stream was assailed by a strong force of enemy fighters.

Looking back from the rear turret Sanderson saw several of the following bombers being attacked and he called over the intercom to warn the pilot that it could only be a matter of time before their number came up. It came a few moments later in the shape of a Ju 88 whose shadowy outline Sanderson spotted lurking under their tail. He called 'Fighter! fighter!' and the pilot began to corkscrew but the German followed the Halifax neatly through every manoeuvre, keeping perfect station below them where none of their guns could reach him. They tried a diving turn hoping to get below the fighter so that Sanderson could get a burst in, but the Ju 88 dived and turned with them. They tried a steep climbing turn; the fighter went up too. And then as a last desperate resort the pilot called that he was going to half roll to give the mid-upper gunner a full downward shot.

The crew braced themselves for this violent manoeuvre; the Halifax dived to pick up speed and then, slowly, with the four engines screaming at full throttle, they climbed and rolled on to their back. For a moment the pilot lost control, and as they wallowed there helpless upside down in the darkness, the fighter raked them with a long burst of cannon fire from amidships to the tail, igniting the incendiaries in the starboard wing bomb-bay. By the time they had righted themselves and regained control, the wing root was ablaze and streaming a long fiery red column. The pilot ordered an emergency bomb jettison but the fire had eaten into the release mechanism and the bombs would not go. Now the fighter came in again for its death thrust; but Sanderson saw him, shouted a warning over the intercom and the pilot weaved away in time.

The inferno on the wing spread quickly to the fuselage and a moment later the crew of 'R' for Robert heard their last flying order of the war – 'Jump! Jump!' The engineer and the mid-upper gunner scrambled back through the flames and out of the main door while the bomb aimer, the navigator, the wireless operator, the Group Captain and the pilot were making their exits through the nose hatch. Presently Sanderson, sitting in the tail with ribbons of flame gushing past his turret, was alone in the aircraft.

One by one he had heard the crew snapping back their acknowledgments of the order to jump. He had added his own cryptic farewell, had collected his parachute pack from its stowage and clipped it on. Then he waited for perhaps half a minute to give the others time to get away, fingering his guns in case the fighter came back. As he sat there with bitter smoke filling his turret he found it hard to accept the fact that they weren't going home that night. It seemed to him grossly unfair that this should happen on the last operation of their tour.

The turret began to tremble violently and he realized that the vibration came from the starboard wing which, weakened by the fire, was beginning to flap. This, and the thought of the bombs still hanging in the bomb-bays, reminded him that it was time to go. The hydraulic system had been damaged so he wound the turret round through 90 degrees by hand until he was facing out to one side of the aircraft with the open back of the turret in the slipstream. Then he leaned back and tried to fall clear.

His body swung down, his back thumped against the outside of the turret – and he hung there, upside down, trapped by his legs. For a moment he dangled there bellowing oaths, angry with himself for his carelessness. There was only one thing to do; climb back and start again. He tried to grasp part of the turret but his hands could not reach it. He tried bouncing up and down, levering his spine against the turret ring, but all the strength seemed to have gone out of his back and after several frantic heavings he gave up and hung there limp and exhausted.

Through his fur-lined flying boots he could not feel precisely how he was trapped, but he assumed that his feet were caught under the dashboard, wedged by the ammunition ducts and control rods. He tried to pull his feet out of his boots but his body was bent backwards like a jack-knife at such an acute angle he had no control over his legs. And all the while he was roasting in the flames which poured back over him, searing his hands and face. Again he tried the bouncing procedure, but he was weak now and with a terrible sense of hopelessness he flopped back knowing he could never get back and knowing that he was going to die.

They had been at 16,000 feet when the bale-out order was given and he wondered which way he would die; whether in the crash, or long before then in the fire – or at any second in the explosion when the bombs went off which he knew they must inevitably do. It was a moonless night and he couldn't see the ground but he could feel that the Halifax was going down very steeply. Of those moments as he was dragged down through the darkness, enveloped in a blast of fire, Sanderson says, 'Strangely enough I felt no terror, had no flashes of my past life. I knew this was the end and I found myself thinking of my widowed mother for I was her only child.'

Ruminating on death Sanderson went down from 16,000 to 1,000 feet. And then came inspiration. Why not pull the ripcord and let his parachute snatch him clear? But then he thought, 'Supposing my feet are too tightly jammed – my legs would be pulled clean off! Life without legs? Surely better to die.'

But almost immediately he had an overpowering urge to live. 'Life is sweet,' he thought – 'with or without legs.' He pulled the ripcord. He didn't know it but he was now below 400 feet.

His chute opened with a crack like a pistol shot, his body suddenly felt as if it had been torn in half, and then with a roaring in his ears he was free, screaming, 'God Almighty, God Almighty' with pain and fear. He looked up, saw that the canopy was fully developed and then, glancing down, saw trees and a second later he knew no more.

He regained consciousness lying on his back in a wood. It was still dark. 'I opened my eyes,' he says, 'but could see nothing. Utter blackness and silence surrounded me – not a star, not a rustle. After the horror of my descent my first thought was "I'm dead". I sincerely believed I had been killed and mixed thoughts crowded through my mind of the soul leaving the body – if a pair of Golden Gates had suddenly appeared it would not have surprised me in my confused state of mind! And then slowly my hearing returned: I heard the sound of water trickling nearby and the drone of an aircraft overhead. My sight came back: out of the blackness I saw a star. The joy of life reclaimed came to me.'

As full consciousness returned, Sanderson's most fearful thoughts were for his legs. He remembered the terrible rending jerk as though he had been torn asunder when he had pulled the ripcord and for a few moments he was afraid to look. He moved his head, then both arms; they were intact, although his shoulder gave him some pain (in fact the jerk which freed him had broken his collar bone) and then he tried to move his legs. But he couldn't and the slow realization came to him that there was no feeling at all below his loins. With growing panic he sat up and looked.

At first in the gloom under the trees he could see nothing where his legs should have been. Then as his eyes focused he saw with horror a tangled twisted mass.

'My legs – oh God!' he cried. Why hadn't he stayed in the turret and died?

Slowly he slid his hand down to explore. He felt his Mae West, then his parachute harness, and inside them, legs and feet, wonderful legs and feet – uninjured. He wanted to shout for joy.

The twisted mess he had mistaken for his legs was his Mae West and harness. The parachute had dragged his feet out of his flying boots and as he had crashed through the trees his Mae West and harness had been torn from his shoulders and had become tightly entwined round his legs. So tightly that all circulation had been stopped, which accounted for the lack of feeling there.

He disentangled himself and stood up. Now that his fears about his legs had been allayed he was conscious for the first time that his face was smarting painfully. Noticing a patch of snow on the ground he picked up a handful and pressed it to his face. The shock cleared his head and relieved the pain; when he looked at the snow he saw that it was stained with blood. He felt his face: it was raw and bleeding from severe burns. And then he saw that the hand holding the snow had what looked like a piece of torn silk glove still hanging on it. He remembered discarding his gloves in the turret and he was puzzled. Only when he began to pull it off did he realize that the 'glove' was a large flap of loose burnt skin.

Painfully he struggled out of his flying suit and because one leg was now giving him pain he crawled on hands and knees towards a clearing he could see some yards away. Beyond the clearing the Halifax was burning and nearby stood four German soldiers. For a few minutes he watched them, enjoying his last moments of freedom. With his burns he knew there could be no question of escape and evasion. He stood up, leaned against a tree for support and shouted:

'Hi! Come here. Englander here, Englander!' The soldiers swung round and ran towards him, rifles at the ready. A lamp was flashed in his face and when the Germans saw the terrible burns there were cluckings and expressions of consternation among them. They picked him up and carried him to a village. And so Sanderson's last operation ended.

In captivity Sanderson met all the others who had baled out of 'R for Robert'; they had landed safely. In prison hospital his face and hands healed and his broken collar bone was set. The pain in his legs was found to be the result of torn ligaments and muscles – the only damage his legs suffered in their violent exit from the turret.

CHAPTER VII

Two principal types of life-saving parachute were used by the men who flew in the last war. They were the seat-type – usually worn by pilots – in which the pack was permanently attached to the harness and hung behind the thighs in such a position that in flight it served as a seat cushion; and the chest type.

With the chest type, the parachute pack was detachable and could be stowed near its owner who merely wore his harness, clipping the pack on his chest only in an emergency. The pack had a pair of metal loops which fitted on to two snap hooks attached to the harness and although it was obviously desirable to engage both loops each of the two connections was strong enough to withstand the opening shock and support a man if for any reason he had to jump with only one loop snapped in position. As the combined weight of harness and pack amounted to more than 22 lb. the chest chute had in one respect an advantage over the other type in that those who used it were not burdened for long hours of flight with a heavy encumbrance.

In other respects though, the chest-type could be a disadvantage. For there were sometimes occasions when disaster struck so swiftly there wasn't even time to reach down and seize it from its stowage – or if it could be reached, no time to clip it on. Usually when this happened the fact of wearing a chute or not didn't make a lot of difference. But there were occasions when bombers exploded and some of those with chutes on were blown clear and pulled their rip-cords. And rarer occasions when men having picked up their packs were blown out – or driven out by fire – still holding them and clipped them on in mid-air.

Flying Officer Rupert North, the navigator of a Ventura of No. 487 (New Zealand) Squadron saved his life in this way on May 3, 1943. It was a disastrous day for the Squadron. Of 11 aircraft which flew out from Methwold in Norfolk to bomb the Amsterdam power station in daylight only one returned; North's Ventura was one of the first to be shot down soon after crossing the Dutch coast.

It was his seventh operation and as it happened he needn't have flown at all that day. He had returned to Methwold the day before from a bombing leaders' course and the navigator who had been taking his place while he had been away was due to fly with his crew. When North discovered this he immediately asked that he be allowed to replace him; his request was granted. As North says, 'For the chap I ousted it was a lucky day.'

With a close escort of Spitfires the Venturas crossed the North Sea in the clear blue afternoon sky; near the Dutch coast they were pounced on by a strong force of enemy fighters. The Spitfires immediately engaged the attackers and in the ensuing battle lost touch with the Venturas. This in itself might not have been disastrous had not another force of fighters, detailed to support the bombers over the target, not reached the area too early and been recalled. Devoid of protection and under orders to press home the attack regardless of the force of opposition the Venturas began their run up to Amsterdam – into the sweep of more enemy fighters. One of the 11 Venturas had already been hit near the coast and turned for home. It was the only one to return. On the run up to the target the other 10 were picked off one by one. The Ventura North was in was one of the first.

Sitting uneasily in the perspex nose waiting to aim his bombs, North knew from the unfriendly cannon that was exploding in the air around them that it could not be long before they were hit. Over the intercom he heard the mid-upper gunner warning the pilot that two Focke-Wulf 190s were coming in from astern and a moment later he heard the mid-upper guns firing. Then he heard a bang and felt the aircraft shudder as a cannon shell ripped into their belly. Abruptly the mid-upper guns stopped firing and he heard the wireless operator/air gunner, Sergeant William Stannard, calling the mid-upper gunner, asking him if he was all right. There was no reply and when North looked back along the narrow gangway past the pilot's compartment, he saw that the whole of the inside of the fuselage was a red mass of flames.

The intercom had gone dead so he unplugged from it, took off his helmet, picked up his parachute pack, and climbed out of the nose. There was no question but that the Ventura was done for and he saw that the pilot was already reaching up to open the escape hatch in the cockpit roof above his head. He didn't relish the prospect of going out that way – there was a good chance of being swept back against the mid-upper turret, and if he missed that, of striking one of the twin fins. But they were now cut off from the main exit door in the fuselage by the fire and he knew that it was the escape hatch or nothing.

As North stepped up into the pilot's compartment the pilot got the hatch open. Immediately the rush of the slipstream sucked the flames forward into the cockpit. North stepped back as if he had been struck a hard blow. Yet although all his hair had been singed off and his whole head and face burnt black, he felt no pain. The fear of being burnt alive seized him; to get out of the hatch became the most important thing in the world. So important that the need to attach his parachute to his harness seemed in comparison unimportant. 'I had read of people jumping from high buildings to certain death to escape from fire even before they had been burnt,' says North. 'I had thought them rather panicky. Now I know that death by fire must be the most terrible death of all.' He picked his chute up by one of its canvas carrying loops, put one foot on the back of the pilot's seat and leapt through the opening in the roof.

The merciful slipstream whisked him away – clear of the turret, clear of the fins. It seemed quiet all of a sudden and the rush of air appeared to have suppressed the fire on his clothing. He couldn't see the ground, didn't know whether he was dropping head or feet first and had no sensation of falling. Once he was clear of the slipstream there was no rush of air around him; all he felt was 'a pleasant relaxed weightless feeling'. And his right hand was still tightly gripping his parachute.

The process of falling was so idyllically soothing it almost deprived him of all perception of danger. But his mind was alert and he knew that it didn't take a man many seconds to plunge down from 11,000 feet. He drew the heavy pack up to his chest and with his left hand took hold of the second holding loop. Coolly he bent his head down to see the snap hooks on his harness. Then he pressed one of the pack's steel rings on to a hook, hearing the click of the spring as clearly as if he had been in a quiet room on the ground.

He drew the second pack ring towards his harness – but it would not reach the second snap-hook. And then he saw why. He had inadvertantly clipped the right ring on to the left snap-hook; to fasten on both sides of his parachute he would have to undo the ring he had already attached and start again. Horrified at what he had done he looked down at the pack lying lopsidedly against his chest. He was afraid to unhook the ring because it called for a two-handed movement and as he fumbled he knew he might drop the pack. Dare he risk pulling the ripcord with only one side attached? He studied the shining metal rings: they looked pitifully slender and inadequate and uppermost in his mind was the thought that if the designer had thought two connections necessary then surely one could not possibly support his weight.

As he fell at terminal velocity losing more than 1,000 feet every five seconds he knew that his life depended on the decision he made – and the speed with which he put it into effect.

He decided to risk a single-connection opening and pulled the ripcord. There was a flurry of silk, the pack jerked up on its solitary link and with a brisk jolt the canopy opened. The tension flowed out of him and after a grateful glance at the white umbrella above him he looked down and for the first time saw the ground. He was surprised to see how far it was still below him; in fact it looked very little nearer than it had done a minute earlier from the nose of the Ventura. He realized then just how quickly he must have half clipped his parachute on and made the decision to pull the ripcord; at the time they had seemed very long seconds indeed.

He saw that he was coming down on to the strip of Holland between the Zuider Zee and the North Sea. There was no sign of the Ventura, no sound of the air battle in which they had been involved – it had moved away eastward towards Amsterdam at 250 miles an hour.

Presently he became aware of an irritation on his hip. He thought nothing of it until the irritation turned to a sharp pain; he looked down and saw that a small fire had broken out on his trousers. He slapped it out. From below came the dismal wail of sirens. Just his luck, he thought, to land in the middle of an air raid. He searched the sky for a sight of approaching aircraft but there was none; then he realized that the raid was the one on which he had been flying.

He noticed that he was drifting towards the North Sea coast and a new worry came to him. But before it became necessary to pull on the rigging lines and spill air out of the canopy to change direction, the ground, which for most of the ten minutes of his descent had appeared as a vast stationary carpet, began to rush towards him. He saw a blaze of colour below and then he dropped into a field of tulips – landing squarely on his feet.

A group of Dutchmen were standing on the edge of the field. He walked over to them and had begun to explain that he was English when one of them pointed towards a road about 50 yards away. North turned to see two uniformed Germans approaching. He was too badly burnt for there to be much sense in trying to escape and he knew he would have to give himself up.

With raised hands he walked over to meet the Germans and at pistol point was escorted into the sidecar of a motor cycle and driven away to captivity where he joined a number of other 487 Squadron men who had been shot down on that fateful raid. Among them was Squadron Leader L. H. Trent, D.F.C., who was subsequently awarded a V.C. for his leadership of the attack. Trent was the only pilot to reach the power stations and drop his bombs in the target area before he was shot down.

During the three months he spent in hospital as a prisoner while his multiple burns healed, North met Sergeant Stannard, his wireless operator/air gunner, the only other survivor from his crew. Until then North had thought the manner of his escape with parachute in hand something of a novelty. But by comparison with the mode of Stannard's descent it became almost commonplace. Stannard's parachute had been destroyed in the fire. He came down from 11,000 feet without one. But that is a story for another chapter.

Probably the luckiest of all men who baled out with their parachute in their hands was Pilot Officer John Vollmer. When he pulled his ripcord he was quite convinced that his parachute was not clipped on – not even by one hook. He pulled the ripcord, holding the pack in his hand as a desperate last resort!

It happened on the night of September 6, 1940, during a raid on Krefeld and it was Vollmer's first operation. A pilot in No. 44 Squadron, he was 26 at the time. On the way home from Krefeld – he was acting as observer on this trip – Vollmer's Hampden was hit by ack-ack near Munster. Here is his story as he described it shortly afterwards from a German prison camp in a letter to his mother.

'I was in the nose when a piece of shrapnel flew right across the compartment; it came in one side and out the other – passing about three inches from my nose.

'We were hit in the wing and the shell went straight into

96

a petrol tank. The wireless operator reported that the starboard engine was on fire. We never heard a word from the rear gunner – I think he was hit by a piece of the shell. The pilot gave the order to jump.

'I had to go about six feet back to reach my parachute pack and the escape hatch, and had just picked my chute up when the aircraft went into a dive. Before I could clip the pack on I was flung back into the nose with my parachute in my hand. The throttles had jammed open and we reached a tremendous speed in the dive. The aircraft was burning like a furnace and I dimly remember the inside being full of smoke. I was quietly preparing for the end – no panic, just sorry that I would not be able to tell you about it.

'Then there was a devil of a bang and a cracking noise. I thought we had hit the ground but in fact the speed of our dive had torn a wing off. This, combined with the explosion as another petrol tank blew up, broke the perspex nose against which I was being pressed.

'Suddenly I found myself hurtling through the air – holding on to my chute which was still not hooked on. I made violent efforts to clip it on as I fell but without success. Then, realizing that I must be very near the ground I decided to hold on to the pack with my right hand and pull the ripcord with my left. I pulled. The chute opened and tore itself out of my hand, breaking two fingers in the process.

'It was then that I really thought the end had come. Imagine my feelings then when I was suddenly jerked up and found that one of the hooks of the parachute pack had caught on to one of the snaphooks of my harness!

'We had been at 12,000 feet when we were hit and by the short time it took me to come down after I pulled the ripcord my chute must have opened between 500 and 1,000 feet. I landed safely in a peat bog and was picked up next morning. The pilot got out when he found it was impossible to control the aircraft in the dive, but the wireless operator and rear gunner were killed.'

It was fortunate for Vollmer that he pulled his ripcord when he did. At the velocity at which he was falling – he got his initial impetus from an aircraft diving at high speed – another two or three seconds spent in the desperate attempt he was making to clip his pack on would have brought him to the ground.

Vollmer is not sure how his parachute got hooked on to one side of his harness. He can only presume that in his struggle to attach the pack by both hooks he was, although he did not know it, half successful. There would certainly have been no question of his being able to hold the parachute had it not been clipped on at least on one side. The shock loading as the chute opened at the speed he was falling could have been anything up to a ton.

Vollmer concluded his letter: 'My escape ranks as about the luckiest in this camp. People do not always realize what it means when an aircraft does not come back. Stories like this might help them to take their hats off to the boys who will never return. Those of us who are alive ask for nothing'.

CHAPTER VIII

Another exclusive little coterie of 'caterpillars' were those who came down safely without pulling the ripcord; their chutes were opened by violent and unorthodox means.

On the night of April 30, 1943, a Stirling of No. 7 Squadron flew out from its base at Oakington in Cambridgeshire bound for Bocholt in the Ruhr. As well as a number of 2,000-lb bombs in its bomb-bays it carried a load of marker flares, for it was an aircraft of Bomber Command's élite Pathfinder Force whose job was to identify and mark the target with coloured flares for the main force of bombers which followed.

But the Stirling, which was one of many flying from Oakington that night, never reached the Ruhr. It was caught by enemy night fighters over Holland and shot down. Only one of its crew of seven survived. He was the flight engineer, Sergeant Fred Painter, and he did not pull his ripcord.

Painter was a regular. He had joined the R.A.F. as an

apprentice at 16 and when war came had been accepted for aircrew. The day he took off on his last operation was the day after his 22nd birthday.

Disaster came swiftly that night. At 2.45 a.m. when the Stirling was at 11,000 feet over Holland heading east, a Ju 88 came up from below and pumped a sustained stream of cannon fire into it. The shells took heavy toll. They ripped through the nose, poured back through the crew positions, severed the cross-balance fuel line and slammed into the two starboard engines, setting the whole wing on fire. The bomb aimer, the pilot and the navigator were killed outright and Painter's left foot was shattered.

When at last the bedlam of crashing cannon stopped Painter heard the rear-gunner shouting over the intercom. It was the last he ever heard of the voices of any of his crew, for almost immediately the intercom went dead. He looked round and saw that the fuselage was ablaze from the broken fuel line. The inside of the aircraft was filling with dense smoke and it was growing unbearably hot. Overcome by the smoke and heat and the shock from his smashed foot, he passed out.

Next thing he remembers was finding himself leaning over the flare chute at the rear of the fuselage. His parachute was clipped to his chest but he did not recall fixing it there, nor, for that matter, making his way aft. The whole aircraft seemed to be burning, he was choking with the hot acrid smoke that caught in his throat and he had a desperate urge to breathe fresh air.

He reeled over to the main entrance door and jettisoned it. Then he lay down on the floor and put his head out in the slipstream, gasping as he filled his lungs with biting cold air.

At first he couldn't see anything in the black void outside but then as his eyes adjusted themselves to the darkness he was shocked to see the outline of the ground moving by a few hundred feet below. He brought his head in to look for the others but there was no sign of them – only a terrifying surging cylinder of flame which blew hotly against him, stinging his face. Quickly he slid out through the door. A second later the Stirling's bomb-load exploded.

Painter's head cracked against the tail plane and a brilliant array of lights burst inside his head. He was sure he had hit the ground and the thought flashed through his mind. 'I'm dead – and it wasn't so bad.' Almost immediately he felt his body toss in the blast as the aircraft blew up not 50 yards away. He hadn't yet had a chance to pull his ripcord but before he could reach the handle he looked up and was astonished to see the silk streaming away above him – blown from the pack by the explosion.

Now what remained of the aircraft was below him, burning on the ground. For a horrible moment it looked as if he would land in the middle of the fire. But once again an explosion saved him. A dazzling orange flash leapt from the pyre on the ground, he felt his descent arrested, and for a second or two he was swept upwards and away from the fire. As he began to sink again he heard a rustling overhead and looking up saw that the explosion had snapped his chute fully open. A moment later he landed safely, 200 yards from the burning Stirling, in his stockinged feet. The first explosion had blown his flying boots off; yet when he sat up to take stock he was surprised to find that in one hand he was still tightly clutching the tools of his airborne trade – a pencil, a calculator and his watch!

Unable to walk because of his injured foot and weak from loss of blood, he crawled away from the vicinity of the wreckage. He didn't want to be there when the Germans came to investigate.

Soon he came to the edge of an irrigation canal. Beyond it he could see a faint light from a house. He wished he could get to the house, but in the starlight the canal looked wide, the water black and deep. After all he had been through he decided it would be an anticlimax to drown, so he spent the long hours until dawn on his hands and knees on a crawling reconnaissance looking for a place to cross.

Soon after daylight he was found by a Dutch boy, a doctor was brought to him and his injured foot was attended to. For most of the day the Dutch kept him from the Germans; Painter didn't know it then but the local Resistance group was divided on whether or not he should be hidden and helped to escape. Throughout the day he was the subject of a succession of secret conferences and in the end the 'noes' had it. They reasoned that (a) too many children had already seen him which made it difficult to keep his presence in the district secret, and (b) that his injury needed hospital attention the Resistance Movement could not easily provide.

So late that afternoon Painter was driven to the local police station and his arrival reported to the Germans. While he lay on a couch at the station waiting to be taken away there was for Painter a touching little interlude. Several dozen villagers came to say good-bye to him. They filed past his couch forming two queues - one of men, the other women – the men to shake his hand, the women to kiss him. 'I leave you to guess which I enjoyed the most!' says Painter.

Seven months after Painter's explosive arrival in Holland, when Lancasters had replaced the Stirlings, another member of the same squadron made an even more startling journey to earth. He came down from 19,500 feet but of that long descent he has no recollection; he does not remember leaving the aircraft or arriving on the ground – nor did he pull his ripcord.

Flight Lieutenant Ted Ansfield was an observer, which in a Pathfinder squadron meant that he was a navigator trained as a bomb aimer and as operator of the air-to-ground radar used for blind marking when the target was under cloud. Casualties among Pathfinders at this time were heavy and on No. 7 Squadron the 'chop rate', as it was called, was less than six trips per crew.

On the afternoon of November 26, 1943, Ansfield lay in a hospital bed at Oakington recovering from burns he had received on an operation earlier in the week. He lay there listening to the roar from the dispersals where the station's Lancasters were being run up and tested for the night's operation and the sound gave him a restless urge to be out of hospital and flying again. He listened to the noise of the

Merlin engines until he could stand it no longer; he called the orderly and demanded his clothes.

At first the orderly, fearful of the consequences, refused. Only when Ansfield climbed out of bed and threatened to go and look for the M.O. in his pyjamas did he relent and fetch his uniform. Five minutes later he was dressed and knocking hopefully on the door of the M.O.'s office.

The M.O. greeted him curtly. 'What the hell are you doing here, Ansfield?' he demanded.

'There's ops tonight, sir, and I want to fly.'

The M.O. said: 'Don't be a bloody fool, man. You're not fit and even if I did discharge you now you know you're compelled to do 48 hours light duty.'

'I fully understand that, sir, but—'

'I'm sorry, boy,' the M.O. said, 'but those are the rules. The best I can do is discharge you from here and let you take it easy in the mess.'

Realizing the pointlessness of arguing against the 'rules', Ansfield saluted and turned to leave. As he opened the door a quiet voice behind him said: 'Ansfield, briefing's at 1500 hours – good luck.'

Ansfield said: 'Thank you, sir, thank you very much,' and ran all the way to the briefing room. The crews were already assembling but he was just in time to get his name down on the list for the night's operation. And the target was worth breaking hospital for – it was Berlin.

Out in the winter darkness in the dispersals the No. 7 Squadron crews sang as they prepared to go aboard their aircraft. They sang 'Silent Night' – not because Christmas was only four weeks away but because the carol had become the squadron's departure theme song. Then as each crew climbed aboard, the singing died away and soon the last voices were drowned in the vibrant crescendo of the engines as one by one the Lancasters started up and taxied out for take-off.

It was six o'clock when Ansfield's Lancaster climbed away from Oakington. Two hours later they were turning over Frankfurt and heading north-east for Berlin. Ansfield heard his pilot warning the two gunners to keep a sharp look-out

102

for fighters and the mid-upper replied that all he could see was another Lancaster about 600 yards away to port. The wireless operator at the airborne interception radar confirmed that the Lancaster and another – which the gunners could not see – were showing as a blip running in line with them, on his screen.

A moment later something else came on to his screen. He just had time to shout over the intercom: 'There's a smaller signal moving fast towards us,' when there was a great crashing, hammering noise which swamped the roar of the engines and the Lancaster lurched as a stream of cannon and machine-gun fire poured out of the darkness into them. The rear gunner saw the fighter, called to the pilot to dive to port, but it was too late. The damage was done. The Lancaster was mortally wounded. The four engines, the petrol tanks and the rear half of the fuselage were afire.

'Get the bombs off,' the pilot shouted. But Ansfield had already thrown the jettison switch; nothing had happened. The electrical release gear had been damaged. He looked into his air-to-ground radar and from it fixed their position. They were 20 miles north-east of Frankfurt-on-Main, at 23,500 feet. He tried to pass on the information but nobody heard him – the intercom wires to his helmet had been shot away. So he leaned out and shouted the position report to the navigator who drew the centre-section curtains aside to relay it to the wireless operator for transmission to base. But the wireless operator was lying dead over his key.

Ansfield went forward. The Lancaster was starting to go down and the pilot gave him a thumb-down sign to bale out. 'Good luck, Ted,' he said, 'see you in hell!'

Down in the nose Ansfield found the sergeant flight engineer crouching over the escape hatch. He looked despairingly at Ansfield. 'The ruddy thing's jammed,' he shouted.

'Put your foot through it,' Ansfield yelled at him and then impatient to get the job done he pushed the engineer aside and kicked it open himself. 'Out you go and good luck – see you below,' he said.

The engineer, who was very young and very frightened, looked down at the black roaring void and backed away. 'I can't, sir,' he said.

'Don't argue, it's your only chance,' Ansfield snapped back. Reluctantly the engineer sat on the edge of the hatch and hung his feet out. Ansfield gave him a push and he disappeared into the night.

Ansfield checked his parachute and was about to follow him when above the noise of tortured engines and the roar of the flames further aft, he heard someone screaming, beseechingly, 'Oxygen! Oxygen!'

He crawled out of the nose back into the cockpit. The navigator told him it was the mid-upper gunner calling from the turret in the burning fuselage. 'The poor devil's in the middle of it. We can't get to him.'

Ansfield knew that oxygen wouldn't help the man in the turret. He could only assume that the gunner believed it might give him added strength to struggle out; so he leaned across the pilot and turned the oxygen lever to 'emergency'.

They were diving now. Standing by the pilot Ansfield saw the airspeed indicator going up towards the danger line and the altimeter unwinding fast from 20,000 to 19,000 feet. He said: 'Can we pull her out together, Skip,' and the pilot shook his head. 'Not a chance in hell – the controls are dead. Out you go. Meet you downstairs.'

Ansfield moved forward into the nose. There was a brilliant flash. The Lancaster's five tons of bombs and flares had exploded and the aircraft disintegrated.

The next thing he knew he was lying on the ground in a forest in the darkness, numb with cold and his face badly frost-bitten. The only sound was the distant barking of a dog.

For several minutes as consciousness ebbed back he lay there while his mind struggled to bring his situation into perspective. At first his last memory was a hospital bed. Then he remembered the trip he needn't have flown on, the fighter, the fire and the flash. He knew he hadn't jumped out and because of that he couldn't at first comprehend why he was alive.

He got to his feet. Apart from his frostbitten face, a thigh wound he had collected in the aircraft and an acute head-ache he was unscathed. Beside him under the trees lay the white spread of the parachute he had not opened. He looked at his watch. It was still going and the luminous hands showed 9.30. The last time he had looked at his watch in the air it had been 8.12 so he had been unconscious for nearly an hour and a half. He could only conclude that the aircraft had blown up, ejecting him and blasting open his parachute pack as it did so. The frostbite, he assumed, he must have got passing through a freezing zone on the way down, for it wasn't freezing on the ground – at least not yet.

Hiding his parachute, harness, and Mae West in the undergrowth he set off to find a way out of the forest. There seemed no end to the trees and he stumbled on through the long hours of the night until, some time after midnight, he collapsed. It was 6 a.m. when he revived. The ground was frozen hard and white with frost and he was stiff with cold. When he stood up he was surprised to see a parachute draped over the undergrowth about 100 yards away. He went over to it and found the body of the flight engineer who had been so unwilling to jump. There was blood on his flying suit and Ansfield saw that he had been killed by a stray piece of flak or night fighter cannon shell on the way down. The irony of his death was that he had left the aircraft with more than a 99 per cent survival chance, yet Ansfield, who had been blasted out into mid air by the explosion of 12,000 lb. of bombs and flares, had come through alive.

Pinpointing his position on his escape map as roughly 35 miles north-east of Frankfurt-on-Main, he stripped all his R.A.F. insignia and rank badges from his uniform, turned his electrically-heated waistcoat inside out to make it look like a brown civilian jacket and set off in the direction of the Rhine which he was anxious to cross before he became too weak. He walked all day, across fields and through woods, carefully avoiding the people he saw working in the open. Towards evening it began to rain and he spent a wet night curled up under some bushes. His only food that day was an energy tablet and a square of chocolate.

It was still raining next morning so after a few hours' trek he hid in an abandoned quarry, staying there for the rest of the day and all that night, cold, wet through and very hungry. His day's ration was two energy tablets and a cigarette.

On the third day he left the quarry and continued on his way. The rain had not stopped and by now the fields were flooded. During the morning he had a narrow escape when a low-flying Fieseler Storch passed overhead, searching for escaping R.A.F. men. Soon afterwards he reached the River Lahn. It was in full brown flood and as the only bridge within reach was carrying an unhealthy volume of traffic, he climbed into a tree and waited until dark before crossing. He stayed on the road after that and passed a number of people who wished him *Gute Nacht* to which he responded with suitably vague mumblings. That day he allowed himself one energy tablet and cigarette and spent the night 2,000 feet up on a hillside – still in heavy rain.

By the fourth day he had almost worn out his flying boots, he was suffering agonizing head pains – although he didn't know it he had been concussed in the explosion – and his injured leg was making walking difficult. He started to take off his clothes to examine the wound but found his underclothes glued to his body with so much dried blood he abandoned the examination. It was raining harder than ever and by dusk he was floundering through flooded fields thigh deep in water. As it grew dark he stumbled on to a wooded slope; halfway up the ground suddenly gave way beneath him and he plunged 30 feet into another disused quarry. He was so shaken by the fall he decided to spend the night where he lay. He ate another energy tablet, smoked a cigarette then fell asleep. He woke some hours later aware of a strange warmth; the rain had turned to snow and he was being slowly buried.

He left the quarry before it was light. He was feeling weak and ill now and he knew that his snow tracks made his evasion chances slimmer. Earlier he had had ambitious plans of reaching Paris where he had friends he knew would help him, but now those hopes were fading. For the first time he found himself thinking of home, of his fiancée, and of the mess back at Oakington. He pictured his name on the notice board under the heading 'The following personnel are missing' – and thought of the padre in his sad task of sorting out his kit and writing the customary letter of sympathy to his family. Someone else would have taken his place in the station soccer team and 'his' groundcrew would be getting to know another Lancaster and a fresh crew.

Plodding across country through mud and snow he came to a railway. According to his map it went to Coblenz on the Rhine. He decided to try and jump a passing freight train. Following the tracks for about a mile he came to a small station. He avoided the railway workers and hid for the rest of the day in the station yard. Soon after eating his daily ration of energy tablets and smoking the day's cigarette he heard a train approaching. He crawled across to the track through deep snow and was heartened to see that it was a freighter and going the way he wanted. The train slowed down passing through the station, and as the trucks went clanking past he stood up and leapt at one. He found a handhold, was dragged off his feet but, before he could haul himself aboard, the strength went out of his arms and he fell off. He lay in the snow listening to the receding clatter of the train, feeling weak and ill, bitterly disappointed at his failure. He now knew how pitifully weak he had become and the realization made him morose and dejected.

Through the falling snow he followed the railway westward hoping that he might find a stationary train at another station. But when after five miles' trudging there was no station he could walk no further and collapsed beside the tracks. He fell asleep and did not waken until dawn. It was still snowing. He left the railway and picked up a road going in the same direction. Presently it brought him to a small town. In all his six days as a fugitive he had never dared walk through a town in daylight. Now he did not care. It was unlikely now that he would get out of Germany and he knew that he couldn't evade capture much longer.

He wrapped his scarf round his head to cover the week's growth on his face and entered the town. In the main street he saw a policeman standing with a civilian in a leather coat who looked very like his conception of a Gestapo man. Opposite them he stopped and turned as nonchalantly as he could to look in a shop window. He watched the reflections of the two men and was dismayed to see that one was pointing at him. Casually he sauntered on down the street. Out of the corner of his eye he saw that the pair were following him. He came to a cinema. Its doors were open. He darted inside, ran down the aisle between the rows of empty seats, out of a rear exit through a network of back streets and into the fields beyond. He did not see the two men again.

On a hillside above the town his legs gave under him and he flopped down in the snow to rest, smoke a cigarette and eat an energy tablet. For six days he had existed on energy tablets. He hadn't wanted to risk stealing and the fields were bare.

Studying his map he decided that he was now only a few miles from the Rhine. In fact, he hoped he might see the river from the top of the hill he was on. It had stopped snowing at last. He had never known continuous snow fall for so long. The countryside was two feet deep in it.

He found a road running up the hill and decided to risk following it. It was the last risk he was to take. Within a few minutes of setting off he met a tough-looking elderly farmer driving a horse-drawn waggon. The German saw him staggering on the road and challenged him. Ansfield tried to bluff it out: he pointed to his mouth, shaking his head, pretending to be dumb. For a fleeting moment he thought of fighting it out but he quickly realized the foolishness of it. Then his legs sagged under him again and he rolled in the snow. The farmer leapt down and picked him up. For Ansfield his strong arms meant the end of a nightmare – and the beginning of captivity. Twelve hours later, well escorted, he was en route to Stalag Luft I.

In November 1944 Group Captain C. T. Weir, D.F.C. was Station Commander of R.A.F. Fulbeck, a Bomber Command Lancaster base in Lincolnshire. Station Commanders were not expected to fly on operations but, from time to time many of them did, and Weir was one.

To do so he had to get special permission each time from his group commander and because he had no aircraft of his own he would take a Lancaster of one of the Fulbeck squadrons and usually a non-squadron crew drawn from the specialist station staff. The station navigation officer would fly as his navigator, the station signals officer as wireless operator, and so on.

On the night of November 22, the two Fulbeck squadrons were ordered to take part in an attack on an aqueduct which carried the Ems-Weser canal over a river about 15 miles north-west of Osnabrück. Weir borrowed a Lancaster of No. 49 Squadron and went along.

The aqueduct was to be bombed by several successive waves of aircraft, each wave arriving over the target at a different height. Weir was first in the bottom wave of 40 Lancasters; they were briefed to attack from 14,000 feet. However, when they neared the target shortly before 9 o'clock, the area was under cloud and the master bomber who was directing the operation from a lone Lancaster low down near the aqueduct called the bottom wave down through the cloud to 4,000 feet. Weir does not remember much more of the raid after that. He found the aqueduct – it had been marked by the Pathfinders – and released his bombs. He heard the bomb-aimer report 'Bombs gone'. A second later the aircraft exploded.

Weir, sitting at the controls, was aware only of a great white flash and a roaring noise in his ears. He remembers no more than that. Three hours later, at about midnight, he regained consciousness, lying in the mud of the Ems-Weser canal a few yards from what remained of the aqueduct. And his only injuries were a gash in each leg and a broken jaw. Stretched out in the mud beside him was his parachute – fully opened and, but for two torn panels, undamaged.

He climbed out of the mud and sat on the canal bank trying to sort out in his mind what had happened. Shivering, he saw that he was soaked to the skin. And then he saw why. He had landed in the canal before the following air-craft had breached the aqueduct. Unconscious, he had floated there until, as the bombs poured down and the aqueduct collapsed, the water had gushed away, the canal had all but dried up and he had been left like a stranded fish in the mud.

Then, as his eyes focused more clearly in the darkness, he began to make out the shapes of the bomb craters. The canal bottom, the banks and the surrounding fields were pockmarked with hundreds of deep ugly holes. For several hundred yards around the area had been saturated with the thousand-pounders of more than 100 Lancasters. Survey-ing this zone of concentrated destruction it gave him a curi-ous eerie feeling to realize that he had lain throughout the bomb deluge in the midst of it all, unconscious and unaware of the man-made earthquakes, the blasts and the flying steel that had not touched him.

Not far away he saw the wreckage of two aircraft still burning in a field. Obviously they were Lancasters and obviously one was his aircraft. At first the presence of two aircraft puzzled him. Then slowly it occurred to him what had happened – the only explanation.

His Lancaster had been hit by a 1,000 lb. bomb dropped from an aircraft in one of the bomber streams attacking from a higher level. Although the various waves had been scheduled to reach the target at one minute intervals it sometimes happened that winds en route from England upset the planned timing and bombs began to fall from the middle or top waves before the lower waves were clear of the target. Even so, although it did occasionally happen, in the wide spaces of the sky the odds were many thousands to one against a lower aircraft being hit. And in this case the tragedy had been doubled. The other Lancaster, which must have been following close behind, had been caught in the explosion and had been destroyed in the same second.

Of the 14 men in the two aircraft Weir alone had sur-vived. He had been blasted bodily out of his seat, up through the perspex cockpit roof; and as he hurtled away amid a shower of wreckage the blast had ripped his neatly folded

110

parachute canopy from the seat-type pack, hanging behind his thighs, and blown it open. He had collected the gashes on the insides of his legs from the control column as he left the seat and his jaw was broken as he burst head-first through the roof.

Weir was at liberty for just 24 hours before being captured by a German policeman.

Somewhere there is an ex-W.A.A.F. who, all her life, will remember his escape with prideful heart. For she it was who packed the parachute that cracked open that fateful night. When Weir came back to England in 1945 she had married and been posted away from Fulbeck. But he traced her, and sent her a cigarette-case which was, as he put it, a small token of his gratitude 'for packing a chute that would open automatically!'

CHAPTER IX

There is a time-worn joke about the parachute that if it fails to operate properly the manufacturer will supply the parachutist with a replacement free of charge! Surprisingly, if the joke had any foundation in fact, which it hasn't, there could have been a number of such claims.

Men have dropped down from the sky on half-opened, and occasionally scarcely opened chutes and survived – some with permanent crippling injuries, others virtually unscathed. In some cases the chutes did not open fully because of battle damage, in others – obviously – because the man jumped too low, and sometimes, fortunately rarely, because of faulty packing. Never in the history of the Caterpillar Club has a chute failed to operate through structural weakness or faulty manufacture.

Sergeant Leonard Smith was one of the lucky members of the part-opened chute brigade. And not only is his story of interest for that, but because it illustrates the dilemma facing an aircraft captain who discovers in an emergency that not all those on board have a parachute.

It happened in September 1940, when Smith was nearing the end of his pilot training on twin-engined Whitley bombers at No. 10 Operational Training Unit at Abingdon in Berkshire. He and four other student pilots, together with a student wireless operator, were detailed for night flying practice at Stanton Harcourt, a satellite airfield near Abingdon.

They flew to Stanton Harcourt at dusk with an instructor, Flight Sergeant L. F. East, D.F.M., but on landing there were told to return to Abingdon immediately as the weather was deteriorating.

It was dark and low cloud was moving in when East and his six students climbed back into the Whitley. They all went up forward into the crew compartment except Smith. There was no room for him up front and as it was only a five minute flight he made himself comfortable on the floor in the back of the aircraft.

Just as they were about to taxi out for the take-off, the door opened and two aircraftmen jumped in. Smith, assuming that East had offered them a ride back to Abingdon, showed them where to sit and for the moment thought no more about them. He felt the Whitley roll out to the flarepath, heard the engines opened to full power, felt the aircraft jolting on its take-off run then lurch into the air. There was nothing he could do so he stretched out on the floor to wait for the landing bump that would tell him they were back at Abingdon.

Five, ten, fifteen minutes droned by without any pre-landing reduction in engine power, and presently Smith went forward to the crew compartment to investigate. He was dismayed to learn that the countryside was now covered in low cloud, that the radio was inoperative, that they couldn't find either Abingdon or Stanton Harcourt and were, in fact, lost. There seemed nothing useful he could contribute to the situation so Smith retreated to the back of the aircraft again and lay down to await developments.

A slow half-hour passed and they were still airborne. Again Smith crawled forward along the narrow tunnel of the fuselage to learn what was happening. He saw that they

112

were flying at 5,000 feet in bright moonlight above an expanse of white stratus cloud whose top lay about 1,000 feet below them. East told him they had been able to find no gap through which to let down and being unsure of their position, he had decided that they should all abandon the aircraft.

Smith went back to put on his parachute and to tell the two aircraftmen to prepare for jumping. The two men looked at him aghast.

'We haven't got parachutes!' they said, miserably.

Appalled, Smith hurried back to the cockpit and told East. East looked at him with astonishment. 'Passengers? What passengers?' he demanded. Smith told him. East swore.

'Stowaways, eh,' he said. 'And tonight of all nights for crying out loud.'

East was silent for a moment, yet he knew there was only one decision. He climbed out of the pilot's seat, took his parachute off and slung it back to Smith. 'Give it to one of them,' he said.

A moment later another chute was passed back. Sergeant John Steel, one of the students who was flying as second pilot, had given it. Both he and East knew that by doing so they were now condemned to stay with the aircraft.

Smith handed the chutes to the stowaways. They looked ashamed and crestfallen as they struggled into them. Then East came scrambling back along the fuselage to speak to them. He knew that he mightn't be alive to see the two men again and he wanted them left in no doubt that if he didn't their thoughtless disregard of flying regulations would have been wholly responsible. There in the dark cone of the fuselage, shouting to make himself heard above the noise of the engines, he told them so in harsh, blunt terms. Then he ordered them to jump.

The door had already been jettisoned and the first stowaway had obediently leapt through. Smith looked out and saw that his chute had opened. He motioned the second man to follow: he refused to go. Stricken with guilt at what he had done and terrified by the prospect of a plunge into

113

space, he was close to tears and pleaded to be allowed to stay. But time was running out and East, growing impatient, took him by the arm, gently steered him to the door, showed him his ripcord handle and pushed him out. Smith shouted 'Good luck' to East, and followed. Then the wireless operator and the two student pilots, who still had chutes, jumped too.

When Smith pulled his ripcord he felt a jolt and found that he was hanging lopsidedly with only one side of his body supported by rigging lines. He looked up and in the moonlight was concerned to see that he was hanging from what he later described as 'about half a chute'. One side of the canopy was fully developed; the other was a useless bunched-up mass of silk and rigging lines.

From the speed at which he was approaching the cloud top he knew that he was dropping dangerously fast. He made frenzied efforts to free the closed portion of his chute by jerking fiercely on the slack lines which hung from it. This released a few square feet of tangled canopy but at the same time the brittle sound of tearing silk came to him; fearful that he might rip the operative half of his chute he stopped pulling and, supported by his elongated 'cottage loaf', sank swiftly into the grey realms of the cloud, convinced that death or at best serious injury awaited him.

It took him only a few minutes to go through the cloud. He broke out suddenly and there below him was a church steeple pointing the longest, sharpest looking lightning conductor he had ever seen. To avoid the spire he risked pulling on the rigging lines to change direction by spilling air from his 'cottage loaf'. But this action resulted in such a violent sideslip he quickly abandoned it. He missed the church by a few yards, saw a row of cottages coming up at him so fast he seemed to be falling without any resistance from his chute, shot past them and crashed into an allotment.

There was only one bush in the whole allotment. It was a clump of elderly gooseberry and Smith thudded seat-first into it. He lay there for a second or two gasping to regain his breath. Then he stood up. At first he couldn't believe it but gradually as he felt his body all over he discovered

114

that, half a chute notwithstanding, he had arrived uninjured.

Smith had landed on the outskirts of Huntingdon – 70 miles from Abingdon. Later that night at No. 2 Group Headquarters, he was reunited with all the others who had baled out of the Whitley, with one exception – the second stowaway who had not wanted to jump. His was a tragic end; he landed in the River Ouse and was drowned. He had made his illicit flight with the intention of spending the evening in Abingdon with his fiancée whom he was to have married the following Saturday.

But, for the other men in the Whitley this sadness was tempered by the news that Flight Sergeant East and Sergeant Steel after flying about for some time above cloud had, when their fuel was nearly exhausted, found a gap through which they let down to make a safe landing in a field near St Neots. Next morning East flew the Whitley out of the field and back to Abingdon. A few weeks later, he was killed in a night flying accident.

In the night sky 18,000 feet above Berlin around midnight on August 31, 1943, a Lancaster of No. 97 Squadron was burning. The victim of a head-on attack by a Focke-Wulf 190, it had been caught a few minutes short of the target. Behind the trail of fire it left, six parachutes floated down in the moonless darkness.

The seventh man, the pilot, was still at the controls. His name was Wing Commander Ken Burns and he was the flight commander. A few moments earlier as the first flames had begun to stream away from the port wing he had called to his crew: 'This is it. Out you go, blokes'. The bomb aimer had asked if he should let the bombs go but Burns had said 'No – leave 'em be and I'll aim the kite where they'll do some good.' A moment later the Wing Commander was alone in the aircraft, trimming it to head down for the already burning centre of Berlin ahead. Then he also prepared to leave.

He unclipped his seat harness and was just raising his hand to take off his helmet when the darkness around him

115

was slashed by a startling great flash as the bombs exploded and the aircraft was blown to pieces.

He woke up lying on soft ground under some pine trees on the outskirts of Berlin. His right hand and half the forearm were missing – blown off in the explosion – and he had a feeling of great lassitude from the blood he had lost. As yet he felt no pain from the pulped mess of flesh and bone below his elbow and had the uncanny feeling – common in these circumstances – that his arm and hand were still there. Strangely, as the numbness wore off, the worst pain came from his right ankle and foot – yet when he looked he saw that the foot was there and seemingly uninjured. He looked at his watch. It was still ticking and he saw by the luminous hands that it was 3.30 – he had been there three-and-a-half hours.

Shakily he got to his feet. He found he could walk. Concerned that if he didn't get help quickly he would bleed to death, he looked around for a sign of habitation. It was then, for the first time, that he became aware of his seat-type parachute still dangling behind his thighs. Of course he must have come down by parachute – how otherwise could he be alive?

But when he released the harness and the parachute fell to the ground he saw that the ripcord was still in position, that only one of the four flaps had burst open and that so little silk had been dragged out, it could only have cut his falling speed to a trifle below terminal velocity. For a moment he stood there while his mind tried to comprehend how he had achieved the apparently impossible, but he was in no condition for rational thought and presently, having dismissed it all from his mind, he staggered away from the spot.

A signalman found Burns lying unconscious near his signal box beside the tracks of a Berlin suburban railway. Still unconscious he was taken to the sick quarters at Tempelhof where he was given an immediate blood transfusion. Then he was rushed to a hospital in north-west Berlin where doctors cleaned up the stump of his arm and drained one of

116

Insignia of the Caterpillar Club: membership card and gold caterpillar pin with ruby eyes

The late Leslie Irvin.
His parachute has
saved over 120,000
lives.

Sir James Martin.
Every week five or six
aircrew, world-wide,
owe their lives to his
ejection seat

The moment of opening–
a flurry of silk as the
small pilot chute draws
out the canopy of the
famous ripcord-operated
Irvin parachute

A new shape in
parachute design – the
GQ Company's
'Aeroconical'. It is fitted
to the latest Martin
Baker ejection seat

Latest in a long line of Martin Baker ejection seats – the Mark 10. Rocket-powered, it can project its occupant clear of the aircraft with parachute fully open, in 2½ seconds

A US Navy pilot hurtles clear of his F-8 Crusader, seconds before it plunges off the deck of the carrier *Franklin D Roosevelt* in October 1961. The pilot's chute opened at 100 feet; he was rescued from the sea by helicopter (*courtesy US Navy*)

Flight Lieutenant Peter de Salis (*left*) and Flying Officer Pat Lowe. Their 1958 ejection from a Canberra at 56,000 feet remained a world altitude escape record for nearly eight years (*courtesy Ministry of Defence – Crown copyright reserved*)

COCKPIT HOOD

SEAT DROGUE

AIRD IN SEAT

The dramatic low-level escape of test pilot George Aird. Watche
by a startled tractor driver, he ejected from a Lightning which h
become uncontrollable a few seconds before landing at Hatfield
in September 1962 (*courtesy Mr J Meads*). The air view (*opposit*
shows the greenhouse in which Aird landed, and the burnt-out
wreckage of the aircraft. Inset, George Aird (*courtesy Hawker
Siddeley Dynamics Ltd*)

Lockheed test pilot Bill Weaver and a USAF SR-71 Mach 3 strategic reconnaissance aircraft of the type from which he established a 78,000 feet world highest escape record in January 1966 (*courtesy Associated Press Ltd*)

An Irvin chute lowers to earth four people and a Cessna aircraft at Ashbourne, Derbyshire, In October 1975. Student parachutist Stewart Avent is hooked up between the canopy and the inverted aircraft (*courtesy Camera Press Ltd*)

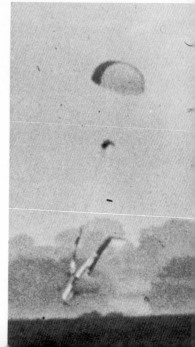

his lungs which had been collapsed by the explosion and had filled with blood.

Some weeks later when he had been moved to a prison camp, it was found that Burns had yet another injury: his back was broken. Such was the extent of his injuries he was selected to join a privileged group of invalid prisoners who were repatriated to England through Sweden in 1944.

Back in England he recovered, was fitted with an artificial arm, and before the end of the war was declared fit for flying again.

Although his was a borderline case, Burns was admitted to the Caterpillar Club. The small amount of silk that the explosion expelled from his pack acted more as a steadying banner than as a parachute as he rushed down. When he crashed through the pine trees, however, it had undoubtedly played a decisive part in slowing him down before he hit the ground. His chute had served him in a highly unorthodox way but it had saved his life in an emergency in the air, and so he gained one of the hardest earned of all gold caterpillars.

CHAPTER X

Shortly before midday on a drowsy warm morning in June, 1945, two Mustangs screamed down out of the sky over R.A.F. Station Bentwaters in Suffolk. They came down in a wide descending turn at high speed, one aircraft above and behind the other. People who paused in their work on the station to watch their noisy approach were suddenly witnesses to a dramatic sequence of events.

They saw the tail unit of the lower Mustang break away. A moment later the other aircraft pulled up and levelled off. Minus its tail, the first Mustang, now about a mile from the airfield, tightened its spiral descent. About 300 feet above the ground the wings broke off and the tiny figure of the pilot was seen to hurtle out. A puff of white appeared behind him as his parachute began to stream – but before more than a few feet of silk emerged, he crashed through an oak tree and hit the ground. That was the last that those watching from the airfield saw of him.

American and R.A.F. ambulances drove to the spot to recover the body. In the oak tree they found tattered fragments of parachute but on the ground below there was no body. A few yards from the tree was a hedge and they saw that a hole had been freshly punched through it. On the other side of the hedge a trail of flattened oats ran for 200 yards across a field. At the end of the trail lay the pilot – Flying Officer Ken Wright. He was alive. So much alive that seven weeks later he was flying again.

With the help of the other Mustang pilot, Flight Lieutenant Dennis Clarke, D.F.C., witnesses on the ground, the scientists of the Royal Aircraft Establishment, Farnborough, who partly rebuilt the aircraft from the wreckage, and from what Wright himself remembered of the incident, it was possible to piece the story together.

Wright, a cheerful extrovert of 27, who had transferred to the R.A.F. from the Army in 1941, was serving at Bentwaters with No. 126 Squadron. The war in Europe had ended a month before and knowing that his R.A.F. days were almost over he was making the most of the routine flying to which the squadron had reverted.

On June 9 his aircraft – a Mustang Mk 3 – was ready for an air test after a major overhaul and, anxious to make the most of a morning's flying, he suggested to Clarke, whom he had known since his schooldays in Sanderstead, that they go up together for a spot of cine gun practice. Clarke readily agreed and at about 11 o'clock they took off together and climbed up into the blue to 12,000 feet over East Anglia where Wright put his Mustang through the routine post-overhaul checks to reassure himself it was handling correctly. When he was satisfied he called up Clarke on the R/T and they began a mock dogfight with camera guns.

They had been 'fighting' for some time when suddenly, down out of the sun, came a squadron formation of American Thunderbolts. It was common, though unofficial, practice for rival formations to engage in mock battle and they

118

quickly broke off their private fight to take on the Americans. Another R.A.F. Mustang pilot, hearing Wright's battle cry on the R/T, called to them that he was on his way to join the fray.

For about 10 minutes the sky around Wright was a zooming whirl of Thunderbolts. They came at him from all directions and he found himself dogfighting with one American after another in a series of friendly but spirited duels. Presently another American Mustang arrived to reinforce the Thunderbolts and made a more than somewhat disconcerting head-on attack on Wright. As the other Mustang came straight for him he thought 'Lord – he's going to hit me' and pushed his stick hard forward. The Mustang flashed over his cockpit so low that he instinctively ducked, missing him by less than inches. He was badly shaken. He enjoyed a mêlée in the sky, but the war for him was almost over, he had a wife and he didn't want to die needlessly. He pressed his transmitter button and called Clarke – 'Nobby, I've had enough. These chaps are crazy.' He rolled on to his back, and dived away from the scene of battle and looking back, saw that Clarke was following him down.

He lost height very quickly. His airspeed indicator wound up to 500 miles an hour and seeing Bentwaters ahead he began to ease out of the dive. It was then he noticed that the aircraft was going into a gentle starboard turn. Automatically, he moved the stick slightly to the left and applied a touch of left rudder – but the Mustang went on turning, slowly but determinedly to starboard. He moved the stick back to come out of the dive. There was a great pressure on the stick but there was no response.

By now he was down to 2,000 feet and his airspeed indicator was showing close to 600 miles an hour. He closed the throttle and tried to bring the nose up with the trim wheel. It had no effect. And now the turn grew tighter, so tight that he was pressed hard down against the seat and everything in his sight began to go grey. He tried to lift his hand off the trim wheel but couldn't: it was held there as if by a great weight it was powerless to lift. To counteract the forces of the turn he lowered his head and took up a crouching attitude.

His indicated airspeed was now above 600 and he saw through the grey haze that the needle had passed the red dangerline. In his last seconds of consciousness he knew that there was nothing he could do to save himself. None of the controls would answer and against them he was powerless to climb out. No kaleidoscopic flashes of his past life came to him. He felt calm and unperturbed in a dull sort of way and his only thoughts were of Nora his wife, serving in the W.A.A.F. Then the greyness became black and he knew no more.

The next few seconds of the story come from Clarke. He was tailing Wright's Mustang down and when it began its uncontrollable starboard turn he turned with it, waiting for Wright to level off. When the other aircraft didn't pull out and its turn grew steeper he realized something was wrong and called Wright on the R/T. He got no answer. He was calling again when he saw the whole of the tail unit detach itself from the fuselage and float away. His own airspeed was now close to the danger mark so he levelled off, turning as he did so to keep the other Mustang in view.

With a taut, empty feeling in his stomach he saw the tailless Mustang go into a tight level turn. Another second and there would be a flash and a great mushroom of smoke. And there was nothing he could do but watch.

When the Mustang was so low that its camouflage had almost merged with the pattern of the countryside below, Clarke saw its wings tear off. Among the shower of debris Wright's slumped body curved forward and downward through the air, trailing a few feet of parachute silk. It crashed through the top branches of the oak, shot through the hedge, hit the ground with a puff of dust some yards beyond, and careered across the field of green oats ploughing a long shallow trench as it went.

Clarke called Bentwaters control tower and circled the far edge of the field where he could see Wright sprawled motionless among the oats. Then to his delight he saw him sit up. It seemed unbelievable to him that any man could have survived after being hurled at such high speed through a tree and for so far along the ground. But as quickly as he had been cheered his spirits sank again a moment later when he saw the figure on the ground roll over and lie still. From the air there was something so final about it that Clarke was convinced Wright had revived only to make a few dying gasps. He waited until he saw the ambulances reach the spot then flew back to the aerodrome. It was sad enough losing a fellow pilot but here the tragedy was doubled by a life-long friendship between their respective families.

When Wright had regained consciousness lying on his back in the field he had no recollection at first of the events of the morning. He felt no pain and for a moment he thought he was lying outside the mess as the squadron pilots sometimes did before lunch. He felt warm and sleepy and lying there the thought suddenly hit him – 'the so-and-so's, they've left me here asleep and sneaked off to lunch without me!' But then he saw the unfamiliar field. He sat up. A sharp pain jabbed him in the chest and he passed out again. When next he came round he was surrounded by Americans and R.A.F. medical orderlies and someone was saying, 'Take it easy, sir, you're all right.'

An R.A.F. ambulance took him to station sick quarters at Bentwaters and there Clarke came to visit him and saw that he was indeed very much alive. The doctors, however, were prepared for the worst and he was taken to Ipswich hospital where it was assumed it would be discovered he had serious internal injuries. But to medical surprise he had none. The total of his injuries was: a fractured sternum (breast bone to which the ribs are attached), a fractured small wrist bone, a few chipped bones elsewhere, severe bruising, and concussion. Within three weeks he was out of hospital.

Before he rejoined the squadron, Wright went down to Farnborough where scientists had gathered the pieces of his Mustang together and, with his help, reconstructed the sequence of events which led to the crash. It had all begun with a starboard elevator hinge. The hinge had broken, the elevator had flicked up into the slipstream and the drag on that side had started the turn from which there was no recovery. And as the speed and *g* had increased beyond the limits the aircraft had been built to withstand, first the tail, where the stress was aggravated by the protruding elevator, and then the wings, had broken off.

It was the wings which, in breaking, had been the first of several factors which combined to save Wright. His seat was attached to the top of the wing centre section and it was here that the wing had fractured. As the two halves had torn away, the seat attachment had broken and he had been shot out in the seat. The safety straps holding him to the seat had snapped, releasing him, and, most fortuitously of all, as he was ejected, unconscious, the cable from the ripcord handle to his parachute pack had caught on the flap lever and been torn off. This opened his chute in the same instant that he left the disintegrating cockpit, but he had hit the tree so soon afterwards the silk had only begun to stream from the pack. Nevertheless this made a further contribution to his salvation and without it he would certainly have been killed.

As he went through the tree, the little silk that had emerged caught in the branches, swiftly ripped out the rest of the canopy and rigging lines and drastically reduced his speed. Most of the canopy and rigging lines then tore off, leaving Wright to continue his journey with only his parachute harness left. Other factors which saved him were that, having been thrown out forward as the Mustang was banked in its final turn at 300 feet he had a wide field free of solid obstructions on which to decelerate relatively gently. Finally was the fact that he was unconscious throughout his violent journey and his body therefore limp; had he been consciously bracing himself en route he would probably have been fatally injured by the severe punishment his body received.

All these things helped to bring Wright back to fly another day. Had just one of them been missing from the swift chain of circumstances then his would have remained another partly explained crash. And because his parachute played a vital, if unusual part in saving his life he was admitted to the Caterpillar Club.

Wright's accident saved other lives. His was one of a number of similar Mustang Mk 3 crashes at that time but none of the other pilots had survived to describe the symptoms. After his accident all R.A.F. Mk 3 Mustangs were grounded until they had been fitted with stronger elevator hinges.

At what speed Wright hit the oak tree it is difficult to say. The last time he saw his airspeed indicator it showed just over 600 miles an hour and he left the aircraft very soon after. This does not mean, however, that his true speed on sailing away from the cockpit was as high as that. It was probably very much lower. The explanation lies in the fact that the pilot's airspeed indicator is calibrated to relate the pressures on the aircraft's leading surfaces during flight to miles-an-hour or knots. The pressure, which increases the faster the aircraft flies, is fed from an open tube, facing into the air stream, to the airspeed indicator in the cockpit. The instrument reads the difference between this pressure and the normal atmospheric pressure at the height at which the aircraft is flying. In many Second World War fighters the tube which fed the atmosphere pressure to the instruments was placed away from the other tube to avoid airflow disturbances, but in such a position on the fuselage that at high airspeeds big negative pressures occurred round the tube. The effect of this was high false readings – sometimes nearly twice that of the aircraft's true airspeed.

Even had Wright's airspeed indicator doubled his true speed, giving him an exit velocity of 300 miles an hour, his must still rank as one of the Club's most sensational escapes of all time.

CHAPTER XI

When his aircraft is in imminent danger, he has ordered his crew to 'Jump! Jump!', and each man is acknowledging the order, the reply which every captain dreads is – 'I can't jump, Skipper – no parachute'.

Sometimes in these circumstances a pilot has, in the highest traditions of his calling, offered up his own parachute knowing that there was a chance he could put the aircraft down, though often such a slender one that giving up his parachute meant giving up his life.

During the Second World War there were times when the man whose chute has been damaged or lost, or destroyed was at a crew station in the rear of the aircraft and cut off from the cockpit by fire amidships. It was then that the captain had to make the terrible decision whether or not to stay at the controls. Sometimes it has happened that the aircraft had been breaking up and his sacrifice was needless; sometimes the pilot stayed only to die in an explosion on the way down or in a crash landing. There have been other occasions when two men have baled out on the same parachute.

During the war aircrew often discussed how they would do this if the need arose. It was agreed that where they were wearing chest-type chutes the safest way was to stand side by side and for each to attach one of the two rings of the pack on to one of the snap hooks on his harness. Since the parachute is designed to take a strain of more than a ton during opening, the prospect of a safe dual descent was considered to be reasonably healthy. The big obstacle, however, was that the escape hatches in most aircraft were too narrow for two men to squeeze through side by side. And so it was that on the few occasions when parachutes were shared, if they couldn't reach the main exit door, the 'passenger' usually rode on the parachutist's back. Unfortunately, in this position it was almost impossible for the 'passenger' to get a firm enough grip that would withstand the opening shock – it has been described as the shock experienced in violently braking a car travelling at 100 miles an hour – and at least in every case the Caterpillar Club has heard of, he fell off when the ripcord was pulled.

If ever a man deserved to survive a dual bale-out it was Flying Officer Dickie Carroll, a 34-year-old Irishman from County Waterford. He was the bomb aimer in a Lancaster of No. 100 Squadron which was badly shot up by a night fighter, returning from a target in France on the night of June 11, 1944. The rear gunner was badly wounded and

124

after the bale-out order Carroll, regardless of his own safety, delayed his exit to go back along the fuselage and help the wireless operator drag the gunner out of his turret which had jammed. He moved the barely conscious man to the main door, put his hand on his ripcord for him, and pushed him out.* Then he went forward again to collect his own parachute, but found that it was missing – presumably fallen out through the open hatch in the nose. The pilot suggested they jump together. With great difficulty, as the Lancaster was now diving steeply Carroll climbed on his back and after a long struggle they squeezed together through the narrow escape hatch and dropped out. As soon as they had fallen clear, the pilot pulled his ripcord. He looked round. The chute was open – but Carroll was no longer with him.

Eight months later, on the other side of the world, two other men tried. A Liberator of No. 358 Squadron had made the 1,200-mile flight from its base at Jessore in Bengal to drop equipment to an Allied team working in Japanese-held territory near Hanoi in what was then Indo-China. The dropping zone had been blanketed by cloud and after fruitless attempts to get below it, the captain had decided to abandon the drop and return to base.

The search for the dropping zone had used up a good deal of precious fuel. There would have been enough to reach base but a monsoon storm over Burma forced them southward off course. About 100 miles from Jessore at 2 o'clock in the morning when they had been airborne for 14½ hours the captain warned the crew that they had insufficient fuel to get home and called them on to the flight deck. Shortly after, the fuel pressure indicators for the two starboard engines began to flicker and the captain gave the order 'to abandon'. As the crew began to leave, the starboard engines cut out.

The second pilot, Flight Sergeant Cyril Collins, an Australian from Deniliquin, New South Wales, was making his way back to the bomb-bay doors which the captain had opened for them to jump through, when he met the first

* The gunner, Sergeant D. R. Foggo, landed safely and was taken prisoner.

125

wireless operator. He had been busy sending out an SOS and he told Collins that he had left his parachute in the rear of the aircraft when he had gone back earlier during a rest period. The Liberator was already losing height, they were below 2,500 feet and Collins knew there was no time to go back for it. He said: 'Hop on my back.'

The wireless operator locked his arms through Collins's harness and crossed his legs round his body. They jumped through the bomb-bay out into the Bengal moonlight, and Collins pulled the ripcord. Despite his fierce clutchings the wireless operator was torn away as the canopy thumped open. Collins heard the swish of his body as it fell away. Then he was alone, left to continue his silent descent, shocked by the tragedy.

But there was at least one 'passenger' whose strong arm resisted the shock of opening. He was the rear gunner of a Halifax and it happened one night over Germany in 1943. Because his parachute had been burnt he went out on the back of the wireless operator who, though wounded, persuaded him to take a chance and join him. They left the burning Halifax at about 15,000 feet. The parachute jerked open and still the gunner clung on. It took about 10 minutes to come down and several times during the descent the wireless operator's injuries caused him to pass out. Each time he revived he was gratified to feel his 'passenger' firmly grasping his harness.

When they were but a few hundred feet from the ground the wireless operator blacked out again briefly. And this time, so nearly at journey's end, he came round to find that the gunner had gone. Seconds later he landed and lost consciousness. The Germans who found him told him that the gunner's body was only a few feet away. The arms that had withstood the tremendous opening shock – made more violent by the double load – had grown tired. Had they jumped from just a thousand feet lower one parachute might have given the Club two members.

The following year, in November 1944, one parachute did just that.

It is difficult to give the story credence – but it did happen.

126

Two men were blown out of a Halifax, 17,000 feet over Germany. One was wearing his parachute, the other was not. Twelve thousand feet down – 5,000 feet above the ground – the man with the parachute pulled his ripcord. As his chute began to open, the other man collided with him in mid-air and grabbed his legs. They continued the journey to earth together.

The players in this mid-air drama were two Australians, Flight Lieutenant Joe Herman and Flight Sergeant John ('Irish') Vivash. They were members of the crew of a Halifax of No. 466 Squadron of the R.A.A.F. Herman, tall and with skin tanned brown from the life he had forsaken back in Queensland first as a cattleman then as a goldminer, was the pilot, Vivash the mid-upper gunner.

They flew out from Driffield at dusk on November 4 to bomb Bochum in the Ruhr. Twice near the target they were coned by searchlights and twice Herman peeled violently away into the protecting darkness before the ack-ack could pick them off. To be caught twice by searchlights within the space of a minute seemed a bad omen to Herman. A great deal of flak was bursting around them and he had such a strong premonition that they would be coned again and not escape, that for the first time in 33 operations he called up his crew and suggested they clip on their parachutes. They did so – all except Herman himself, who was too preoccupied with the run up to the target to have his own pack brought to him from its rack in the engineer's compartment behind.

A minute later the bomb aimer reported from the nose that the bombs were away; they flew on out of the worst of the flak and searchlights, then turned west for home. As soon as they had settled down on the new course Herman began to let down from 18,000 to 10,000 feet as he had been briefed. He had scarcely begun his descent when he felt a frightening thud from behind – they had received a direct flak hit in the fuselage just behind the rear spar of the wing.

Immediately Herman took evasive action, swinging the Halifax to port. But as they pulled away he felt two more

127

heavy thuds from behind and knew they had been hit again. The second and third hits were in the wings; they set alight the fuel tanks on both sides and, in seconds, the port and starboard wings were burning from root to tip.

Herman knew that they had at most a minute before the wings weakened and folded back. He shouted over the intercom: 'Bale out! Bale out! Bale out!' He held the aircraft straight and level and one by one the crew dropped out into the night. Presently, only Vivash and the engineer, Sergeant Harry Knott, were left. Herman wondered why Vivash hadn't gone and then over the fading intercom he recognized his voice.

'I think my leg's broken, Skip. Can you help me?'

'Can't leave my seat, Irish,' Herman called back. 'Get Harry to give you a hand.'

Looking back along the fuselage, Herman saw the stocky figure of Knott directing the fire extinguisher at the flames around the rear spar. Seeing that he was no longer connected to the intercom he tried to wiggle the wings to attract his attention and tell him about Vivash. But the aileron controls had been burnt through and he got no response from the control wheel. There was no elevator response either, so, as he had lost all control over the aircraft, there was no point in remaining in the cockpit. He undid his seat harness and went back to get the others out and to collect his parachute.

He was relieved to see Vivash crawling along the fuselage towards him, dragging his injured leg. Before helping him he decided to collect his parachute from the engineer's compartment. He stepped up on to the raised floor of the compartment, pulled his helmet off and was about to reach down for the parachute when, out of the corner of his eye, he saw the starboard wing fold back in a great shower of fire.

The Halifax flicked over on to its back and before Herman could reach his parachute the aircraft had started to spin and he was flung against the side of the fuselage. He thrust both hands up to brace himself against the roof and at that moment the Halifax exploded. The roof disappeared

128

and Herman found himself falling through the cold night air amid a shower of debris.

He was fully conscious – conscious most of all of the fact that he had no parachute. The knowledge brought a chill to his heart and for a second or two he panicked, struggling violently in the air because he wanted desperately to do something and that was all he could do.

And then realization of the dreadful inevitability of it all came to him and he relaxed his body, resigned to die somewhere far below, very soon. He remembered that they had been at about 17,500 feet when the aircraft blew up. He didn't know how long it took a man to fall 17,500 feet but guessed it wasn't much more than a minute,

It wasn't pitch dark. A three-quarter moon bathed the countryside below in its pale glow and not far away the long white beams of several searchlights moved, exploringly, about the sky. He noticed that various broken metal pieces of the aircraft were apparently stationary a few yards from him and then he realized why: they were falling at the same rate as he was. He had left the Halifax in a shower of debris and presently he would hit the ground and die in that same debris.

Looking at the shapes of the wreckage around him it occurred to him with a flash of hope that perhaps his parachute was falling nearby. But when he looked closer he saw nothing that resembled the oblong of the chute pack, saw, too, that in any case none of the falling metal chunks was within reach.

Although he was slowly rotating there was no sensation of falling. One moment he was looking at the stars, then the ground, then the stars again. It felt as if he was being gently swung round on a feather bed. He was surprised to find that the ground didn't appear to get any closer. And there were moments when, because there was no discomfort about his mode of descent, he had a sudden sense of detachment from it all, a feeling that he was a witness not the participant. But these were brief moments, quickly overshadowed by the terror he felt at the prospect of the final crunch. He knew he wouldn't know anything about it when

129

it came; it was thinking about it and waiting for it that was so demoralizing.

Far below he saw the meandering ribbon of a river, silver in the moonlight. With another glimmer of hope he wondered if he might land in it, saving himself by cleaving the water cleanly head first like a high diver. He knew that water could be as hard as dry land and he would be killed just as surely in the river, yet he clung to the hope for the meagre comfort it gave him.

Several times when his emotions got the better of him and he thought how little time was left to him he wanted to scream, 'Oh God – don't let me die like this.' He cannot recall whether he did cry out, but the prayer was turning fiercely in his mind.

Suddenly his body hit something with a great thump. 'This is it,' he thought. And then with a sort of mental somersault he knew that conscious thought was still with him and that he wasn't dead after all.

The thump had winded him and as he fought for his breath he became aware that he was clinging to an object with both arms. And then a few feet away he was startled to hear a voice. He knew the voice. It was his mid-upper gunner's, 'Irish' Vivash's – *and he was gripping Vivash's legs*. Above them was a parachute, fully open.

If Vivash had been a character in aeronautical fiction, his creator would hardly have let him meet Herman with less than, 'Good God! It can't be possible!' Or in lighter vein, 'Hello, old chap – fancy meeting you here.' But truth, it is said, is stranger than fiction. Both men were still dazed by the explosion that had flung them into mid-air. For them in that moment there was no drama, no miracle. Later, when they reconstructed the incident and between them recalled the conversation they agreed that this was the dialogue—

Vivash: 'Is there anybody around?'

Herman: 'Yes, I'm down here.'

Vivash: 'Where? Where are you?'

Herman: 'Here, just below. I'm hanging on to your legs.'

Vivash (by now he had recognized Herman's voice): 'Be careful of my right leg, Joe. I think it's broken (in fact his leg wasn't broken. Both legs had been badly punctured in seven places by shrapnel and were numb which, plus the fact that he was still suffering from the shock of the explosion, explains why he couldn't feel Herman hanging there).

Herman: 'O.K.' (and after a pause) 'Are any of the crew around, do you know?'

Vivash: 'I think the navigator and wireless op are above somewhere.'

Herman: 'Good show.'

They fell some distance in silence, neither man fully comprehending the situation, Herman aware – if he wasn't dreaming it all – only that his life had been, at least temporarily, spared and that for its prolongment he must not for an instant relax his grip, Vivash more concerned with his damaged leg than with the uninvited fellow traveller who had joined him out of the darkness.

Presently Vivash spoke again.

'When we get near the deck, d'you think you'll be able to drop off?'

Herman, whose arms were aching and who was beginning to wonder if he could hang on for much longer, said, 'Maybe'. Then he saw the black bowl of the horizon going up around them, then the tops of trees.

'Look out,' he shouted. 'The deck's coming up.' He felt the leaves of a tree brush past but before he could release his grip and fall clear, his feet hit the ground, he rolled over, and Vivash landed heavily on top of his chest – breaking two ribs.

For a few minutes they lay gasping on the ground. Then Herman, who recovered first, got up. He saw that they had come down in a small clearing in a pine wood; the parachute hung above them, hooked up on a tree. Slowly, in the darkness, he examined himself. Until then he hadn't been aware of any injuries but now, as well as the broken ribs, which were painfully stabbing his chest, he found that his face and ears were split open and bleeding, his left leg was cut and he was bruised from head to feet. His left flying boot was missing and the left leg of his trousers was in tatters. But to Herman who had, a few minutes earlier, been plunging

131

down through mid-air, resigned to death, these injuries seemed for the moment trivial. He was alive; he could walk. He asked for no more.

As the numbness in his legs wore off, Vivash began to feel the full agony of his wounds. But after Herman had stopped the bleeding and bandaged his legs with strips of silk torn from the parachute, he was able to walk after a fashion. In fact he managed to walk, with Herman, evading capture for four days. But on November 8, when they were well on their way to Holland, they were caught and taken prisoner.

During their days of liberty, as the shock wore off and they were able to revive the fantastic events of that night coldly and factually, Herman and Vivash tried to analyse the events that culminated in the mid-air miracle.

When the Halifax had exploded at about 17,500 feet, they had both been blown out. Apart from a few seconds' mental void after the explosion, Herman had been fully conscious as he fell. Fortunately for Herman, Vivash had blacked out in the explosion – otherwise he would have pulled his ripcord much sooner than he did and there would have been no mid-air reunion. They had fallen, therefore, for what they estimated must have been about 12,000 feet, dropping through the darkness at around 175 feet a second, amid a shower of debris, keeping perfect station a few yards from each other. Vivash would not have seen Herman for he was unconscious for the greater part of his free fall; Herman, on the other hand, realized later that one of the objects he could see falling near him might well have been Vivash.

About 5,000 feet above the ground (they estimated this height from the time they judged it took them to descend together) Vivash had partly recovered consciousness, and pulled the ripcord. He did not remember pulling it but did so half automatically in the mists of semi-consciousness.

As his chute streamed out of the pack on his chest he began to swing out under it like a pendulum. This oscillation at the moment of opening is normal. Herman owes his life to it. For, and here the odds were piled against him, at the

132

end of his first swing towards Herman, it just happened that Herman was at a point in his head over heels tumbling cycle where he was face down and almost horizontal. In this position he smashed on to Vivash's legs which were also nearly horizontal at the end of his swing. A second or so later, Vivash's parachute would have been fully developed, Vivash would have decelerated from 120 to about 11 miles an hour and Herman still falling at 120 m.p.h. would merely have bounced off. But at the moment they collided, Vivash was still falling fast. Herman's grip above his knees held, and as the canopy bumped fully open they both decelerated together.

Before they met they had fallen more than two miles, which took them just over a minute. Herman worked it out that at that point he would have had less than half a minute of life left to him. Instead, thanks to Vivash, he covered the last mile to the ground in three to four minutes.

All of Herman's crew came down safely that night. Both Herman and Vivash returned to Australia after the war and became civilians again. But Vivash had survived the explosion over Germany only to die subsequently by other means; a few years after the war he was killed in a motor cycle accident in New South Wales.

Paratroops are rarely eligible for membership of the Caterpillar Club because they don't often jump to save their lives; jumping is their job. Sergeant Tom Spencer, of the 11th Parachute Battalion, was an exception. He met his emergency after he went out on a routine jump – and another parachute saved his life. It all happened in the space of 400 feet and less than 15 seconds.

In the latter half of 1943 the 11th Parachute Battalion was forming at Ramat David, a parachute training school near Haifa. The battalion was nearing the end of training when Spencer volunteered to join a platoon of trainees to repeat a particularly arduous exercise he had already done once. It was a jump on to a dropping zone on the Plain of Acre, about 20 miles from Ramat David, after which the platoon had to make the long march back to base.

There were 20 men in the stick of which Spencer was

133

number 16. Four containers packed with Bren guns and ammunition were to be dropped at the same time; they were carried in racks under the fuselage and were released automatically, two by No. 7 and two by No. 15. To avoid colliding with the container parachute numbers 8 and 16, who followed them, had to pause at the exit door for a few seconds before jumping.

They took off from Ramat David in a Dakota soon after 8 o'clock and reached the dropping zone about 10 minutes later, flying at 400 feet. One behind the other the paratroopers filed up to the open door and in swift succession on the command 'Go!' began jumping. They had no rip-cords to pull: a static line linking each parachute with the aircraft opened the parachutes automatically as they fell away.

When Spencer reached the door he paused to count five to allow the container chutes to drop clear, then with stomach fluttering as his always did at that moment, he leaped smartly out. Out of the corner of one eye he saw the aircraft's tail plane pass quickly over his head. Then, glancing down, he saw the coloured container chutes, one blue, one orange, with their cylindrical cargoes pendulum-swinging about 50 feet below him and beyond, the white chutes of the men who had preceded him, descending in a long diagonal row. Instinctively he put his hands up to grip his lift webs. They weren't there. His parachute hadn't opened.

It takes only about four or five seconds to fall 400 feet.* And that is how quickly Spencer would have hit the ground – had fate not decreed otherwise. Had his jumping sequence number been any other than 16 – except perhaps 8 – events would have been tragically different. But as No. 16 he was close behind the container chutes. It was one of these that saved him.

* A paratrooper, whose chute has not opened, does not fall at the same terminal velocity as a free-falling man. The 'squidded', undeveloped canopy offers enough resistance sometimes to reduce his rate of descent to as much as ½-terminal velocity – about 60 m.p.h. It is not *much* consolation – although a few paratroopers have survived falls with unopened chutes for this reason.

It happened so quickly that it had hardly registered in Spencer's mind that his own chute had failed him when he fell feet-first into the rigging lines of the orange container chute. Having just opened, it was still oscillating and at the moment he arrived it had conveniently swung out under him. A half-second earlier or later and he would have missed it.

His clutching hands grabbed two handfuls of rigging lines and he felt a sear of pain as the lines bit into the flesh of his bare legs below his shorts, entangling him, a few feet above the supply cylinder, as effectively as a fly in a web. Above him, the orange canopy began to flap and the side he was suspended from crumpled and folded up. With the weight of its new burden and because he had partly collapsed the canopy, the chute began to go down at dangerous speed.

Spencer found he was hanging in a crouching attitude with his knees drawn up. He struggled to release his legs to avoid landing on the base of his spine. He could see the blur of the ground coming up fast and knew that he had only a few seconds – less than 200 feet – in which to change position.

He tried grappling with one hand, tearing at the silk cords and fiercely wriggling his left boot. At last the leg came free. But time had run out. The hazy brown flat of the ground was now less than 20 feet away. Grasping the rigging lines above him he drew his body up as high as his strength would take him. The container clanged on to the ground and he hit beside it.

His left leg twisted under him and as it snapped up behind him his boot cracked into his back, fracturing his spine. He was taken to hopital in Haifa. Despite the seriousness of his injuries – spine, leg and pelvis fractured, and leg burns from his violent impact with the container rigging lines – he recovered quickly. Three months later, by which time he was able to get about with crutches, he was discharged; after another four months he could walk normally again. He went back to the Parachute Regiment – but on medical orders not to jump again.

Although it wasn't a man-carrying parachute that save
his life, Spencer's escape made him eligible for membershi
of the Caterpillar Club because the container chute was o
Irvin design. And he is the only one of the Europea
Branch's 30,000 members to have saved his life in this way

CHAPTER XII

When the war ended in 1945, the Letchworth branch of th
Caterpillar Club was 27,000 strong. Twenty-three thou
sand had been wartime enrolments, 13,000 of them in th
last year of the war. Gradually, as squadrons were dis
banded, and the air forces contracted, the flood of appli
cations subsided. By the end of 1945 the management o
the Club was no longer a full-time job and Mary Loft
found she could cope with the trickle of enrolments in he
spare moments.

Irvin went back to his company's headquarters at Buffalo
leaving Captain Cyril Turner, a First World War test pilo
and an airline captain of the early twenties, in charge o
the Letchworth factory. Before he left England, Irvin mad
his last parachute jump. He made it from a Dakota of th
Parachute Training School at Ringway, near Mancheste

He had been invited to attend one of the School's partie
During the war he had been a frequent visitor to Ringwa
where 60,000 British and Allied parachutists had bee
trained, and at its staff parties had acquired a reputatio
for a parlour trick he could sometimes be prevailed upo
to perform. The trick, which he had learnt in his circus day
as a youth, was to stand on his head against a piano an
play 'I want to be happy' while drinking a glass of beer.

At the height of this particular party Irvin was invited t
join some of the instructors the following morning in a loca
ceremony known as 'The Mortification of the Flesh'. I
simple terms it meant parachuting from 700 feet into th
cold water of Rostherne Mere, a nearby lake. Lightheart
edly, Irvin agreed. And next morning, although he was the

somewhat less enthusiastic about the ritual, he joined the instructors and General Crawford, Director of Air at the War Office, in an icy plunge into the lake where they were picked up by a waiting launch. Irvin was then in his fiftieth year. He had lost count of the number of times he had jumped in all, but he knew it was well over 300. He had resolved that many of the jumps he had made in the previous five years would be his last, but somehow he had always been tempted again. But this time, he decided, his jumping days were over. He never jumped again.

The 34 years of Irvin's active parachuting career, which ended at Rostherne Mere, had spanned an era in aviation in which aircraft speeds had crept from 50 to more than 400 miles an hour. It had been the era of the piston-engined aeroplane, and the parachute which he had designed 27 years before had served that age faithfully. But now, in 1945, the smell of paraffin was already in the air and a new age was in lusty infancy. Jet propulsion was bringing level-flight speeds of 600 miles an hour and more. And aircrew now needed more than a silk umbrella to help them in an emergency. The rush of the airflow and *g* forces were becoming so great that they could not always struggle out: they were liable to be pressed back, helplessly, into their cockpits. The time had come for some forceful means of ejection. Fortunately that means was on the way.

It had been on the way since January 1944. At Farnborough, early that month, there had been an accident that tragically underlined the urgency of some form of safe ejection from jet aircraft in an emergency.

A Royal Aircraft Establishment test pilot was testing an early version of the Gloster Meteor, when engine failure made it necessary for him to bale out. But in his attempts to leave the cockpit he was battered by the airflow, lost consciousness and, shortly afterwards, was flung out. Still unconscious, he crashed to the ground and was killed.

As a result of this accident an escape device became the subject of urgent investigation and by the spring of 1944, preliminary experiments were begun at the Royal Aircraft Establishment to discover how the human body reacted to the violent accelerations and decelerations that ejection would require.

The doctors of the R.A.F. Institute of Aviation Medicine, many of whom were also qualified aircrew, whose assignment this was, were their own 'guinea pigs'. They used a 2,000-ft long rocket track, on Laffan's Plain at Farnborough, which had been built earlier in the war for tests with balloon cable cutting devices. A rocket-propelled trolley, on which the doctors were strapped, was fired along the rails of the track at about 40 to 50 m.p.h. Most of the trials were done by Squadron Leader William K. Stewart, who was to become Director of the Institute. To simulate the attitude and forces of sudden ejection from a cockpit, he lay on his back with legs drawn up and bent at the knees – as they would be in a seat. At the end of its journey the trolley was abruptly stopped by hydraulic rams which could be adjusted to vary the rate of deceleration.

In the course of more than 12 rides down the track, Stewart found that he could tolerate decelerations of up to 12g without injury, so long as the peak of 12g was not imposed on him for longer than a tenth of a second. Above 7g his head was uncontrollably flicked forward, and to prevent injury on deceleration at higher g it was necessary to lie on the trolley with his head supported and strapped down. Although these were *decelerative* forces and those which would be experienced at the moment of ejection would be *accelerative*, for the purpose of human toleration they were treated as the same.

The Aerodynamics Department of the R.A.E. was now in a position to relate the forces that a man could take, to the realities of sudden expulsion from a cockpit into a high-speed airflow. Basing his calculations on the newly acquired rocket track data, Professor A. D. Young of that Department worked out the fundamental mathematics of ejection. He declared that the basic requirement for a seat, or other device, that would take its occupant upwards out of the cockpit without injury, and clear of the tail unit, at the same time imposing a maximum acceleration of 12g for no more

han a tenth of a second, was one with an ejection velocity
of about 40 feet per second.

While the scientists and aviation doctors were laying these
foundations at Farnborough in the early summer of 1944,
plans, and a small-scale model, of a pilot ejector were taking
shape in a small factory at Higher Denham, near Uxbridge.
It was the factory of the Martin-Baker Aircraft Company
and the ejector was the inspiration of the Company's managing director and chief designer, James Martin, a nuggety,
dynamic, sandy-haired Ulsterman.

Martin had become interested in the escape project as a
result of a conversation with Wing Commander John Jewell,
a Fighter Command technical staff officer (eight years later
when he retired from the R.A.F. Jewell was to join Martin's
staff). Martin's inventive genius was well recognized by the
Command's technical officers and they had been in the habit
of seeking his advice, unofficially, on various fighter
modification problems which arose from time to time. Jewell had consulted him several times and when, in the spring
of 1944, medical and technical staff officers at Fighter Command Headquarters began to address themselves in earnest
to the bale-out problem, Jewell inevitably turned to Martin.

The challenge so appealed to Martin that he determined
forthwith to design a cockpit escape device as a private
venture. The outcome was a swinging arm ejector which
would hurl the pilot upwards and backwards out of his seat,
flinging him clear of the tail unit. He suggested that the arm
be mounted along the top of the fuselage with its rear end
hinged just forward of the fin and the front end hooked on
to the pilot's parachute harness. To eject, the pilot would
merely have to jettison his canopy, undo his seat straps and
release the spring. Whereupon he would be whisked out of
the cockpit, the arm, having received its initial impetus from
the spring, being caught by the airflow and swinging him
up to a point where he would fly off the end of the hook
and be left to pull his ripcord.

Martin showed the model of his ejector to the Ministry
of Aircraft Production. The Ministry were interested enough

to agree to lend him a Defiant, a piston-engined night fighter in which to install a full-scale version.

By now, better escape methods had officially become an R.A.F. operational requirement. In July, the first Meteor – Mark 1s – had entered squadron service and almost immediately had tackled their first operational assignment – the interception of German flying bombs. During investigations which Fighter Command had made to discover ways of improving the performance of the Meteors against the flying bombs, Jewell had visited the first jet squadron No. 616, and talked to the pilots. While he discovered universal enthusiasm for the Meteors, he was quick to detect an underlying concern which some of the pilots felt about their escape chances at the new high speeds at which they were flying.

Although the Meteor Mk 1, with a top speed of 445 m.p.h. at 30,000 feet, was not a lot faster than some of its contemporary piston fighters, faster versions capable of 500 and 600 m.p.h. were coming along and Jewell, aware of the effect these misgivings could have on morale and fighting efficiency, had written a report for his Commander-in-Chief Air Marshal Sir Roderic Hill, in which he urged the introduction of some means of 'assisted escape'.

Sir Roderic had endorsed the recommendation and sent the report to the Air Ministry where it had given further impetus to the cause – impetus now sharpened by reports from R.A.F. pilots that German aircrew were 'popping out' of disabled aircraft in their seats, discarding the seats in mid-air, then opening their parachutes.

The truth was that the Germans were a great deal more far-sighted in the matter of high-speed escape than were the British. As far back as 1938 they had foreseen the need for it and their first experiments had begun that year. They did not leave development until the arrival of jet aircraft made it a necessity: they built an ejection seat and promptly began to make use of it in some of their piston, and later, jet aircraft.

The early German ejection seats were fired by compressed air guns and the first aircraft to be fitted was a Junkers 88 in 1939. By 1940 more than 200 test ejections had been made by firing seats up rails on ground test rigs – about 70 of them with human subjects. Four of the big aircraft companies, Dornier, Focke-Wulf, Junkers and Heinkel, were engaged on ejection projects, and among the aircraft to have seats installed were the Heinkel 219, a twin piston-engined night fighter in which both crew members – pilot and navigator – were catered for, the Heinkel 177, a four-engined piston bomber, and several jet fighters, including the Me 262, the He 280, and the He 162 – the *Volksjäger*.

The *Luftwaffe* first began to use ejection seats in 1941 and by 1943 German aircrew were using the seat in battle emergencies; the first such escape was from a night fighter over Venlo in Holland in the autumn of that year. There is no record of the precise number of successful *Luftwaffe* escapes, but it is known that in the last two years of the war more than 60 pilots made emergency ejections.

Although the compressed air guns effectively shot the seats clear of the aircraft, most of the early German models went out with such a violent 'kick' that the occupant was liable to have his spine injured. In fact, by 1944, when the German Air Ministry issued a directive that all front-line fighters were to be provided with ejection seats, the injury rate had given rise to such concern that a full-scale investigation of the physiological limitations was ordered. However, before the medical research had proceeded very far the war had ended.

Nevertheless, before Germany faded out of the high-speed ejection field, at least one company, Heinkels, had built a seat fired by an explosive charge and had experimented with the use of a small drogue parachute to prevent the seat from spinning after ejection. The drogue was eventually discarded in favour of metal stabilizing fins attached to the seat, but the fact of its conception is interesting in view of the vital part drogues were to play in British ejection seats several years later.

But in October 1944, when the Ministry of Aircraft Production held a meeting at which designers of the aircraft firms were told about the new escape needs, little was known of the German research, apart from the isolated reports that *Luftwaffe* pilots had been seen 'baling out in their seats'. And when Germany had surrendered the following year and full details of the German seats were available, British development had so advanced that we had little to learn from them.*

As a result of the October meeting, Martin's private venture gained official support, and another company, R. Malcolm Ltd, also embarked on the ejection project. For the Martin-Baker Company, then scarcely known outside the aircraft industry, the decision to pioneer this new field was to lead to fame. Within five years, over much of the world, its name was to become a byword among pilots who rode the sky in its tall angular quick-exit seats.

Martin had already made several contributions to the R.A.F.'s war effort. He had designed and built an explosive balloon cable cutter which had become a standard fitting on the wings of many Bomber Command aircraft, a jettisonable cockpit hood for the Spitfire, and in 1940 when there had been a shortage of suitable night fighters, had converted the nose of the Douglas Havoc to accommodate 12 forward-firing guns where normally there were only four.

When he had set up his factory at Higher Denham in 1929 with a total staff of two, he had called the business Martin Aircraft Works, for his ambition was to build aeroplanes. That ambition was fulfilled, but to his bitter disappointment it was not for his aircraft that his company was to become celebrated. They were remarkable aircraft some of them, but none ever went into production.

There was the M.B.1, a light two-seater monoplane, and, in 1938, its successor, the M.B.2, an eight-gun, 350-m.p.h. fixed undercarriage fighter. Then, in 1942 came the M.B.3 – and disaster. The M.B.3 was a high performance fighter, powered by a 2,000-h.p. Napier Sabre engine, capable of more than 400 m.p.h. and armed with six 20 mm. cannon

---

* In Sweden, the Saab Company had built an explosive ejection seat for the Swedish Air Force in 1943, but little was known about it in England when our own development began.

guns. Martin had high hopes that the R.A.F. would want
it, but the prototype hadn't been flying long when, at Wing,
on September 12, 1942, it crashed after engine failure on
take-off, killing the pilot, Captain Valentine Baker – Martin's co-director, whose name had been added to the company's title. For a small firm this was a crippling blow. It
was too late in the fighter design race to rebuild the M.B.3
and, after some preliminary investigation of an M.B.4, which
was discontinued, Martin had set to work on his M.B.5.
The M.B.5, powered by a Rolls-Royce Griffon engine driving a pair of triple-bladed counter-rotating propellers, was
designed for a top speed of 460 m.p.h. and was one of the
most powerful single-engined piston fighters ever built. But
it came at the dawn of the jet age and was too late. Martin
probably wouldn't have given up there: he would almost
certainly have launched a jet M.B.6 – had the ejection seat
project not come along.

Although they worked independently, both the Martin-
Baker Aircraft Company and R. Malcolm Ltd. maintained close liaison with the R.A.E. and the Institute of
Aviation Medicine at Farnborough where 'assisted escape'
research had certainly not ended with the Laffan's Plain
rocket trials. In those early days consideration was given
to ejecting aircrew downwards, sideways and upwards; one
suggestion was for a big braking parachute, attached to
the aircraft's tail, which could be opened in an emergency
to reduce speed and allow the crew to bale out without
difficulty, and another, a more dramatic proposal, was
for a system that would progressively disintegrate the
aircraft around the pilot, in such a way that he was eventually left sitting alone in mid-air, free to pull his ripcord!
But upward ejection was finally chosen as the best way
out.

Although Martin had been offered a Defiant for trials
with his swinging arm ejector, this startling device was never
built. Before it progressed beyond the model stage it became
clear that the most effective way of getting the pilot out was
by explosive methods. And so, in the autumn of 1944, all
efforts were directed towards the development of an explo-

sive ejection seat.* Although the Ministry had made available to him all the test data which the rocket trolley trials had yielded, Martin set out to learn still more about the body's capacity to withstand the sudden upward thrust he planned.

In his factory at Denham he built a test rig. It was a tubular steel affair, 15 feet high, with a pair of guide rails sloping up one corner. Between the rails a seat was fixed. The seat was loaded with bags of ballast of the weight of an average man and, with cameras recording it all, the seat was shot up the rails with a small explosive charge detonated by remote control.

After many experiments with charges of varying power Martin was satisfied that the accelerations were within the endurance of the human body. The time had come for tests with a human subject. Bernard Lynch, one of the company's experimental fitters, volunteered.

Lynch was 27 and in every respect an ideal subject. Thick-set and powerfully built, he had the sort of body that looked as if it could take a great deal of punishment. At the same time he was well suited by temperament for the experiment, being exceptionally cool and unflappable.

It was thought best to begin the human tests with short rides. On January 24, 1945, Lynch was firmly strapped on to the seat with a supporting band across his forehead and knees drawn up, which was then thought to be the best bracing position. The charge was exploded and Lynch shot abruptly up the rig to a height of 4 feet 8 inches. It happened so quickly he had scarcely any sensation of going up. He reported no undue discomfort and subsequently repeated the test three more times, each higher than the last. On his fourth ride up the rails when he was shot up to 9 feet 11 inches, however, Lynch complained of 'considerable physical discomfort'. As a result Martin limited the tests pending further investigation.

* R. Malcolm Ltd. were to build an explosive seat but subsequently discontinued ejection seat work. The only other British ejection seat manufacturer at present is Folland Aircraft Ltd, whose seat is fitted in the company's light fighter, the Gnat, of Red Arrows fame.

Meanwhile a number of R.A.F. and Royal Navy pilots and medical officers came to Denham for test rides. In all 180 live 'ejections' were made by various volunteers and a great deal of valuable information resulted. But of all these short violent journeys the most significant was that made by Mr C. F. Andrews, a representative of the aeronautical magazine, *The Aeroplane*. Andrews made the fourteenth ride. Next day, Martin heard that he was in hospital at Weybridge with crushed spinal vertebrae.

Martin went quickly to the hospital to visit Andrews and was shown the X-ray plates. He saw how the sudden burst of acceleration had jerked the vertebrae together and damaged them. Here, Martin realized, was a serious stumbling block to further development. An ejection seat liable to inflict injury on those who used it was clearly not good enough. He determined forthwith to learn more about the spine and its limitations under high g. He got permission to visit a hospital theatre and watched a number of spinal operations. Then he acquired part of a human skeleton on which he made acceleration tests at Denham. From these tests he learned two very important things. He found that the spine could tolerate relatively high acceleration without injury provided that the vertebrae were square to one another, and that the explosion pressure in the ejection gun came on relatively slowly before being increased to its maximum pressure.

The first of these requirements was quickly taken care of by redesigning the seat. Until then the volunteers had sat with knees well drawn up in such a way that the spine was curved and the vertebrae butted together. Now the footrest was lowered, the knees were not so high, the spine was straighter with more clearance between the vertebrae, and was thus less prone to damage from the sudden thrust of ejection. The other points Martin remedied by introducing an ingenious gun to shoot the seat out less violently. Instead of one cartridge he fitted two in such a way that the first ignited the second after the seat had begun to rise; the moment of sudden thrust was thus made smoother although the force which shot the seat well clear of the tail unit remained.

Martin was now convinced that he had the makings of a safe ejection seat and was anxious to proceed with trials in the air. A seat embodying all that he had so far learnt was fitted in the turret position of a modified Defiant, a dummy was strapped in and at R.A.F. Wittering on May 11, 1945, the seat was successfully ejected and floated down on a parachute opened by a time release device. After further dummy ejections from the Defiant up to speeds of 300 m.p.h. Martin asked the Ministry of Aircraft Production for a Meteor for high-speed trials. He was loaned a Meteor Mk 3 into which he fitted an ejection seat in the space behind the pilot normally occupied by the ammunition tanks, and on June 24, 1946, trials with dummies began at speeds above 400 m.p.h.

It was during these trials that a further refinement was added. To steady and decelerate the seat after ejection, Martin had fitted a small drogue parachute which streamed out behind as soon as it cleared the aircraft. During the high-speed trials it was found that the drogue was being drawn into the wake of the seat and was tangling with it. Martin saw that somehow the drogue must be made to shoot clear. He fitted a small gun to the seat to fire it out and after that the drogue never tangled again. All that remained now was for the seat to prove itself in a live ejection. And for that there was no shortage of volunteers.

Several R.A.F. pilots were keen to do it but Martin wanted the risk to stay with the company until the seat had made its supreme test. He didn't have to ask Lynch if he was interested. From the day he had ridden the first seat five feet up the test rig Lynch had secretly hoped that the first live ejection would be his.

After a short course in jumping, at the Parachute Training School, he made it from the Meteor, 8,000 feet over Chalgrove aerodrome near Benson on July 24, 1946, ejecting himself with a jerk of the face blind which fired the charge, protected his face from the blast of the airstream and prevented his head from jerking forward – the danger which Squadron Leader Stewart had discovered on the rocket trolley two years earlier.

The Meteor was travelling at 320 m.p.h. and those watching on the airfield below saw a small black bundle suddenly hurtle out and curve up and away behind the aircraft with the white speck of the stabilizing drogue streaming close to it. A few moments later they saw Lynch drop clear of the seat, fall a few hundred feet, then open his parachute. He landed unhurt near his seat, which had crashed down several minutes ahead of him. Like April 28, 1919, the day Irvin had made the first jump with a manual parachute, it was an historic day for Anglo-American military aviation. And in a sense Irvin played a part in both events, for the parachute on which Lynch continued his journey to earth was one of his.

The report which Lynch gave of his ejection couldn't have been more satisfactory. As he had pulled the blind over his face he had heard a bang, had only been vaguely aware of leaving the cockpit before he found himself sailing through the sky in his seat. He had waited a few seconds to slow down, then unfastened the straps and fallen head first out of the seat. After that it had just been a matter of pulling his ripcord. He had felt no sudden jar on ejecting, the blind had protected his face from the pummelling of the 300 miles-an-hour airstream and he had suffered no injury.

Subsequently Lynch made more than 30 ejections for the Martin-Baker Company – more than any other man. His last ejection in 1953 was from 30,000 feet, at that time the highest ever made in Britain. On landing he got caught up in a barbed wire fence and broke an ankle; it was the only injury he ever received in his eight dangerous years of ejection testing. He was a voluntary 'guinea pig' in a hazardous new sphere and the outcome of his bravery has been a device which, in 1947, was officially adopted by the R.A.F. and Royal Navy as standard equipment in most of their jet aircraft. By 1956 it had saved more than one hundred lives.

Since 1947 Martin has worked continuously to improve his life-saving seat. The first model which he gave the Services did just what the Services had asked – but it was a manual seat in that the pilot, after ejection, had to get himself out of it and open his parachute. This all took time and it meant that the seat couldn't be used with any guarantee of safety at heights below about 1,500 feet. It also meant that if the pilot became unconscious after ejection as a result of battle injuries, or lack of oxygen at high altitude, he might not revive in time to separate from the seat. Martin began designing again. The result, in 1951, was an automatic seat.

It incorporated an aneroid-controlled clock mechanism which, at any pre-set altitude and after any predetermined delay, operated a device which unfastened the seat harness, freed the pilot from the seat and opened his parachute for him. Below the pre-set altitude all these things happened almost immediately after ejection in such rapid sequence that safe ejection was possible down to 500 feet. All the pilot had to do was to jettison his cockpit hood and pull the ejection blind to fire his seat. If he passed out after that and all went well he would wake up safely on the ground. Both Services adopted the new seat and in many aircraft the manual seats already installed were converted to automatic operation. For aircraft flying over Britain the barostat was set to function at 10,000 feet (The Swiss Air Force – for obvious alpine reasons – set theirs at 17,000 feet) which brought seat and occupant quickly down through the cold, rarefied air of the higher levels to a more comfortable height before the parachute slowed things down. The possibility of failure of the automatic system through damage was provided for with an over-ride control by which the man in the seat could free himself manually. And for the free falling phase of the descent above 10,000 feet, there was a 10-minute supply of oxygen.

But Martin was still not satisfied. He wanted to make safe escape possible from heights even lower than 500 feet. And he achieved it.

The reason why the automatic seat could not be guaranteed to get the pilot safely into the silk below about 500 feet was because of the time taken to complete the sequence

148

of ejection. About five to six seconds elapsed from the time the firing blind was pulled until the parachute was fully developed. This delay was deliberately arranged because at high speeds immediate opening of the parachute is liable to burst the canopy and the drastic shock is more than the human body can take. The seat, therefore, embodied two timing controls. One was fitted to the drogue gun and set for one second's delay to allow the seat to clear the cockpit before the drogue deployed; the other, set for five seconds' delay, was built into the mechanism which separated the occupant from his seat and opened his parachute. The effect of all this was to give the seat time to decelerate to a safe parachute opening speed – but in the process, depending on the aircraft's speed, several hundred feet of height was lost.

If he was still to provide for the pilot who had to get out at 600 miles an hour and more, Martin knew that he couldn't reduce the time delays and make lower ejection possible without somehow cushioning the tremendous parachute opening shocks which quicker opening would often mean. The answer, he decided, lay in the business of decleration, in the drogue – a drogue that would slow the seat down smoothly, yet faster than it had been doing, was wanted.

In the end he solved the problem by using two drogues in tandem. The first, which was shot out by the drogue gun, was nearly two feet in diameter and as it hit the airflow it pulled out a much bigger drogue, five feet across, and, at the same time, tilted the seat on to its back so that the pilot's body took the deceleration forces in the safest position – longitudinally. Then, as he zipped forward through the air rapidly losing speed, the separating mechanism transferred the nylon drogue line from the seat to the pilot's parachute, pulling the parachute smoothly out of its pack and the pilot away from the seat with it.

With this duplex drogue system, Martin found that he could now safely reduce the time delays to half-a-second for the drogue gun and three seconds for the separating mechanism. This meant that within 3½ seconds of ejection the parachute was fully developed. If the aircraft was flying straight and level at the time, the seat would continue travelling forward in the first vital seconds with no great loss of height, and ejection as low as 100 – or even 50 feet, Martin claimed, was possible up to 600 m.p.h.

Having proved the 50 foot ejection with more than 50 tests, using dummies at speeds up to 650 m.p.h., Martin's next ambition was to provide for the last 50 feet – and right down to ground level if need be. He did so by reducing the separating time delay still further – to one-and-a-half seconds. And in a demonstration at Chalgrove on September 3, 1955, one of his test pilots, Squadron Leader J. S. Fifield, showed the world that Martin's claim to make bale-outs at nought feet possible was no extravagant boast. Using a seat fitted with a telescopic ejection gun* Fifield ejected himself from the rear cockpit of a Meteor 7 travelling at 140 m.p.h. while it was still on the ground. He shot up to a height of 80 feet where the two drogues were already drawing his parachute out, and landed 6½ seconds after ejecting, his chute having been fully developed for the last 35 feet of his descent.

Fifield's grasshopper act was a gallant demonstration of the remarkable versatility of the seat which Martin's genius had given the jet age pilot. But this same versatility posed a new problem.

The 'deck level' bale-out was only possible with the one-

* The supersonic speeds and high tail assemblies of some of the new generation military aircraft called for a seat with a higher ejection trajectory. The simplest way of doing this would have been to increase the explosive charge. But the objection to this was that it would also increase the acceleration beyond reasonable human toleration. The problem was solved with a telescopic gun which has three tubes inside one another. When the primary charge is fired the pressure generated takes the inner tube together with the middle tube and the seat on the start of its journey out of the cockpit. After it has gone 16 inches two ports are uncovered allowing the flame to ignite a pair of secondary charges, and as the telescope extends further, two more auxiliary charges are fired to boost the inner tube and seat on its way. By spreading the charges in this way the seat is made to eject without any greater acceleration forces than normally but they are applied for slightly longer and a higher ejection speed is achieved. The early guns expelled the seat at 50 or 60 feet a second: the telescopic gun does so at 80 feet a second.

and-a-half second time delay, which meant that it was only safe at relatively low speeds; at high speeds the drogues and parachute could burst if deployed so quickly. Yet, ideally, the seat must be able to save its occupant's life whether he pulls the blind a few feet after take-off or at 40,000 feet.

However, Martin, never at a loss for a design remedy, was again to solve the problem. He was to develop a seat with ingenious automatic controls that would permit safe ejection across the whole range of operations, from stationary on a runway or carrier deck, to high-speed flight at high altitude. The sophistication the seat was to achieve is described in Chapter XVI.

Meanwhile, by the 1950's, the roll of names of aircrew who owed their lives to Martin's invention was steadily growing.

A few pilots had already been saved twice with the seat, one had escaped in it in supersonic flight, another went out at 500 feet and one, Lieutenant B. D. Macfarlane, of the Fleet Air Arm, used his seat in highly unconventional circumstances to eject from his Wyvern when it lost power and plunged off the catapult of H.M.S. *Albion* into the Mediterranean. Macfarlane, trapped in the cockpit, began to go down with his aircraft. Somewhere between 10 and 20 feet below the surface as a desperate resort he pulled the blind. He was fired out and after 40 seconds under water, surfaced and was rescued by helicopter.

For the Caterpillar Club there had now begun an era in which many of the members arrived by the joint courtesy of Irvin's parachute and Martin's ubiquitous seat.

CHAPTER XIII

It was not until three years after Lynch made the first 'live' ejection that the Martin-Baker seat was called on to prove itself in a real emergency.

An Armstrong Whitworth test pilot, Mr J. O. Lancaster, was testing the company's second prototype Flying Wing, the A.W.A.52, at 5,000 feet near Coventry on May 30, 1949, when a violent and uncontrollable oscillation developed. The control column began to move rapidly backwards and forwards and as it did so the nose pitched up and down so fiercely that Lancaster began to blackout. The bucking was soon of such extreme violence that he knew the aircraft was hopelessly out of control.

In a grey state of half consciousness, Lancaster jettisoned the cockpit hood, pulled the face blind and ejected. The aircraft was then travelling at 320 knots.

When he let go of the blind and looked around he found himself falling, tilting forward at about 45 degrees. He lost no time in unfastening the straps, falling clear of the seat and pulling his ripcord. His parachute opened about 2,000 feet above the ground and a moment later the empty seat dropped past him a few yards away.

Lancaster, a big man weighing nearly 15 stone, landed heavily in a stiff breeze beside a canal near Coventry.

Another two years passed before the 'hot seat', as pilots now called it, saved its second life. In March 1951, a Royal Navy pilot, Lieutenant P. L. McDermot, ejected from an Attacker when its engine failed at 7,500 feet near West Raynham. By 1951 the seat had been fitted to most frontline jet aircraft and was a novelty no longer: by the end of the year six more pilots had made emergency rides.

The first R.A.F. pilot to save his life with the seat was Sergeant Bill Tollitt, a lean six-footer of 23 from Manchester. It happened on July 3, 1951, when he was serving with No. 65 Squadron at Linton-on-Ouse in Yorkshire and very nearly ended tragically – though through no fault of the seat.

That morning, the squadron – equipped with Meteor 8s – was taking part in an interception exercise over northeast England. Meteors of another squadron had been sent up to represent high-flying enemy bombers and at 4 a.m., just as dawn was breaking, Tollitt's section of four aircraft was scrambled to intercept four of these 'bombers' whose approach had been spotted by early warning radar.

Taxiing out to the runway, Tollitt found that his cockpit

hood would not close properly so he turned away from the section to fix it. A minute later when he had managed to close it the other three Meteors had taken off; he roared off after them hoping to catch them up.

It was still only half light and he couldn't see the three Meteors but the ground radar controller directed him towards them and presently, after climbing up through a layer of high cloud, he saw their white condensation trails against the blue sky ahead. When he caught up with them at 35,000 feet he found there were only two aircraft, one having returned to base with mechanical trouble.

Now the formation was a threesome again and a few minutes later the controller brought them within sight of the four 'enemy' Meteors which were over the North Sea heading for the coast and flying a few thousand feet lower down. Tollitt's leader called over the R/T for a high quarter attack from starboard and the three Meteors dived down, one after the other, to make their mock kill. Then to 'finish' the formation off they pulled up and turned to deliver another attack from port. During this attack Tollitt, who was No. 3, lost sight of the attacking aircraft ahead of him, and as he pulled up over the target Meteors, he felt his aircraft suddenly lurch – he had collided with his No. 2.

Immediately, his Meteor flicked over on to its back and went into a tight inverted spin. Tollitt snapped the throttles closed and stabbed on opposite rudder, but it had no effect and he went on spinning. And being an inverted spin with high negative forces, blood was soon forced up into his head, spots danced before his eyes and the details of the cockpit began to swim in a red mist. A voice which seemed to come from a long way away was calling over the R/T, 'Two aircraft collided and spinning.'

In what would have been his last seconds of consciousness, Tollitt leaned forward and pulled the hood jettison handle. His sight was fading and his eyes felt as if they were standing out on stalks. The hood flew off and a great inrush of freezing air tore his helmet and oxygen mask from his head and swept them away. He reached up above his head with both hands and grasped the firing handle, pulling the blind down over his face with the last of his strength.

For a fraction of a second nothing happened and, having been led to expect instantaneous results, he thought the seat had failed him. Then with a bang which he only dimly heard above the noise of the air blast, the seat fired and out he went – ejected downwards because the aircraft was spinning upside down. But that didn't matter because he was still nearly six miles above the ground.

He felt himself tumbling through the air. He was still suffering from the effects of his partial 'red-out' and his bloodshot eyes still felt as if they were half out of their sockets; he could neither see properly, nor orientate himself in space. It was a manual seat and he knew that he must lose no time getting out of it, but his mind was working sluggishly and he found the concentration needed to undo the straps temporarily beyond him. Presently, still in a pink haze, he began to fumble with the release box. All it needed was a sharp twist and the straps would be undone. But now he discovered that he had lost his gloves during ejection; his fingers had lost all feeling and he couldn't grip the release point. He tried hard to shake off the lassitude but the determination with which he drove his jet about the sky had been sapped from him, first by the negative g and now by the anoxic effects of lack of oxygen.

From time to time he was aware of the hazy spread of the ground below him – or was it cloud? He wasn't sure. He glanced up and saw the small white stabilizing drogue parachute ballooned out above the seat. He thought of his own parachute, useless in its pack underneath him. If he couldn't get clear at least he could pull the ripcord.

With numbed hands he felt for the ripcord D-ring. Hazily he pulled it. From under him silk, then rigging lines, poured out between his legs and with a loud crack the canopy blossomed out. As it opened and the parachute took up his weight, the seat tilted over backwards and he hung upside down. And as it did so a tremendous pressure came on his chest as the parachute pulled him against the harness which held him to 110 lb of metal seat. It felt as if he was being crushed by some giant steel spring, as if life was being inexorably squeezed from him.

He tried to brace his chest against the compressing straps but suddenly all the breath seemed to go out of him and he lost consciousness.

A farmer bringing in his cows on his farm near Mablethorpe in Lincolnshire soon after 4.30 that morning heard the shrill whine of an aircraft and looked up just in time to see a Meteor dive out of the sky and crash with a great explosion into one of his fields. Some minutes later he was surprised to see a parachute bearing a man upside down in a large black seat, coming down into the next field. He ran over to where Tollitt lay, spattered with a great deal of blood. His face and hands had turned blue, and the farmer, taking him for dead, hurried off to telephone the news to the R.A.F. Station at Strubby a few miles away.

While he was gone Tollitt regained consciousness. Several cows were gazing soulfully down at him. The pressure was still on his chest and he found it difficult to breathe. Squirming to relieve the pressure, he shouted for help. Nobody came, and soon the tightness came back again and his breathing became so restricted he thought he was dying.

After some time the farmer returned. He was startled when Tollitt called out and beseeched him to undo the straps. He did so and Tollitt rolled on to the ground, gulping in lungfuls of air. Soon the blueness – caused by the inability of his lungs to oxygenate his bloodstream fully – disappeared, and his body regained its normal colour. Feeling much better, he looked to see where all the blood had come from and found it was from nothing more serious than a small gash on his nose.

In hospital later that morning it was discovered that Tollitt had fractured his skull on landing. His only other injuries were frostbitten fingers caused by the freezing air at 30,000 feet where he ejected, and bruised eyes – the result of the negative g he had been subjected to. The whites of his eyes were red and the eyeballs were painfully swollen for a week, during which he had to lie in a darkened room.

But he recovered quickly and three months later was flying again.

The Meteor with which he collided that morning also spun down. The pilot ejected and released himself from the seat but, either because he was injured or disorientated as Tollitt had been, he did not pull his ripcord and was killed. A sad pointer to the value of the automatic seat – at that stage not in service.

Tollitt was more than lucky to have survived. In normal circumstances, pulling the ripcord while still in the seat as he had done, would not have opened the parachute. In the manual seat the pilot sat on his chute pack which fitted snugly into a metal pan under him, leaving no space through which the silk could emerge. But by a trick of fate, Tollitt's seat had been damaged in the process of ejection. Technical officers who examined it afterwards found that the front wall of the pan had been torn off. It was through this gap that the parachute had streamed.

Two weeks after Tollitt's unorthodox descent, Sergeant Herbert Tickner became the second R.A.F. pilot to make an ejection escape. He went out at 11,000 feet over Germany – and was grateful for every one of those eleven thousand feet.

Tickner took off in a Meteor from Bückeburg in Westphalia on a three-leg high-level cross-country training flight. The first leg of the triangle was to be north-west to Hage, the second south-east to Hamm and the final one northeast back to Bückeburg. He had been briefed to fly at 30,000 feet but there was a towering mass of cumulo-nimbus cloud over north-west Germany that morning and, as at 30,000 feet he was still inside it, he went on climbing. At 33,000 feet the cloud began to thin and soon he broke out into dazzling sunshine.

Above cloud he flew to Hage, confirmed his position there with a radio fix and flew to Hamm where, after another radio position check, he set course back to Bückeburg, presently calling Bückeburg on R/T to request a radio controlled descent through the cloud. Passing him courses to steer, the Bückeburg controller brought him over the airfield at

33,000 feet, then directed him to descend to 25,000 feet on a heading of 330° which took him into the safety lane clear of hills.

Easing back the throttle and with air brakes out, Tickner nosed the Meteor down out of the sunshine into the gloom of the cloud. There was a good deal of turbulence and he had to concentrate hard on his instruments as the aircraft twitched and shuddered. At 25,000 feet when he was several miles north of the airfield he called the controller to report his altitude and was told to turn left on to 140° – back towards the runway – and to let down to 1,000 feet. He acknowledged the instruction; it was the last the controller heard from him.

Tickner had almost completed the gentle descending turn towards the runway and was beginning to straighten up when suddenly the aircraft hit an extremely violent patch of turbulence in the cloud. Huge hailstones crashed against the hood like showers of gravel, there was a moment of fierce juddering, then all control was snatched from him as the Meteor was flung upside down. Tickner saw his gyro artificial horizon – the instrument upon which he was most dependent – topple and cavort uselessly about the dial. The next thing he knew the aircraft was diving and the airspeed indicator had swung quickly up to 400 knots. He saw the altimeter unwinding faster than he had ever seen it do before and felt himself pressed heavily down in his seat by increasing g.

With the speed he had built up he knew it would take him more than 10,000 feet to pull out of the dive. Recovery would have taken that in a clear sky – but diving blind in cloud which he guessed lay to within 1,000 feet of the ground, and with his artificial horizon out of action, he knew he would need a lot more height than that. And now his altimeter was racing past the 12,000 mark. He decided to get out.

It wasn't easy. First he had to get rid of the hood and that meant pulling the black and yellow striped jettison handle up on the top right of the instrument panel in front of him. But there was so much g weighing him down by now that he had great difficulty raising his right hand to reach it. It was as if invisible bonds had tied it down and only by concentrating all the effort in his body on the task did he eventually manage to reach the handle with two clawing fingers.* He pulled, and with a whoof the hood, helped on its way by the cockpit pressurization, was sucked away.

A great roaring noise filled the cockpit and an icy blast of air poured in with such force that before he could bring his right hand back to the firing blind his arm was flicked out into the airflow. It was held there against the side of his seat so firmly that for a moment he seemed to lack the strength to pull it in.

After a struggle he got it back. Then with both elbows drawn tightly together against his chest, he seized the handle above his head and hauled the blind down. There was a bang, a second of blackness, and then he felt himself cartwheeling head over heels through cloud.

The air blast ripped the protective blind from his face and he felt his cheeks burning painfully in the airflow. Hailstones pelted against his head, and blood began to trickle down his face from the savage cuts they made around his nose and lips.

Slowly the giddy cartwheeling began to stop and the rush of air grew less. The change of environment from warm cockpit to violent gyrations in the cold damp topsy-turvy world of the cloud had been so drastically sudden that his senses weren't immediately ready to deal with the situation. Parachutes are an older institution than ejection seats and ingrained habits, especially when they relate to survival, die hard. Instead of freeing himself from his seat, Tickner instinctively, automatically, felt for his ripcord and pulled it. The handle came away normally in his hand – but his parachute didn't open. It couldn't.

Sergeant Tollitt's chute had streamed out because, by a chance in a million, his seat pan had been torn open. But

* Hood jettisoning later ceased to be a problem. Escape systems were introduced in which the action of firing the seat automatically exploded the hood away – or the seat was able to blast out safely through the hood.

Tickner's had been a faultless ejection; his seat was intact and his parachute was held firmly closed under him. For several seconds as he fell through cloud he was puzzled because his chute hadn't opened. Then with horror he remembered that he was still strapped to his seat.

Still clutching the ripcord handle in his right hand, he felt for the seat harness release box with his left; he twisted the knob and the straps came loose. It was at that moment that he broke cloud, less than 1,000 feet above ground. Abruptly his world became three-dimensional again and he saw the countryside, looking strangely colourful after his sojourn in cloud, rising very quickly towards him. But there was nothing he could do now but wait and hope.

Painfully slowly, almost unwillingly, the big seat which had saved his life but which now could take it from him if it didn't go quickly, fell away. And as it went, his parachute, the ripcord pins already withdrawn, sprang out from under him and began faithfully to unfurl in a gush of white above him. With less than a hundred feet to go the canopy was only at the swirling half open stage, his fall had been only partly arrested and he appeared to have little hope of survival.

He might have been killed, would certainly have been seriously injured, but for the intervention of a tree. The tree wasn't directly below him; it was several yards to one side when he first saw it. But near the ground a strong wind began to drift him sideways, drifted him straight for it.

The flapping half-open canopy hooked in the branches, he felt his lower harness straps snap into his loins, twigs and leaves showered down on him, and with a crunch that shuddered right through his body, he hit the mercifully springy turf of a peat bog.

The next thing Tickner remembers is running across the bog for help. He met a German girl who took him to a farmhouse and telephoned the squadron for him. Except for bruises, severe wind burn, and facial cuts from the hailstones, he was unhurt. Within a few weeks he was fit for flying again.

Tickner's escape re-emphasized the fallibility of man and

the need to tax him in an emergency, when his senses are
confused, with the least possible number of tasks. For as
Tollitt and Tickner – and others after them – demonstrated
the normally powerful instincts of self-preservation were
not always enough to make the vital move from seat to sill.

The fifth emergency ejection was an historic one. It was
the first in real battle and it gave the Caterpillar Club what
was, at that time, its highest bale-out. The man who made
it was a young Royal Australian Air Force Meteor pilot
Flying Officer Ron Guthrie, and his half-hour descent was
the longest in the history of the Club.

It happened in Korea on August 29, 1951, when Guthrie,
who came from Kingsgrove, Sydney, was serving with No
77 Squadron, R.A.A.F. The squadron had been sent up on
combat patrol above the Manchuria/Korea frontier at the
Yalu River to intercept Chinese MIG jet fighters. Pilots had
named the area 'MIG Alley' and it was here that the first
ever jet versus jet air battles had been fought. Several
squadrons of MIGs were based at the Chinese airfield of
Antung just over the border on the north side of the Yalu
And Australian and American pilots who often saw them
taking off from the unsealed runways in clouds of dust
cursed the ruling which banned United Nations aircraft
from crossing the frontier and destroying the MIGs when
they were at their most vulnerable.

The advantage then was strongly in the enemy's favour.
Not only could he gain height for missions into Korea
unmolested, he could, if faced with unfavourable odds south
of the Yalu, scuttle northwards into the convenient sanc-
tuary beyond the river.

On this particular morning Guthrie, for whom it was his
15th mission, was in one of eight Meteors which in two
formations had been allotted the 35,000 to 40,000 foot
patrol level. Below them, at 30,000 feet, eight other Meteors
were flying. It was a hot cloudless morning with exceptionally good visibility.

The squadron had almost finished its patrol and was about
to return to base at Kimpo-Seoul when two MIGs appeared
below, travelling fast across the river into Korea. Immedi-

ely the four Meteors in Guthrie's formation wheeled round
dive and attack. They were still turning when they were
mped from above by more MIGs.

With guns spewing cannon fire which even in the bright
inshine was visible, streaming past like red ping-pong balls,
e MIGs came down steeply from 6 o'clock high. Guthrie
w the red shells pouring over his wings; he broke to port
id shouted a warning over the R/T. But his call never went
ut. At the same moment a shell exploded into his fuselage
ist behind the cockpit, destroying his radio.

Two MIGs, so close that he had a clear, photographic
impse of the pilots' heads, flashed past in front of him.
e turned in pursuit, and presently had one of them in his
ghts. He pressed the firing button and heard his guns chat-
ring.

Suddenly his aircraft shook convulsively. Another MIG
ehind him had hit his Meteor with a 37 mm. shell. It felt
s if he had flown smack into a brick wall and for a fraction
f a second it seemed as if he stood still. The MIG at which
e had been firing swung out of his sights as the Meteor
ick-rolled to port. When he tried to recover he found that
is elevator controls had been shot away, and he went on
olling tightly and uncontrollably to the left.

Before he ejected he had a last look at his altimeter and
ach-meter: he was at an indicated height of 38,300 feet
avelling at Mach .84. He jettisoned the hood without
ifficulty and pulled the firing blind over his face. A moment
ater he was alone in his seat falling through the sky, 7½
niles above Korea.

The drogue had streamed out to steady his seat and slow
down and soon having quickly lost all the forward
nomentum of the 580 miles an hour with which he had
egun his ride, he was descending vertically with the seat
n a comfortably upright position. He noticed that his oxygen
nask had been blown off his face and had fetched up round
is throat; he pulled it back, seeing as he did so that both
is gloves had been ripped off, and was gratified to feel a
,entle stream of oxygen playing softly and coldly against
is face.

It felt oddly unreal sitting there, strapped to a seat in the silence of the sub-stratosphere without any apparent earthward movement. He felt secure and utterly detached from the vast panoramic stretch of land and sea which lay below him, felt no sensation of falling and was aware of no airflow slipping past him. It was as if he had been hung up there in the sky on some invisible support to stay, poised above the earth in perpetuity.

After the noise of the battle from which he had so suddenly departed it was the infinite silence that fascinated him most. He could see no sign of his aircraft and the mêlée of Meteors and MIGs had moved away out of sight.

But for the cold he would have liked to have prolonged his stay at his lofty space station. The fact of summer made little difference at that height and he knew that the temperature must be all of 50° or 60° Fahrenheit below zero. He was wearing only a thin cotton summer flying suit over his underclothes, yet despite the intense cold he was to discover later that he had escaped frostbite.

He saw that he was coming down over the west coast of North Korea and that his line of descent looked as if it might take him into the sea. He hoped he would land in the sea because he was wearing a Mae West with an inflatable rubber dinghy strapped to it, and he knew that his only chance of rescue would be by American amphibian, for the land below was enemy territory. With his parachute open he would at least have some control of his descent. It meant exposing himself for a longer period to the cold of high altitude, but he decided the end justified the risk.

And so, at about 35,000 feet (he worked this out afterwards from the time his descent took) Guthrie undid his seat straps, kicked the seat away and pulled his ripcord. His parachute snapped open – the highest emergency deployment of an Irvin chute – and the seat, with its drogue flying above it, dropped away below.

Hanging there under the silk, he spent his last half-hour as a free man drinking in the view below him. It was no novelty for him to look down from above 30,000 feet, but in the cockpit he was usually much too preoccupied with more vital matters than scenery gazing. On this still, blue morning the visibility was so scintillatingly clear that he could see the curvature of the earth. The cold did not worry him unduly and, slowly, as the minutes passed and he sank lower, it grew warmer.

His horizon shrank and he became more aware of his descent path in relation to the North Korean coast immediately below. Since he had opened his parachute he had been disappointed to see that he hadn't drifted seawards from the coast. In fact now as he got down towards the last 10,000 feet he found that a westerly wind was drifting him steadily inland. He didn't want to land far inland – escape by boat, if he could get one, was easier on the coast – so he tried to arrest his easterly drift by pulling on the west-side rigging lines to slip in that direction.

This wasn't very successful and after a while, when he estimated he was more than 15 miles inland, he resigned himself to landing just where wind and silk elected. At about 1,500 feet he got a foretaste of what awaited him below: North Korean troops began firing at him and with some uneasiness he heard bullets zipping past very close. But he wasn't hit and a few minutes later – 28 minutes after ejection – he landed softly and damply in a paddy field.

When he discarded his parachute and stood up he saw North Korean soldiers approaching from three directions. There was no escape. Within a few minutes he was a prisoner.

Not every pilot who has ridden the 'hot' seat to safety, needed an ejection seat to get clear. Some ejections – those prompted by fuel shortage in bad weather, for instance – have been made in ideal circumstances from undamaged aircraft at comparatively low speeds: the pilots ejected because it was the safest and most convenient way out. In many cases, however, it has been shown that but for the means of explosive exit the pilot would certainly have perished. Few ejections proved this more dramatically than Pilot Officer Peter Poppe's on June 17, 1952.

Twenty-three years old, he had abandoned a mechanical engineering apprenticeship at Shoreham in Sussex two years

earlier to join the R.A.F. and by June 1952 was a fully
fledged Meteor pilot serving with No. 208 Squadron at Abu
Sueir in the Canal Zone of Egypt.

Poppe was already a member of the Club, he and his
instructor having baled out of a Meteor 7 when they got
into a flat inverted spin over North-East England a few
months earlier. The Meteor 7, a two seat jet trainer, is not
fitted with ejection seats, but they climbed out without
difficulty and landed safely, Poppe in a muddy field, his
instructor squarely on the back of a young bullock which
promptly tipped him off and fled.

On June 17, when he hit the silk for the second time,
Poppe was flying over the Canal Zone desert on a formation
exercise with two other 208 Squadron Meteors. To end the
exercise and lose height for return to Abu Sueir they started
a tail chase in which, one behind the other, numbers 2 and
3 try to follow the leader doggedly through every manoeuvre he makes.

Poppe's leader, Master Pilot Jock Pratt, led them into a
loop. In line astern the two other Meteors followed him,
diving, then pulling up past the vertical and over the top.
As he zoomed over the top, Poppe, who was No. 3, saw
that No. 2 was leaving him behind.

So, instead of reducing power on the downward side of
the loop, he kept his throttle open to catch up. He picked
up speed so quickly that he soon had to open his air brakes
to slow down; he was about 200 yards behind No. 2, when
with a thump, he hit the other aircraft's slipstream.

Immediately, his starboard wing dropped and his aircraft
flicked upside down; he felt a sudden onrush of g and blacked
into unconsciousness. A few seconds later he partly revived
to see, through eyes blurred by a hazy greyness, an object
hurtling away through the sky ahead of him. He thought it
was an engine cowling that had broken loose. In fact it was
the whole starboard engine: his aircraft was breaking up.
The starboard wing minus its engine, which had shot ahead,
detached itself from the fuselage and was swept away. About
the same time, the port wing, engine and all, folded back
and tore off. A moment later, the whole tail unit and the

164

rear part of the fuselage sheared off. But Poppe, plunging down in a giddily spinning, wingless, tail-less fuselage, knew none of this.

All he knew was that his rudder bar and control column were flopping about uselessly, and that he was being subjected to violent *g* which held him in a state of semi-inert part consciousness. He was unaware of sky or ground, could see only the vague shapes of the objects in the cockpit around him as if he were viewing them from the recesses of a long dark tunnel.

Somehow he reached the hood jettison handle and pulled it. Nothing happened. He began pushing at the hood with his hands. Suddenly it flew away. His face was battered by the air blast and his helmet and oxygen mask were torn from his head.

He put his hands up to feel for the blind. It wasn't there. The grey-out seemed to sap his situation of all urgency and he explored the space above his head with slow graspings. But still he couldn't feel the blind handle.

With a great effort he twisted his head round and looked up. It was then he saw that he was pressed to one side of the seat and the blind was no longer directly above him. He reached up and dragged it down.

A second later the cockpit had disappeared and he knew, although his vision was still blurred, that his seat had taken him out. Slowly he turned the release knob on his chest and the straps loosened. He leaned forward as he had been taught, but the seat didn't leave him and he experienced a moment's vague perplexity as he wondered helplessly what he should do. His sluggish mind was still trying to cope with the impasse when he felt himself tilt forward and leave the seat. With a jerk of the ripcord, Poppe opened his parachute. As the canopy filled out and he was jerked upright he let go of the now loose ripcord handle.

And then almost simultaneously several things happened. The handle dropped a few feet and plopped into the desert sand. Before he could absorb the shattering fact of his proximity to the ground his feet hit the sand; and, as if in doing so he had triggered off the explosion, the fuselage of his Meteor crashed into the desert less than 150 yards away, exploding with a great orange blast.

The price of a heavy landing was a compression fracture of two vertebrae – the parachutist's traditional injury. But Poppe wasn't long in hospital and 18 weeks later he was back with the squadron.

If Poppe's hood hadn't jettisoned he could probably have saved himself by pulling the blind and ejecting through the hood. But at that time, although many pilots had declared their intention of exploding themselves out that way as a last resort, none who had tried it had survived.

There was nothing new about bursting through plastic hoods in emergency. Spitfire pilots had done it during the war by undoing their seat harness and kicking the stick forward so that as the aircraft bunted, the negative g hurled them out.

But for several years after the ejection seat came into service many of the aircraft in which it was fitted had hoods strengthened by a metal fairing behind the pilot's head. This didn't necessarily prevent the seat from bursting through, but it could damage the seat and injure the pilot in the process. However, most of the peril went out of this seemingly drastic mode of ejection with the introduction of the plastic 'bubble' type hood, which had no obstructing metal, and with the general issue of crash helmets – renamed 'bone domes' by the men who wore them. Not that the bone dome took the brunt of the impact with the hood. The top of the seat did that, shattering the plastic bubble into hundreds of pieces, but the bone dome protected the pilot's head against plastic splinters.

Two thousand feet – and that in straight and level flight – was reckoned to be the minimum safe height for escape with the manual seat. It was proved that the average pilot, experiencing the swift bewildering processes of ejection for the first time, could get himself safely into the silk with a few hundred feet to spare from this height. If he kept his head and worked quickly he could get away with it below 2,000 feet, although even Bernard Lynch who has made more ejections than any other man, has said that, despite all his experience, he wouldn't care to try it below 1,500 feet.

It was, therefore, with a certain amount of disbelief that Martin heard on December 16, 1953, that a young R.A.F. Meteor pilot of the same name had saved his life with an ejection from less then 900 feet. But the report was correct.

Flying Officer Alan Martin was one of three 56 Squadron pilots all of whom had ejected that day within the space of ten minutes.

They and a fourth pilot had taken off from Waterbeach in Cambridgeshire to practise cine gun attacks at 15,000 feet. Low cloud hung to within 400 feet of the ground and below the gloomy stratus, mist and drizzling rain reduced visibility to less than a mile.

On their return, the four Meteors – they were flying in independent formation pairs – diverted to Duxford, another Cambridgeshire R.A.F. station, about 14 miles from Waterbeach. They were all low on fuel by this time and it was imperative that they be landed within a few minutes.

But this was to be 56 Squadron's black day. Permanent echoes – returns from the surrounding terrain – on the radar screens made it difficult for Duxford's radio talkdown operators to identify the blips of the aircraft they were trying to help, and after one abortive attempt to land, both pilots in the first formation, their fuel almost exhausted, climbed up above the cloud and ejected.

Meanwhile Martin and his leader had arrived overhead at Duxford. They fared no better. On their first attempt they broke cloud too far to one side of the runway to land. They climbed up above cloud to 2,000 feet for a second attempt. Martin now had only 60 gallons of fuel left – enough for barely five minutes' flying. He knew that if he didn't land this time there could be no third attempt.

In close formation the two Meteors dropped back into the cloud, the leader following the directions chanted over the R/T by the controller, Martin keeping close beside him. When they were down to 500 feet, with flaps and under-carriages down, the controller reported that they were over the airfield. But they were still in thick cloud, and Martin, glancing down at the fuel gauges for his two tanks, saw that they were showing zero/zero. He could never land now. All he could do was to scramble for as much height as his last drops of fuel would give him, and get out.

He broke formation, snapped up flaps and undercarriage, opened up both engines to full power and began to climb back through the cloud, calling over the R/T, 'Pulling up and jumping.'

Desperately low on speed, the Meteor had gained barely a hundred feet when the port engine stopped. Immediately he reduced power on the live engine to prevent the aircraft turning, and pressed on full starboard rudder. He knew it would only be seconds before the starboard engine dried up too, yet he had only drifted up to 700 feet – a suicidal height for ejection. He tried to get rid of the hood but when he pulled the jettison handle nothing happened. He banged it fiercely with his hand and pressed the electric unwind button but the hood wouldn't budge.

The altimeter, reading height above sea level, showed 900 feet now – just 700 feet above the ground. It seemed to have stopped there and he realized that at his feeble rate of climb he would be lucky to gain another 50 feet before the inevitable happened. His airspeed had dropped to 130 knots and the aircraft was beginning to wallow. Again he thumped at the hood. It didn't move.

He was on the point of reaching for the blind and ejecting through the hood when, with a gentle pop, it flew off. He closed the starboard throttle – miraculously the engine was still running – to prevent the aircraft swinging when he took his feet off the rudder bar, brought his feet back, drew his elbows together in front of his face and pulled the blind.

For a brief moment he blacked out. When he opened his eyes he was tumbling head over heels through cloud. Even as he tumbled his hand was on the harness release box. As he felt the seat begin to steady under the influence of the drogue, he flipped the knob, planted his right hand on his ripcord – he didn't have to look for it; he had practised the movement so often – and fell forward, pulling the ripcord as he went. He couldn't see, or care, if he was clear of the seat.

As he fell forward, the cloud thinned, the brown square of a freshly ploughed field loomed hugely in his vision, his parachute bumped open and, in the same bump, his feet dug into the soft furrowed soil and he passed out.

He came round to awareness of pain and peacefulness. He had injured his back and couldn't stand up. So he just lay where he had landed, fascinated by the two deep holes his feet had punched in the ground, enjoying the hush after the noisy bedlam of the last half-hour. The only sounds were the hiss of escaping oxygen from the cylinder on his seat which lay about six yards away, and the distant putter-putter of a tractor.

When he looked around he saw how lucky he had been. He had landed in a hollow. On either side of the field, the ground sloped up – so far that it went up into the misty base of the cloud.

Later that day as he began a six week spell in hospital with a compression fracture of the spine, he learnt that his leader had crashed and been seriously injured when he ran out of fuel on his third attempt to land.

When Martin came to write up his report of the incident the senior R.A.F. officer who signed it wrote on it pithily, 'A very lucky gentleman!'

CHAPTER XIV

By the middle of 1954 automatic ejection seats had almost entirely replaced the manual type, and escape from as low as 500 feet soon came to be nonchalantly accepted as quite normal.* But it wasn't long before a pilot came along to show that, but for the fact of his seat leaving him, and his

* The first man to save his life with the Martin-Baker automatic seat was a Fleet Air Arm pilot, Lieutenant Bushe. He ejected from an Attacker, 2,000 feet over the Channel following a structural failure.

parachute opening, automatically, he probably wouldn't have survived.

Desmond Melaniphy, an Irishman, was a Pilot Officer who had trained as a pilot during his National Service and, finding that he much preferred a cockpit to the desk he had left behind at the Board of Trade, had decided to stay on in the R.A.F.

On October 4, 1954, when he was training at a Meteor conversion unit at Stradishall in Suffolk, he was involved in a collision with another Meteor at 30,000 feet. Both aircraft went down out of control, Melaniphy's with a buckled wing tip, the other minus its tail.

Melaniphy found himself in a near-vertical spiral dive. At 20,000 feet, having lost 10,000 feet in less than four spiralling turns, and having failed, despite frantic efforts, to reach the hood jettison handle, he decided to blast out through the perspex.

He couldn't get both hands up to the blind against the *g* which was making black spots dance in his eyes and dragging him to within a shade of total blackout, but his ingenuity did not fail him. Gripping his left elbow with his right hand, he prised his left arm up past his face until his hand could clutch at the firing handle, and wrench it down.

As he burst through the hood, his head (he wasn't wearing a helmet) struck a jagged piece of perspex and, after momentarily feeling a slap of cold air round his ears, he lost consciousness. It did not matter, for he had no further part to play. The automatic mechanism of the seat looked after him from then on.

For several thousand feet he fell, safely strapped in his seat, which was held upright and slowed down to about 110 miles an hour by the small drogue parachute, trailing several feet above it. And as he went down a small barostatic capsule was slowly contracting as the atmospheric pressure of the surrounding air increased with loss of height. It went on contracting until, 10,000 feet above the ground, a tiny projection on the capsule case, which had been engaged between the teeth of a starwheel, disengaged. The moment it did so the starwheel, under the impetus of a spring, began to turn and to set in motion an array of spring-loaded plungers, gears and levers.

Within five seconds, the drogue line had been uncoupled from the seat, the seat harness had been undone and a nylon cord attached to the drogue line had withdrawn Melaniphy's parachute from its pack, at the same time tipping him forward out of the seat. As the drogue pulled his parachute fully open, the seat, its job done, fell away.

Of all these automatic wonders, Melaniphy knew nothing. He revived for a few seconds when it was all over and saw his seat receding towards the cloud tops below him. He had no idea what he was doing there in mid-air, had no recollection of the collision or even of having taken off at all that morning, felt utterly unconcerned by his circumstances, and, almost immediately, blacked out again.

It was some minutes before he revived and by now he was descending through cloud. He was swinging, sickeningly, from side to side, his hands were numb with cold, and blood from the cut on his head was running down his face. Still he had no idea what had happened, but aware now that he was on the end of a parachute, he began to wonder anxiously whether he would break cloud over land or sea.

Presently, with some relief, he dropped out of cloud and saw fields about 2,000 feet below him, looking colourless and dull after the brilliance of the reflected light from the cloud tops higher up. The Meteor had been heading northeast across London just before the collision and, being above cloud and not able to pinpoint their position precisely, the formation leader had the sudden terrible thought that the two aircraft might be plunging into a crowded London street. In fact, however, they had passed over London and both pilots – the other pilot had ejected successfully – came down near Chelmsford in Essex.

After his reassuring glimpse of the ground, Melaniphy passed out for the third time and was still unconscious when he landed a few minutes later in a stubbled field. Although the landing shock is equivalent to that in jumping from a seven or eight foot wall, he was relaxed in unconsciousness

171

and suffered no injury from the impact. Presently he woke up, feeling groggy from loss of blood, and walked across the field to a road where a passing motorist picked him up and took him to hospital in Chelmsford.

Two hours later, with 20 stitches in the back of his head, he was on his way back to Stradishall. He remembered the formation exercises and the collision now, remembered pulling the ejection blind, remembered his two brief returns to consciousness. And as the details came back, he realized in full measure his debt to the automatic seat, which had eased his limp body safely into the silk and which now lay smashed in a field some miles from where he had landed.

Just how vital were the design features intended to forestall deployment of the parachute until the seat had slowed down was forcefully demonstrated towards the end of 1954. Duplex drogues – two drogues in tandem – had not then been fitted to the R.A.F.'s ejection seats and at high subsonic speeds below 10,000 feet, the single 24-inch drogue then in use could not always decelerate the seat to a safe parachute opening speed in the five seconds which was the automatic delay between ejection and chute deployment. (At higher altitude, the speed of ejection, if all went well, did not matter, for the barostat mechanism delayed opening until the seat descended to 10,000 feet, by which time it had lost all forward momentum.)

On December 5, 1954, Pilot Officer Brian Cross ejected at about 14,000 feet over the Thames Estuary from a Meteor travelling at 500 knots – 580 miles an hour; his parachute cracked open five seconds later with drastic results. One side of the canopy exploded and instead of a normal 10 to 15 minute descent he came down in two minutes.

A telephone engineer, Cross was a part-time pilot serving with No. 604 (County of Middlesex) Squadron of the Royal Auxiliary Air Force, based at North Weald in Essex. He had trained as a pilot during his National Service and when he returned to civilian life had joined No. 604 Squadron with whom he flew at week-ends.

It was a cold, dreary, grey Sunday morning when Cross took off from North Weald in company with another Meteor for interception practice at 30,000 feet with two other Meteors which had gone off ahead of them. For the first part of the exercise Cross's formation represented the target aircraft and the other pair the attackers. Then they reversed roles and Cross and his No. 2 were vectored in pursuit by ground radar control.

The interception course took them eastward across Essex. Near Southend, Cross sighted the target Meteors below and a few miles to port. He called 'Tally ho' over the R/T to the ground controller, and led his formation in to the attack in a steep diving turn.

It was a tight turn and soon, as his airspeed built up to Mach .8 his aircraft began to judder near the stall. To rectify this he momentarily reduced his rate of turn, opened the throttles wider, then retightened the turn. But in his enthusiasm he inadvertently pulled too much g thereby accelerating the effects of compressibility.

He was closing on the target aircraft, which were flying at 25,000 feet, when, without warning, the Meteor flicked over on to its back and went into a steep spiral dive.

Quickly, he throttled back, opened his air brakes and tried to recover. He could not. The Essex coastline, towards which he was rapidly screwing down, just went on revolving round him, so, deciding to abandon the aircraft while time was still on his side, he jettisoned the hood.

The first time he lifted his hands to the blind, the fierce air torrent prevented him raising them higher than his mouth. So he stretched his hands forwards and up behind the shelter of the windscreen, let the blast blow them back on to the firing handle, and pulled it. He was then at around 14,000 feet.

His first emotion on regaining his equilibrium in space after the customary whirlwind business of ejection was relief at being out of the cockpit. His second was surprise that his seat, which was supposed to convey him down to 10,000 feet, had disappeared. The third, on looking above him, was sheer fright; his parachute had streamed but hadn't opened.

In fact the parachute had opened. The barostat control,

which has a nominal setting of 10,000 feet but which may, in practice, operate at anything between 10,000 and 13,000 feet, had snatched his seat away and opened his chute while he was still travelling at such high speed that it had burst nearly half the canopy, whereupon the chute had collapsed.

Gripping the rigging lines he tugged with all the desperation of a man who believes he is about to die. And almost immediately the canopy obligingly unfurled and he felt a jerk as the air filled it – filled part of it, that is, for although the skirt to which the rigging lines were attached was still a complete circle, one side of the canopy had a great hole punched in it. The nylon that should have been there had been torn into dozens of long strips and these were flapping furiously upwards in the air which the canopy displaced. But at least his fall was being partly checked and although he knew he would make a heavy landing he felt intensely relieved.

Looking down, he saw his aircraft a long way below him, still spiralling. It was heading for the sea off the coast of Foulness Island and it looked as if he was going into the sea, too. But before he could be sure on that point he felt a sudden upsurge of air around him and, looking up, saw that the canopy had collapsed again.

With an empty, twisted feeling in his stomach he tugged at the rigging lines. 'My brain kept repeating to me over and over again, "I've got to keep the chute open or I've had it",' he said afterwards.

In that second plunge he fell about 5,000 feet before his desperate jerkings filled the canopy out again and once more he slowed down. He took a quick look below him, estimated that he had about seven or eight thousand feet to go, then turned his head up again, for he was afraid now to take his eyes off his parachute.

And so, when for the third time the canopy crumpled up and the air began rushing past him again, he saw it happen and was able in the same instant to seize the lines. But this time not only had the canopy collapsed, the rigging lines had twisted, and his jerkings were no longer transmitted to the canopy. Frantically, he tried untwisting them, but the more he pulled and prised, the tighter the lines wound round one another.

There seemed nothing more he could do now and with a feeling of morbid depression he resigned himself to sudden oblivion. He looked down to see where he was going to die. It was to be in the sea and he had less than 2,000 feet to go. He glanced up again. The canopy was still a useless bunch and the rigging lines looked more tightly twisted than ever. He looked down once more to watch the grey sea rushing towards him.

He didn't see the lines untwisting in those last 2,000 feet when he had given up all hope. Even if he had, nothing he could have done would have speeded up the slow, deliberate process of unravelling which went on to within a few hundred feet of the water. But at last they were free and before they could retwist, the canopy bumped open.

Cross felt a jerk on his harness, and in the same instant he hit the sea with a fearful smack and went under.

Noises roared in his ears and a moment later he was lying on his back on the sea bed. Struggling to his feet he started, with furious strokes, to swim to the surface. But, almost immediately, as he straightened his body, he was surprised and delighted to find that the water was only about three feet deep and reached only to his waist.

He saw that he was about a mile from the shore but less than 100 yards from a small steel tower on the top of which was an observation platform. It looked like the answer to the ditched airman's prayer and, discarding his parachute, he set off to wade across to it. But wading was not the simple matter it looked: a strong off-shore current was running and he soon found that against it he could make little progress.

By now reaction had set in and he started to shiver uncontrollably. The water was so cold he began to wonder how long he would survive in it and he couldn't get out of his head a remark he had once heard – 'You only last ten minutes in the North Sea in winter out of a dinghy – and only a few hours if you're in one.' Well, at least he had a dinghy. He unclipped it from his Mae West, inflated it and climbed aboard.

Cross spent less than 20 minutes in his dinghy. His descent from 14,000 feet had taken scarcely two minutes (he estimated later that the parachute was open for no more than 30 seconds of this time) but before he was half-way down a distress call radioed by his No. 2 had alerted the air/sea rescue service and soon a United States Air Force Albatross amphibian was airborne from Manston in Kent and heading across the Thames Estuary towards him. It landed beside him and picked him up; 50 minutes after ejecting he was in hospital at Manston, having qualified for membership of three exclusive clubs and having established a high-speed ejection record – 580 miles an hour.*

That record didn't stand for long. A fortnight later it was broken, first by a Canberra pilot who ejected through the hood at nearly 600 miles an hour, and again, the following day, by a Meteor pilot who popped out of his aircraft in an uncontrollable spiral dive at 630 miles an hour.

With the arrival of supersonic fighters in squadron service it was inevitable that before long the seat would have to prove itself at even higher speeds.

It did so – faultlessly – on August 3, 1955, when 22-year-old Flying Officer Hedley Molland, pulling the blind at 760 miles an hour, became the first R.A.F. pilot to eject at a speed faster than sound.

Molland was serving at Wattisham in Suffolk with No. 263 Squadron which, a few months earlier, had been re-equipped with Hawker Hunters. The Hunter is not super-

* The three clubs for which Pilot Officer Cross qualified in the space of a few minutes were the Caterpillar Club, the Martin Baker Club for life saved by the ejection seat, and the Goldfish Club. Formed in 1942 by Charles Robertson, then chief draughtsman of P. B. Cow and Company, air-sea rescue equipment manufacturers, the Goldfish Club is for those who, in aircrew wartime slang, go 'down in the drink'. Eligible are aircrew who have had to ditch their aircraft in the sea or who have made an emergency bale-out into the sea. Members can buy a club tie with goldfish motif, and car and blazer badges. The club's headquarters are at the Pathfinder Association, the Sesame Pioneer and Lyceum Club, 49 Grosvenor Street, London W1. Membership at the beginning of 1977 stood at 450.

sonic in level flight but can exceed Mach 1 in a fairly shallow dive.

It was in a dive, although a far from shallow one, that Molland faced his emergency, between 30,000 and 40,000 feet over the North Sea, several miles off the Suffolk Coast. He was tail-chasing another Hunter, trailing it at high speed and stationed about 400 yards behind. The first Hunter went into a gentle dive. Molland followed.

In the next few seconds both aircraft slipped smoothly through the sound barrier and continued diving, still gently, at a shade over Mach 1. Very soon afterwards Molland noticed that he was catching up with the other Hunter and dipped underneath it.

He pulled back on the stick. At that speed it should have been fairly stiff, and he was surprised, therefore, at how easily he was able to move it. But although he moved it fully back, the aircraft went on diving, no longer gently, but very steeply now. He tried all the normal recovery actions, without success, and as he was now losing height faster than he had ever done before, and with little apparent hope of recovery, he decided it was high time he and the aircraft parted company.

Being in no doubt about the ferocity of the air blast that would hit the cockpit the moment he got rid of the hood, he took the precaution of gripping the firing blind with his left hand before he pulled the jettison handle with his right. Just before he pulled it, at 25,000 feet, he had a last quick glance at his mach-meter and saw that it was registering Mach 1.1.*

As the hood swept away, the supersonic blast roared into the cockpit, sucking away all his loose maps and blurring his vision. The noise wasn't as great as he had expected – 'a rushing noise like a passing train', was how he described it – but the most startling effect was the rapid failure of his

---

* The speed of sound at sea level is about 760 m.p.h. It decreases as the temperature drops with increase in altitude and above 36,000 feet is about 660 m.p.h. – 100 m.p.h. lower. Mach 1.1, Molland's indicated Mach number, meant that he was travelling at one and one-tenth the speed of sound, which at 25,000 feet is about 760 m.p.h.

sight. In a few seconds he was temporarily totally blind, but the blast hadn't blown his left hand off the firing handle and he managed to haul the protecting blind down over his face and eject.

When he came to, his sight had returned, the seat had stopped spinning and was descending to the accompaniment of a high-pitched whistling noise. A circle of foam on the sea below showed where the Hunter had ended its last dive, taking with it, incidentally, all evidence of the cause of the accident. Above him, the two drogues, one flying above the other, were steadying the seat; they were undamaged. His seat had only been fitted with the duplex drogue a few days earlier. That was fortunate because a single drogue would have burst at the speed he went out.

Slowly, as he became less dazed, he began to examine himself. The first rather alarming discovery he made was the apparent absence of his left arm. Only by fishing with his right arm did he eventually find it – twisted limply round the side of the seat; it had apparently flailed during ejection for it was broken. He pulled it back but as soon as he let go of it, it blew back round the edge of the seat again. After two further attempts to get it back he gave up and left it there.

Continuing his inspection he began to appreciate the full fury of the blast he had ridden through on his violent journey. His helmet, oxygen mask and gloves had gone. His watch had been torn from his wrist, his left shoe and sock had been blown off and the attachment which held his dinghy to his Mae West had been undone.

He managed to refasten one of the dinghy attachments just before he was abruptly tipped forward out of the seat and his parachute opened. The seat quickly dropped away out of sight and he was left swinging on the end of his parachute, 10,000 feet above the North Sea, about three miles out from Felixstowe.

His next worry was the fact that he couldn't swim. However, he drew comfort from the thought of his Mae West and as he got down near the sea he inflated it to guarantee his means of flotation. Ten minutes later after drifting

178

another five miles seawards, he dropped into the water, went under once, and bobbed to the surface. He tried to inflate his dinghy but couldn't manage it with one hand. Happily it didn't matter, for he was quickly rescued by a passing tug.

Few bale-outs have been accorded as much publicity as Molland's. His ejection made front-page news and at least one banner headline described it as a 'Supersonic Miracle!'

In truth it was nothing of the kind. Molland went out at a true airspeed of about 760 m.p.h. – but from the ejection point of view, the true airspeed is of minor importance. It is *indicated* air-speed that matters, and Molland's indicated airspeed, although high, was, however, considerably less than 760 m.p.h. It was in the region of 480 knots – 560 m.p.h.

Indicated airspeed is the speed registered by the pilot's airspeed indicator which measures the air pressure on the aircraft's leading surfaces. However, as the density of the atmosphere decreases with height, the progressively 'thinner' air being fed to the airspeed indicator gives progressively lower readings. Only at sea level does true airspeed – the speed at which an aircraft in level flight moves over the ground, in still air – equal the indicated speed; the higher an aircraft climbs, the greater the disparity. For instance, an aircraft flying at an indicated airspeed of 200 m.p.h. near sea level will be doing a true airspeed of about the same value. But, if the pilot maintains 200 m.p.h., and climbs to 20,000 feet, his true airspeed will have increased to about 275 m.p.h.; at 30,000 feet it will be nearly 330 m.p.h., and at 40,000 feet, 400 m.p.h. – he will then be travelling twice as fast as his indicator shows because the density of the air through which the aircraft is flying at 40,000 feet is a great deal less than at sea level.

By the same token, the greater the altitude at which a pilot ejects, the less dense the airflow and the less violent, comparatively, its impact on the seat hurtling through it. Thus, a pilot who ejects from an aircraft doing, say, 400 m.p.h. (true airspeed) at 10,000 feet will encounter a much more punishing air blast than a pilot who ejects at the same true airspeed at 40,000 feet. A pilot who pulled the blind at 1,000 m.p.h. at 60,000 feet would face no greater slam of air than he would if he had ejected at 360 m.p.h. near sea level. And, if the pilot of a space capsule travelling at several thousand miles an hour far beyond the earth's atmosphere could put his hand out, he would feel no blast at all.

Molland was fortunate, therefore, in getting out at 25,000 feet – much more fortunate than George Smith, until then one of the few other men to have made a faster-than-sound ejection.

Smith, a North American Aviation Company test pilot, ejected from a Super Sabre on February 26, 1955, on a test flight near Los Angeles. The aircraft went out of control at 35,000 feet and had dived to about 6,500 feet before he fired himself out. Just before he left the cockpit his machmeter was showing Mach 1.05 and it was estimated that he ejected at a true airspeed of nearly 780 m.p.h.

This was not a lot faster than Molland's true bale-out speed, but it was at a much lower altitude and amounted to an indicated airspeed of close on 720 m.p.h. Smith's was an American type automatic seat without drogues: when his parachute opened four seconds after ejection the canopy was ripped and he made a rapid descent into the sea where some fishermen picked him up, unconscious.

On his quick, damaging journey through the most ferocious air blast any man had then been subjected to – it even tore the ring off his finger – Smith suffered multiple injuries. He was unconscious for five days; yet within three months he was out of hospital and flying again.

CHAPTER XV

The Caterpillars, despite their considerable numbers, are an exclusive brotherhood and few could envy them the process of initiation. But even the most terrifying bale-outs, the most frightening descents that ended with a merciful dangle in the silk, pale into insignificance in comparison with the air-to-ground journeys of a small band of men who, although they fell out of the sky, will never wear a caterpillar pin on their lapels. They are ineligible for membership for a simple reason – they came down without parachutes.

It is not known just how many men have survived chuteless descents but there are at least six cases on record. And, although, strictly, they have no place in the chronicle of the Caterpillar Club they are such remarkable escapes that some deserve recording.

The classic among these rare tales is that of an R.A.F. rear gunner, Flight Sergeant Nicholas Alkemade. He jumped out of a Lancaster of No. 115 Squadron, 18,000 feet over Germany without a parachute, yet he survived, and without a single broken bone.

Alkemade, who had been a market gardener at Loughborough before joining the R.A.F., was 21 at the time. It happened on his 15th operation on March 23, 1944, when he and his crew were returning to their base at Witchford in Norfolk from a raid on Berlin.

Over the Ruhr, shortly before midnight, the Lancaster was caught by a German night fighter, the starboard wing was ripped open like a tin of beans and the aircraft caught fire. Alkemade saw flames begin to pour back past his turret and before long he heard the pilot's voice on the intercom say, 'Sorry, boys, I can't hold her. Bale out! Bale out!'

As the crew began individually to acknowledge the order with, 'Baling out,' he unplugged his intercom lead, centralized the turret and opened the swing doors, which led back into the fuselage, to reach for his parachute which was in a metal container on the other side.

He was too late. The fuselage interior was ablaze from end to end. It looked like the barrel of a giant blow-lamp and in the brief seconds during which he saw his parachute pack burning in its stowage, his face and wrists were scorched, and his rubber oxygen mask began to melt on his face.

Quickly, he slid back into the turret and closed the doors. The terrible discovery brought a hollow contracting sensation to the bottom of his stomach, yet in those moments it was very much a subsidiary feeling; the merciless skinshrivelling heat terrified him far more than the loss of his parachute.

And now the turret, too, was burning. He ripped off his melting mask and as it came away from his face the oxygen that was streaming into it began to feed the flames. Then the fluid in the turret hydraulic lines caught fire and the flames spread to his clothes.

Far better, he decided, to die cleanly – better than a slow frying death.

With the hand control he rotated the turret on to the beam. Then he fell out backwards into the night. He had scarcely left the aircraft when in a fiery flash it exploded above him.

He found himself falling head-first, rigidly to attention. It was a clear, dark night and all he saw during the minute-and-a-half of his three-and-a-half mile descent were the stars beyond his feet. He had no sensation of falling and his body made only a slight breeze as it dropped.

After the inferno he had escaped from, the cool night air was peacefully soothing and he found himself thinking, 'If this is dying, it's not at all strange.'

No memories of his past life flashed before him. He felt no fear, no panic. There was just nothing he could do to save himself and he knew that he would know nothing of the end when it came. He decided not to turn his head and look down; he didn't want any warning of the end.

And that was his last recollection of his descent – inverted in space, the stars below his flying boots, and a sensation, which persisted to the end, that he was stationary.

It had been close to midnight when they were attacked. Three hours later, Alkemade regained consciousness lying on his back in snow in a small pine wood. When he opened his eyes and looked up he could see the stars through the hole he had made in the trees above.

'Jesus Christ,' he murmured to himself, 'I'm alive!' And it was not an expression of blasphemy, but heartfelt thanks.

To make quite sure, he wriggled his toes and with his hands began systematically to feel himself all over. Incredibly, fantastically, apart from severe bruising, numerous small cuts and scratches and the burns he had received in the aircraft, he was in one piece.

He suffered no loss of memory, remembered clearly his descent without parachute, yet strangely, after his initial discovery of the fact, he felt no great surprise that he was alive. It was not until several hours later that his emotional numbness was to wear off and his senses were to grasp fully the significance of the miracle. For the moment his mind was unable to appreciate the enormity of his experience; he could not regard his deliverance as much more than extraordinarily good luck.

Groping in the pockets of his Irvin suit he found his watch. It was still ticking and by its luminous hands he saw that it was 3.10 a.m. He put the watch back, pulled out a crumpled packet of cigarettes and lit one.

For several minutes he lay smoking peacefully. Then, as his eyes grew accustomed to the dark he stood up and examined himself more thoroughly.

Both boots, which he had been wearing when he left the aircraft, were missing, presumably torn off when he had crashed at the 120 m.p.h. of terminal velocity through the branches of the pine trees. The trouser legs of his flying suit were charred and torn. His harness (it was a chest type on which the parachute pack had to be clipped) was still firmly in position, the lift webs still neatly folded. Not realizing then the part it was to play in corroborating his story he took the harness off and dropped it in the snow.

The snow, he saw, was no more than 18 inches deep. It had drifted in under the trees from open ground which bordered the pine wood. Out in the open there was no snow. If he had fallen just 20 yards to one side of the wood nothing could have saved him. And so to two simple facts he owed his life. First to the springy branches of the pines, which were young and supple, and secondly to the snow which had received him as he dropped out of the branches.

When he tried to walk out of the wood, one leg crumpled under him and he had to sit down again. He remembered that he had twisted it as he flipped himself out of the turret. The reaction was setting in now and the cold began to creep

through his bruised limbs. He knew he would have to giv
himself up, so he pulled up the whistle hooked on to h
battledress lapel and blew a series of long blasts.

Soon he heard voices and the sound of crashing throug
the trees. A torch shone in his face and he saw that h
captors were German Home Guardsmen.

The Germans were more interested in his cigarettes, whic
they promptly relieved him of, than in Alkemade. The
brought a tarpaulin, laid him on it and dragged him like
sack of potatoes to a cottage where an elderly woman fe
him brandy egg-nogs. Then some Gestapo men arrived an
he was taken by car to hospital at Maschede, where doctor
removed a large quantity of perspex splinters and twig
from his flesh, and treated his burns.

Next morning the interrogation began. The German
wanted to know what had become of his parachute. Whe
Alkemade said he had come down without one his inter
rogators laughed disbelievingly, accused him of being a sp
and of hiding his parachute.

'If you don't believe me then,' said Alkemade indig
nantly, 'go and find my parachute harness.'

In due course the harness was collected from the pine
woods. And when his accusers saw it they were partly con
vinced, for the lift webs which extend when the parachute
opens were, of course, clipped down. A few days later, from
being a suspect spy Alkemade became a minor hero; in the
burnt-out wreckage of the Lancaster which had fallen twent
miles away, with four members of the crew who did not ge
out, the metal remains of his parachute – the ripcord handle
and cable – were found still in the stowage.

So impressed were the Germans that when Alkemade was
delivered to prison camp, the 200 Allied prisoners there
were paraded to hear a Luftwaffe officer recite the details
of his incredible descent. And so that he would not be
doubted again he was given a certificate. It read:

'It has been investigated and corroborated by the German authorities that the claim of Sergeant Alkemade,
No. 1431537, is true in all respects, namely, that he has

made a descent from 18,000 feet without a parachute and made a safe landing without injuries, the parachute having been on fire in the aircraft. He landed in deep snow among fir trees.

'Corroboration witnessed by:

(Signed) Flight Lieut. H. J. Moore (Senior British Officer)
          Flight Sergeant R. R. Lamb
          Flight Sergeant T. A. Jones

(25/4/44).'

After the Luftwaffe officer's speech a young United States Army Air Corps pilot, who had been a clergyman before joining up, came up to Alkemade and shook hands.

'I thought my escape just about as lucky as they can get,' he said, 'but yours beats mine. The stage is yours.'

The American, it appeared, had been the captain of a Flying Fortress which had been shot down on a raid over Germany. The aircraft had broken up and, in the process, he had been flung out and was caught up on one of the detached wings. Jammed there he had come down on the wing to within 1,000 feet of the ground when his parachute opened and pulled him off with only seconds to spare.

Nor was the American the only fellow prisoner who Alkemade found had an experience to rival his own. By a strange coincidence he was later to share a hut at Stalag Luft III with the rear gunner of a Sunderland flying boat which had been shot up over Norway: an explosion had blown his turret clean off. It fell, with him inside it, into a deep snow drift. Several hours later some Norwegians found him nearly frozen to death – but alive!

Perhaps these three men were merely incredibly lucky; or was it, as Alkemade stoutly believes in his case, divine intervention? His three-and-a-half mile fall was only the first of a series of narrow escapes from violent death. The next was in 1946 when, soon after demobilization, he was working in a chemical factory at Loughborough. One day he had to enter a sump hole to pump out a quantity of liquid chemical that was generating poisonous chlorine gas. Halfway through the operation he received a severe electric shock from the pump he was holding and, as he stumbled, his gas mask fell off. It was fifteen minutes before his cries brought help and he was hauled out, nearly asphyxiated by the chlorine fumes.

A few weeks later, in the same factory, he was syphoning sulphuric acid. A pipe burst and his face and arms were drenched in the acid. But for a 40 gallon drum of limewash which was standing nearby he might well have been fatally burned. With lightning presence of mind he dived headfirst into the lime drum; the acid was neutralized and he escaped with first degree burns. And, having recovered from that, he went back to work to be knocked flat by a nine-foot tall steel door channel which broke off and fell on top of him. The men who prised the channel up and pulled him out were sure he was dead. Not Alkemade. He had suffered only slight bruising. But even *he* felt he had tempted providence often enough. Deciding to seek work in a less dangerous environment he became a furniture salesman.

When Flying Officer Rupert North's 487 Squadron Ventura had been shot down during the Amsterdam raid of May 3, 1943, he had clipped his parachute on in mid-air (Chapter VII). His wireless operator/air gunner, Sergeant Stannard, came down without a parachute.

When war broke out Stannard, a Southwark man who was a packer in the publishing department of the London *Daily Telegraph*, applied to join the R.A.F. At first came bitter disappointment. He was then 30 and the recruiting officer told him he was too old for pilot training, too old, in fact, for any aircrew duties. Stannard said that if he could not fly then he wouldn't join the R.A.F., he'd sign on with the Army. But the R.A.F. relented when it was discovered that he had some knowledge of radio. The age limit was waived and he went off to train as a wireless operator/air gunner.

And so it happened that, on May 3, 1943, Stannard, with 20 operations behind him, flew out across the North Sea on what was to be his last flight.

There were three others in the crew – the pilot, the mid-upper gunner, and the navigator, Rupert North. Stannard had two responsibilities – radio and gunnery, but as they neared the Dutch coast he gave all his attention to the defensive role, going back and taking up his station behind the twin Browning guns which, in the rear ventral position, were the Ventura's defence against attack from below.

But the guns of the 11 Venturas on this heroic raid were no match for the cannon-firing Focke-Wulf 190s which swept down on them in vastly superior numbers.

Lying spread-eagled on the floor, gripping his guns and scanning the sky below, Stannard heard the mid-upper gunner's warning that two enemy fighters were attacking from above. He heard the mid-upper guns fire, then stop as a stream of cannon thumped into the fuselage. He called to the mid-upper gunner on the intercom to ask if he was all right. There was no answer, so he quickly stood up and went forward to the turret – the gunner was dead.

Back at his guns, Stannard saw two 190s coming in to attack from below. He fired, but they broke away before he could hit them. He tried to call the pilot on the intercom but as the circuit was dead he looked round to see if the two men up forward had survived the first attack. To his dismay he saw that the fuselage was a blazing red holocaust and, in the same instant, he realized with a feeling of anguished helplessness that his parachute, which was stowed in a rack by the main door, was in the middle of the fire.

But as he crouched there, slightly stupefied by this personal tragedy, the flames were suddenly sucked forward away from the main door. Through the fire he saw North leap out through the escape hatch in the cockpit roof and knew then that it was the draught from the hatch that had drawn the fire forward.

With a burst of hope he went forward to the door, shielding his face from the cruel heat with his gloved hands. His parachute pack was still there in the rack and although the cover was badly charred, he snatched it up eagerly. He was about to clip it on to his harness and open the door, when the flames surged back again and he had to retreat to the rear of the fuselage. As he stumbled back, the silk poured out of the pack and he accidentally dropped it. He stooped down to gather up the folds, but he was then swamped by a wave of such intense heat he had to abandon it and got back into the narrow recess of the tail. With his chute now burning and useless, it no longer mattered that he was cut off from the door that was his only exit.

Huddled as far into the tail as he could squeeze, Stannard waited for the end he knew could not be far away. He prayed that it would be quick.

Slowly the fire ate its way towards him. He could no longer see the cockpit through the flames and black smoke, could not hear above the crackling and the roaring whether or not the engines were still running. With awesome fascination he watched the fuselage metal a few feet away from him begin to melt and run in molten rivulets. He drew his knees up and buried his face to stave off the heat for a few more seconds, and tried to wriggle back an inch or two further. But his back was already hard against the tail wall.

And that, a moment or two later, is how he would have died – a small bunched-up figure, burnt to death – if the aircraft hadn't blown up.

Stannard heard an explosion which seemed to come from the depths of the inferno in front of him. He looked up and was just in time to see the whole of the Ventura forward of the tail unit, fall slowly away below him in a great flower of flame.

The roaring faded away, the heat subsided, and he found himself sitting in the broken-off tail unit in a clear blue sky – 9,000 feet above the coast of Holland. It suddenly felt unnaturally quiet and cool – and after the terror of the fire it was the coolness, the softness of the gentle breeze that swirled into his stubby, truncated piece of fuselage, that he relished most. This, he told himself, was an infinitely preferable way to die – a quick plunge to earth in a ready-made coffin.

But, for simple aerodynamic reasons, the tail unit did not plunge down. The tail plane gave a certain amount of lift, and the twin fins and rudders contributed a further element of stability. The result was that it came spiralling down like a sycamore leaf.

Sitting there with his back against one wall of the fuselage and his feet touching the other, Stannard made himself comfortable. He crossed his legs, folded his arms and began, as far as he could, to study his vehicle and its method of descent. He examined it slowly, deliberately and unhurriedly, for death which a minute ago had appeared so imminent, so final, now seemed, in this silent peaceful limbo, strangely remote.

He saw that the fuselage had broken off about ten feet from the tip of the tail. It was not a jagged break but surprisingly clean-edged; it looked almost as if the cylinder of the fuselage had been methodically cut through, all the way round, with a blow torch, an illusion that was heightened in places where the tarnished edges had apparently melted and lumpily resolidified.

The two Browning guns hung on the edge of his platform, bouncing gently up and down on their elastic suspension lines which ran up to the top of the fuselage. From where he sat it was about 18 inches to the broken edge of the tail and, looking out past the guns, he could see that he was slowly revolving. One moment he could see the line of the North Sea horizon, then a hazy blur of land, then the sea again. It was a gentle, not unpleasant motion and he felt no giddiness.

Of his rate of descent he could make no estimate at first. In fact, for several thousand feet, there was no impression of descending at all. There was no uprush of wind; just a delicate breeze which sighed, almost soundlessly, past the entrance of his eyrie.

Stannard is not an emotional man. He has always taken life as he finds it, and in the three or four minutes he spent in that spiralling tail unit believing it to be his last let-down, he says he felt calm and unafraid. And that is not an heroic boast after the event. For, as he realized later, on looking back at it all, from the moment he knew he had been spared death by fire, that relief transcended all other emotions.

It was not his own end that upset him in those minutes

189

but the thought, which accompanied him all the way down, of the shock it would be to his mother.

'I thought a great deal of my mother,' he says, 'and was the apple of her eye. I was her only surviving son and there was an exceptionally strong bond between us. She was the only person I thought about as I came down and I thought about very little else.'

Because his view extended outwards and he could not see vertically downwards, it was not until the last 1,000 feet that Stannard saw for certain that he was coming down over land. He could see the North Sea, but there were now green fields between him and the coast. And as the Dutch landscape began rapidly to expand into details of canals, houses and dykes he saw for the first time that he was descending a great deal faster than the gently spilling air had led him to believe.

He had hardly absorbed the fact of his swift deceptive rate of descent, and estimated that he still had at least 500 feet to go, when the tail crashed through the top branches of a tall pine tree.

Totally unprepared, Stannard was still sitting relaxed, with legs crossed and arms folded, when he felt the tail tilt slightly and heard the crashing and squealing of metal against wood. It was not a violent impact, for the top branches were thin and springy, but as the tail carved its way down through the tree he heard big boughs splintering and snapping, and the sound of tortured timber amplified by his metal shell.

The moment he hit, Stannard braced himself, wedging his body tightly between the fuselage walls, expecting to be hurled out. But, extraordinarily, for the full 100 feet of its journey as it ploughed through the tree, the tail did not topple and he stayed inside, unharmed.

Only when it broke through the last branches and, all momentum spent, dropped gently on to the ground, did it turn over. As he was tipped out, the elastic gun straps twisted round his neck. For a moment he felt too dazed to release himself and began slowly to choke. But he rallied in time, forced the straps apart, and pulled his head out.

Staggering away from the tree he was suddenly obsessed

with the idea that the rest of his crew had come down with him and that at all costs he must find them. He saw that he was on the lawn of a large well-kept garden and in a vague semi-delirious state he began staggering about calling the names of his crew.

The next thing he remembers is standing in a vast, luxuriously furnished room, reaching out for a glass of red wine that a little, elderly, regal looking woman was handing him. There were several other people in the room and in a big wall mirror he suddenly caught sight of a man with two ugly black eyes, whose head and one hand were swathed in bandages. After a few seconds' bafflement he recognized the reflection as his own and heard himself saying 'thank you very much' for the wine he had been handed. The little elderly woman then introduced herself as Miss Willink van Bennebroek and told him, in English, that her gardener had found him wandering about her garden, and that she had sent for her doctor who had treated and bandaged his burnt left hand and face.

Although he was mildly concussed and still utterly bewildered by his presence in this big luxurious house, he sensed a tension among the people in the room. Presently he knew why. Not all those who stood watching him sip his wine were Dutch. One was a German and although he was in civilian clothes he guessed correctly that he was a member of the Gestapo.

Presently a Luftwaffe officer arrived, spoke a few words to the Gestapo man and beckoned to Stannard to follow him. It was the beginning of a long journey to Stalag Luft VI near the Lithuanian/Russian border and two years' captivity.

His injuries, from which he had completely recovered within a few months, fell into two categories: those he received in the aircraft before the tail broke off, and those caused by his crash through the tree. In the first group were a badly burned left hand and forehead, and two flesh wounds where he had been hit in the leg by exploding bullets when the fire reached the ammunition belts for the Browning

191

guns. In the second, incredibly, were only slight concussion and a cut on the head.

In 1948, Stannard went back to Holland to visit the graves of the two members of his crew who died in the aircraft – and to find and thank Miss van Bennebroek. She was still living in her big house near Bennebroek village and gave him a warm welcome. This time he was able to sip the red wine she offered him, without interruption. He met the doctor who had bandaged his burns and the gardener who had, on that day five years before, seen the burning Ventura explode, had seen the wreckage shower down, had seen the tail piece decimate the finest tree in his garden and crash on to the lawn and had watched unbelievingly as a man scrambled out of it and ran away.

In the memory of Peter Underdown nearly three days are missing. They have been excised from his mind and are probably lost for ever. For the knowledge he now has of what happened to him between nine minutes past two on the afternoon of Friday, October 29, 1954 and 10 o'clock on the morning of Monday, November 1, he has had to accept the word of others – among them the Dutch people who saw his aircraft disintegrate and watched him hurtle to the ground, unchecked by parachute or drogue, in his ejection seat.

Underdown was a Flying Officer in No. 234 Squadron, then based at Geilenkirchen in Germany and equipped with Sabres – supersonic American jet fighters. Although he was only 23 he was a little older than many of his fellow pilots and had already been seven years in the R.A.F., having joined as an apprentice at 16 and subsequently graduated from the Royal Air Force College, Cranwell, with his 'wings' and a commission.

After lunch on that Friday afternoon, the pilot attack instructor in Underdown's flight found himself too busy to do an air test on his personal Sabre and asked Underdown if he would do it for him. It was only a routine test following a minor inspection of the aircraft and Underdown immediately agreed.

He pulled on his flying overalls, collected his helmet,

192

gloves and maps, and went across to the aircraft servicing flight hangar. There, after a few words with the technical flight sergeant, he signed the aircraft servicing form, walked out to the Sabre which was standing in front of the hangar and climbed in. He started up, spoke to the control tower on R/T and after the customary clearances taxied out to the runway, took off and climbed away westward across the Dutch/German border into Holland.

That was at seven minutes past two. Sixty-eight hours later, at 10 o'clock the following Monday morning, Underdown was astonished to find himself lying in a hospital bed at Sittard in Holland. His ribs felt sore and he couldn't see properly with his right eye, but otherwise he was intact. He demanded to know why he was there and what day it was. A Dutch doctor told him that his aircraft had crashed and that he had been found, still strapped to his ejection seat, in a tree – three days earlier.

Underdown thought back. He could remember no crash, no tree. At first, all memory of Friday eluded him. Then slowly, in fragments he recalled the events of Friday morning. He remembered the lunch in the mess, remembered going back with the others to the crew room, remembered being asked to do an air test. He remembered saying, 'Yes, I'll do it,' but that was his last conscious recollection of Friday.

Later on Monday some R.A.F. officers came to visit him. They told him his aircraft had disintegrated two minutes after take-off and were anxious to know what had caused it. Underdown couldn't help them.

The story had to be pieced together without his help. It was fortunate, therefore, that a large number of Dutch people in villages near the German border had seen the crash.

They had heard the Sabre coming from the direction of Geilenkirchen and had looked up as it approached, travelling fast at about 2,000 feet and leaving behind it the usual brown trail of partly burnt fuel – then a characteristic of the Sabre. About five miles from Geilenkirchen, over the village of Wintraak, its nose was seen suddenly to pitch

193

steeply, first up, then down. At the same moment flames spurted out of the starboard wing root, both wings folded upwards, there was a series of explosions in rapid succession and within a few seconds there was only a mass of flying wreckage where the Sabre had been.

Among the falling wreckage was the ejection seat with Underdown in it. It curved forward ahead of the main debris, described a long arc through the sky and was seen to disappear behind a wooded slope.

A Dutch policeman found it in an orchard a few minutes later, perched a few feet above the ground, lodged in the branches of an apple tree. He pulled it down and was amazed to find that the man in it was not only alive but shouting. Having no English he could not understand what Underdown was saying, but he quickly undid his harness, helped him out and took off his parachute, which was unopened and had the ripcord still in position.

Within half an hour, Underdown was in Sittard hospital. He was still conscious, and still talking, though somewhat incoherently. The Dutch doctors who examined him expected to find, at the very least, serious internal injuries. But soon they were shaking their heads incredulously for these were his only injuries: mild concussion, bruises, five broken ribs, dislocated shoulder, strained right eye muscle, one of the smaller pelvis bones fractured. In four weeks he was out of hospital – still with no memory of that lost weekend.

Meanwhile the accident investigators had collected all the wreckage of the Sabre that could be found. They estimated that it had been travelling at about 350 knots when the break-up started. It had happened so swiftly that Underdown had had no time to eject, for the seat gun had not been fired. Instead, as the nose pitched violently down, the seat had broken from its mounting and had been bunted out through the plastic hood. It was an American type manual seat and, unlike the Martin-Baker seat, employed no drogue. In consequence there had been nothing to slow it down as it shot away from the cockpit at more than 400 miles an hour.

It was the orchard that saved Underdown. The trees were on sloping ground and, by rare chance, it just happened that the angle of the seat's trajectory coincided with the angle of the slope. The seat hurtled down the slope, about ten feet above the ground, crashing through tree after tree, until finally having lost speed, it came to rest in a stout fork.

Not only did a fortuitous combination of angles save him: there was also the attitude of the seat at the moment it began to punch its bulldozing trail through the trees. Had he gone through facing forward, his body would have been pounded by the branches. But the seat, in its spinning passage, had hit the first tree upright and back first; he had thus swept through the orchard protected by the metal structure behind him.

But, whereas the effects of the break-up had been dramatically obvious, the cause could not be established. One theory was that a mounting bracket in the tail plane actuating mechanism had failed from metal fatigue, causing a fully nose-down trim change which had sent the aircraft into the start of an outside loop and overstressed the airframe. But it was only a theory and the only person who could have confirmed it was Underdown and he had no recollection of the flight.

Doctors and technical experts questioned him closely trying to help him recall his lost hours – without success. No matter how desperately he tried, he could not shape the smallest picture of the events of those 68 hours on the blank canvas of his mind.

As a last resort hypnosis was suggested. The R.A.F.'s consultant neuro-psychiatrist was called in and although he pointed out that there was little more than a one-in-ten prospect of success, it was decided that it was worth trying.

The Services have no power to hypnotize a man against his will and it was made clear to Underdown that he need only make the test if he wished to. But he was as eager as the investigating officers to have his memory of those three days restored, and offered immediately to co-operate. And so, after the permission of his Commander-in-Chief in Germany had been obtained, he went down to the R.A.F. hos-

195

pital at Halton in Buckinghamshire and submitted to pentothal hypnosis.

The outcome was only partial success. Under hypnosis his 68-hour amnesia gap was reduced by less than half an hour. He was able to remember collecting the aircraft from the hangar, taxiing out to the runway and taking off. That was all. The vital moments immediately preceding and during disintegration, hypnosis failed to reveal. They must remain – if, that is, he was conscious, and he may not have been after the break-up started – a secret for ever in the recesses of his mind.

CHAPTER XVI

Since the mid-1950s when *Into the Silk* was first published there have been dramatic advances in aviation and in the technology of aircrew escape. Military aircraft fly faster and higher than ever before. Sustained supersonic flight is now routine for many of the world's air forces. Speeds of more than 2,000 miles an hour – three times the speed of sound – and cruising levels of 80,000 feet and above have become commonplace for some squadrons. And at the other end of the spectrum vertical take-off aircraft, which can operate from zero forward speed to Mach 1, have long been in service.

To keep pace with the increased range of operational speeds and heights the techniques of escape have become vastly more sophisticated. They have had to respond on the one hand to the need to bring safely back to earth crews whose aircraft break up at Mach 3, 16 miles up in the stratosphere, and on the other to recover pilots who may be caught in life or death emergency situations while their aircraft are stationary on runways or carrier decks.

The days when military aircrew in aircraft on fire or out of control struggled to release themselves from seat harnesses, fought to open escape hatches and hoods, battled with the slipstream and fell out into mid-air, counting the necessary seconds before fumbling for ripcords they often couldn't find, are now virtually part of history. The era of the 'escape system' has arrived.

Parachutes, ejection seats and life support equipment now more than ever before have become interdependent, working together to preserve life in critical situations and dangerous environments. And with every development the systems of escape have added new refinements, more automation, to the point where an injured pilot can descend unconscious through the freezing upper atmosphere, thin in pressure and oxygen, land in the sea and be kept afloat by automatically inflated life-jackets and rescued by courtesy of homing radio beacons automatically triggered to transmit.

Central to escape from military aircraft remains the ejection seat. And supreme in this field are the ingenious range of seats which continue to come from the factory at Higher Denham of the Martin-Baker Aircraft Company. They remain the inspiration of the company's Managing Director and Chief Designer, James Martin, who was knighted in 1965 for his personal inventor's contribution to the development of escape equipment.

Now in his early eighties, Sir James is still the driving force behind the company he began – initially to make aeroplanes – with a staff of two back in 1929. His is the tireless, still energetically probing mind of the gifted inventor. He is in his office every morning at 7.30, rarely leaves before 7 in the evening, and works a full day on Saturday. He is a perfectionist and a legend among the air forces of the world to whom, since his first model proved itself with a human test ejection in 1946, he has delivered 46,000 of his increasingly more versatile seats. But despite the scores of different versions of the seat he has designed and built for use in 58 countries, despite his introduction in 1961 of rocket propulsion, and a constant flow of technical refinements from his drawing board, Sir James is never satisfied.

His latest, the remarkable Mark 10, is, he admits, 'the

best I've ever designed'. But, he adds immediately: 'I've got to improve on it. I can make it even better'.

Two of the men who worked in the immediate post-war years on the pioneer seats are still with the company. Wing Commander John Jewell, who as a wartime Fighter Command technical staff officer, had first put the R.A.F.'s needs for a new escape system to Martin in 1944, is now Consultant Engineer.

Squadron Leader John Fifield, who in 1955, before the days of the rocket seat, made the world's first 'nought feet' ejection from a Meteor travelling at 140 m.p.h. on the runway, is today Chief Pilot of the company's fleet of two Meteors, a Dove and a Dakota.

Bernard Lynch, the man who volunteered to make that first ever live ejection in 1946, has retired. By the time he left the company he had made more than 30 test ejections.

An earlier chapter in this book recorded that, in 1956, the Martin-Baker seat had saved just over 100 lives. At the gate of his factory Sir James has now erected a large board. Day by day it indicates to his 2,000 staff the rising tally of lives owed to the seats they have built. At the beginning of March, 1977 the number on the board was 4,153. And the total grows at the rate of five or six a week.

Many of the men saved have become members of the Martin-Baker Club, receiving a silver wing brooch and a tie with the inverted red triangle symbol of the company.

Although seats of American manufacture exist it is a tribute to Sir James that the Martin-Baker seat has become standard equipment in a number of U.S.A.F. and U.S. Navy combat aircraft. In fact American military aircrew represent more than half the lives saved by his seat.

Since Korea the seat has proved itself again in combat. In wars in South-East Asia and the Middle East over 750 successful ejections were made.

The escape systems of the 'seventies have evolved to the point where they can blast aircrew out of trouble and 'into the silk' at almost any speed and any altitude. In every case the journey begins in the seat and ends on a parachute. In between, survival, for escape from high altitude, depends on a third element – the protective clothing and life support system worn.

Outside their warm pressurized cockpits pilots climbing to the upper levels of the earth's atmosphere, and beyond, are faced in emergency with an environment in which, unprotected, they would swiftly die.

Emergencies can come in many ways. From mid-air collision, on-board explosions, control failures, battle damage – all of which can cause explosive decompression of the cockpit, suddenly exposing the crew to the very real perils of the outside atmosphere. Alternatively damage or loss of control, without decompressing the cockpit, can necessitate rapid ejection into the high altitude environment.

The human body, among other things, needs warmth and oxygen. And it needs oxygen under pressure for adequate oxygenation of the blood through the lungs. At sea level this occurs efficiently at a pressure of 14.7 pounds per square inch. The pressure decreases progressively with altitude. At 10,000 feet it is only 10 p.s.i.; at 30,000 feet, 4.35 p.s.i.; at 50,000 feet, 1.7 p.s.i.; at 70,000 feet, 0.63 p.s.i.; at 100,000 feet a mere 0.15 p.s.i.

In rapid ascent to high altitude, unless oxygen is supplied artificially under pressure, the consequences are dramatic if man is directly exposed to the atmosphere. Above 10,000 feet the effects of anoxia – oxygen lack – begin to be felt. Reactions slow down, speech becomes slurred followed, higher up, by dizziness and sickness. Between 20,000 and 30,000 feet lack of oxygen leads to vaporization of nitrogen in the blood, concentrating bubbles in the joints and causing the painful symptons called 'the bends' – well known to deep-sea divers adjusting, on ascent, to decreasing water pressure.

At 40,000 feet the air is so low on pressure and oxygen that the unprotected body becomes unconscious. At 63,000 feet, because of the diminished oxygen pressure in the blood, only about 6% of that at sea level, the body fluids begin to boil.

Military aircrew are protected from the rigours of high flight by oxygen masks, pressure helmets, pressure jerkins,

G-suits and pressure suits. The helmets and suits are normally of a 'partial pressure' type in that they do not encase the entire body, leaving the back of the head, neck, hands and feet without artificial pressure to permit freedom of movement. Through the helmets the crew breathe oxygen supplied under pressure, automatically controlled by a barostatic regulator which increases the pressure with altitude. Oxygen at the same pressure is fed to the special clothing; it inflates the suits through tubes or bladders tightening the garments round the body. This is essential to counteract the swelling which pressure breathing would cause in an unsupported body. The pressurized oxygen would drive the blood to the lower parts of the body, thereby reducing the supply to the brain and inducing unconsciousness.

G-suits help the crew to withstand the blacking-out effects of high levels of *g* imposed during tightly pulled manoeuvres which would otherwise drain the blood from the brain and lead to temporary unconsciousness. An automatic sensing device reacts to *g* forces and feeds pressurized air to the suits which inflate, thereby supporting the abdomen and lower limbs, preventing the blood draining from the brain towards the body's lower extremities. Some suits perform the dual function of reaction to *g* forces and providing the pressure to counter the swelling caused by breathing oxygen under pressure.

Full pressure helmets and suits which totally encase the body, providing complete isolation from the environment, are worn by test pilots and the operational aircrews of ultra-high-level flying aircraft such as the SR-71 Blackbird, the U.S.A.F.'s Mach 3 strategic reconnaissance aircraft. It flies routinely at altitudes above 70,000 feet, where no man was designed to survive.

Today's ejection seats therefore have to do a great deal more than fire aircrew out of an aircraft in trouble. They have to keep him alive until he drops down to low altitude and is no longer in need of artificial life support. And they must be capable of plucking a man into his parachute at supersonic speeds at extreme low level through punishing ir blasts in diving attitudes, possibly inverted – as well as getting him out even before he has left the runway.

This is how the Martin-Baker Mark 10 seat does all these things, if necessary where fractions of a second count, in a sequence of actions at incredible speed.

When the pilot, clad in partial pressure helmet and suit, climbs aboard his high-performance aircraft, his parachute is already stowed in a container behind his head-rest. His harness is connected to the chute. Packed with the parachute are two small miniature parachutes called drogues. They are linked to the top of the seat through a scissor shackle controlled by a barostat which continuously senses the altitude. The barostat is pre-set to a height, usually 10,000 feet – but higher for use over mountainous country – at which the main parachute is required to open.

As instant deployment of the parachute is essential only for low level escape there is another device which eliminates unnecessarily high g stress on the occupant's body at higher altitudes. It is a barostatically controlled 'G-limiter'. As chute-opening deceleration forces at altitude can exceed 25g, close to safe human limits, the mechanism delays parachute deployment for ejection above 6,000 feet until the loads have fallen to a comfortable 3g.

Subject to the G-limiter's control, at the pre-set barostat height, or immediately if ejection is below 6,000 feet, the shackle opens allowing the drogues to draw the main chute out. But a lot of other ingenious complex automation goes into action before that happens.

Let's assume that our pilot is airborne and cruising at Mach 2 – 1,350 m.p.h. – over the sea at the inhospitable altitude of 60,000 feet. His cockpit is pressurized and he is able to breathe normally without the aid of the emergency equipment surrounding him.

Suddenly he comes under attack from an enemy fighter. The cockpit is pierced, causing instant explosive decompression. The artificially high cabin pressure in which he has been cruising drops to the slender 1.05 lb per square inch of the outside atmosphere, and the temperature around him plunges to −56 degrees Centigrade.

Immediately the barostatic sensor attached to his partial pressure helmet reacts. The helmet visor snaps shut, sealing off his face. In the same split second the oxygen regulator switches on a flow of pressurised oxygen from the aircraft's supply, inflating the partial pressure suit and feeding his lungs through his oxygen mask. Boots and gloves protect his extremities from the sudden piercing cold.

But the equipment that has kept him alive in a suddenly hostile world is only designed to maintain the pilot's faculties so that he can get himself quickly down to a lower and safer altitude. Unfortunately this is not possible. His flying controls have been damaged and the aircraft will no longer respond. He has no alternative but to eject.

By now the aircraft is performing a violent manoeuvre imposing severe g forces which threaten to black him out and his arms have become leaden weights. The G-sensor responds by inflating the G-suit to the necessary pressure limiting the rush of blood away from his head to the lower part of his body.

There is no need, as with earlier model ejection seats, for the pilot to force his arms up to pull the face-blind firing handle. The handle is within easy reach between his legs. He pulls it. It is the only action he has to take. From here on automation takes over.

The cockpit hood is exploded away. Within one-fifth of a second his shoulder harness tightens to secure him for exit and to straighten his spine for the best position to take the high g loads of ejection thrust. The telescopic ejection gun is fired by a series of explosive charges. The gun begins to extend, driving the seat upwards. As it lifts, restraint garters tighten round the pilot's legs and arms to prevent injury should his limbs flail when he hits the air blast outside. The seat disconnects from the aircraft's oxygen system which is immediately replaced without interruption by another pressurized supply from a cylinder attached to the seat.

As the seat clears the cockpit there is a smooth transfer of thrust from the ejection gun to a rocket motor. It burns for only ¼ second but speeds the seat up and well clear of the tail at 160 feet per second.

Half a second from the start of ejection the rocket motor has burned out, the two drogues have been fired to stabilize the seat, and the pilot is on his own, decelerating behind his receding aircraft. It all happened so fast. One moment he was in his cockpit, the next he was alone with his seat in space.

And although he ejected at over 1,300 miles an hour, the blast forces that hit him, reduced by the low air density, were only the equivalent of 550 m.p.h.

It is suddenly very quiet as he descends, breathing pressurized oxygen, his suit inflated, dropping through the upper atmosphere at over 16,000 feet a minute. It takes him something like three minutes to reach 10,000 feet where the air is warmer and has adequate oxygen to offer.

As the barostat registers 10,000 feet it operates a mechanism which opens the shackle coupling on top of the seat. The drogue line disengages from the seat and draws the parachute from its container. The limb restrainers are released and as the canopy develops and the pilot swings beneath it, the seat falls away. The action of separation can trigger his personal radio locator beacon which begins to transmit his position to searching aircraft even before he reaches the sea. All this would happen even if the pilot were unconscious.

The remainder of the journey is a normal parachute descent at a gentle 22 feet per second, taking about seven minutes. As he drops into the sea the final acts of automated escape can come to his aid. If the equipment is fitted, his lifejacket will inflate on contact with the water – and so will the dinghy that has travelled down with him.

For escape at low level the sequence of events in the operation of the Mark 10 seat are spectacularly fast. Here the barostat does not need to postpone separation from the seat until descent to less extreme atmospheric conditions. The need very often is to get a man from cockpit to parachute in the quickest possible time. And to do so without imposing deceleration loads beyond human limitation to survive without injury.

To help a process which had to be both powerfully swift yet

relatively smooth, Sir James Martin decided that the standard flat disc-shaped 24-foot Irvin chute, which had served all his previous model seats, did not have the right rapid inflation characteristics. The GQ Parachute Company, of Woking, did however have a suitable chute. It was called the 'Aeroconical' and has been fitted to the Mark 10 seat.

In 1976 the Mark 10/Aeroconical combination saved its first life in highly international circumstances. He was a pilot of the Pakistan Air Force. He was saved by a British seat and parachute fitted to a supersonic Russian-designed MIG-19F6 built in China. The Pakistani was the first to experience in an emergency ejection the low swinging characteristics of the aeroconical chute on the descent, and its ability, through air-spilling gauze 'windows' in the canopy to drive forwards – a feature which may be developed to provide a manual steering facility in service.

The Pakistani Air Force pilot, Flying Officer Zahid H Malik, was the 890th life saved with a GQ parachute. The company has a small counterpart of the Caterpillar Club. Known as the GQ Club, it was formed in 1940. Members many of whom are Swedish Air Force Saab Lansen, Drake, and Viggen pilots, are presented with a pair of small gold wings and a colourful scroll.*

* The most unusual admission to the GQ Club was a pilot who never left his cockpit. The aircraft was a Victor V-bomber and it was being flown to Woomera by John Baker, Chief Test Pilot of the South Australia Weapons Research Division of the A. V. Roe company on August 17, 1962. The flight was to test a Blue Steel missile. At 47,000 feet Baker and his co-pilot, Flight Lieutenant Jimmy Catlin, noticed a large discrepancy in the readings of their duplicated flight instruments, particularly between the machmeters and the airspeed indicators. The fault was never satisfactorily explained but its immediate consequence was that the pilots suddenly had no idea whether they had high or low airspeed. While trying to resolve the problem the aircraft stalled, pitched up and went into a spin. Standard recovery methods failed and the Victor continued 'in a very rough man oeuvre' to head for the sea about 50 miles off the South Australian coast. As a last resort Baker decided to release the aircraft's GQ braking para chute normally used on landing. It worked. After a prolonged spin through 30,000 feet Baker recovered control at 17,000 feet. With the help of a Royal Australian Air Force aircraft which flew in formation with the Victor radioing correct airspeed, he landed safely. Baker has since retired from flying. He is a travel agent in Adelaide in South Australia.

At low level (whether at high or low speed) during an emergency while stationary, or at the moment of take-off or landing, the latest Martin-Baker rocket seat can whisk a man from the moment he pulls the handle to the point where he is suspended under a fully opened parachute in just 2½ seconds. This was demonstrated early in 1977 on a rocket-sled track test at Langford Lodge in Northern Ireland with an ejection at 600 knots – nearly 700 miles an hour. 'This,' says Sir James, 'is by any standards fairly spectacular.'

Spectacular, too, is the performance of Martin-Baker rocket seats from slow moving naval aircraft facing emergencies on carrier decks – as the two-man crew of a runaway U.S. Navy Grumman F-14 'Tomcat' found off the far northern coast of Scotland in 1976. The aircraft was taxi-ing out for take-off when an 'engine malfunction' occurred and the F-14 began a short but relentless roll towards the edge and over the side of the deck of the carrier, the *John F Kennedy*. The pilot and his Naval Flight Officer ejected. They rocketed up to nearly 300 feet. Their chutes were open on the way down at 280 feet, five seconds from ejection. Ten seconds later they were back on the carrier deck.

The two men in the Tomcat crew went out almost simultaneously, although they did not eject themselves individually. The Naval Flight Officer operated the system that fired *both* men out.

This technique is known as dual or 'command' ejection. Its aim, in two-crew aircraft, is to get both men out quickly and provide, in the event of injury to one crew member, the ability of the other to fire him out. To avoid collision the ejections are phased to allow a short interval between the two exits. And the directions of thrust of the rockets are slightly angled to blast one seat to port and the other to starboard.

The system has been introduced into the new European Tornado multi-role combat aircraft. Should the pilot initiate ejection his navigator will go a split second first. The navigator has the option of either ejecting himself only or, by moving a selector valve to the 'dual' position, ejectin[g] his injured pilot, as well as himself. But in the tradition o[f] the service, the system is so arranged that irrespective o[f] who takes the action, the pilot will always be last to go.

A variation of the procedure operates in the new R.A.F[.] Hawk jet trainer. Here there is a built-in safeguard to pre[-] vent an inexperienced but well-intentioned – or mayb[e] exasperated – student from ejecting his instructor. The stu[-] dent can eject himself. Only the instructor has the facilit[y] to take them both into the silk.

On a larger scale a system for multiple ejection exists i[n] the U.S. Navy's Grumman EA6B Prowler. It operates wit[h] a four-man crew. All four can be fired out in emergency b[y] the captain in just over a second.

CHAPTER XVII

The last 20 years have brought into the Caterpillar Clu[b] pilots who have escaped from sudden disaster in the air a[t] extremes of low and high level and at speeds which woul[d] have seemed sheer fantasy to those who earned their gol[d] caterpillars in leaps from piston-engined fighters and bombers in the Second World War.

One such escape, made all the more graphic by the fac[t] that it was photographed (see illustrated section) as it hap- pened, was that of de Havilland test pilot George Aird. He was 34 at the time and was flying a supersonic Lightning fighter which the company was using to test missile equip- ment.

On September 13, 1962 he flew off from the de Havilland (now Hawker Siddeley) airfield at Hatfield, in Hertford- shire, to air-test the aircraft following an engine change and, in particular, to check the operation of the reheat sys- tem, in which fuel is burned in the engine exhaust to provide extra thrust.

The air test completed, Aird turned back to Hatfield and began his descent from the north-east towards the airfield.

t was a bright early autumn day with a cool north-easterly breeze. The direction of the wind was to contribute to near-disaster for Aird.

Descending through 15,000 feet, a warning light flickered on in the cockpit. It indicated a fire in the reheat area of he exhaust of the new engine. The Lightning was then only 20 miles and a few minutes out of Hatfield. As there was no fire extinguisher in the reheat zone there was little that Aird could do but hope that the warning, as sometimes occurs, was spurious through a fault. Unfortunately, the warning was real: the engine was on fire.

But unable to see this from the cockpit Aird's main concern was to get the aircraft down quickly. 'The idea of abandoning a valuable research and development aircraft, with the risk to people on the ground, I hardly considered at that stage,' he says.

He called the Hatfield air-traffic controller, told him of the fire warning, and requested a priority landing. His normal approach into the prevailing westerly wind would have been straight in to a landing on the south-west heading of the single runway. But because the wind was from the east he had to make a time-consuming circuit to head for runway 06 for a north-easterly landing. But for this he would have landed normally.

The extra minutes he spent in circling the airfield were long enough for the fire to destroy the hydraulically powered jack which operated the Lightning's moving tail. Only half a mile and ten seconds from touchdown the aircraft suddenly pitched up.

'I reacted instinctively with forward stick,' says Aird. There was no response. The stick felt disconnected. I waggled it fore and aft in utter disbelief. A hundred feet above the ground the aircraft was totally out of control.'

The Lightning was now beginning to make its final nose-down plunge. There was only one course left. Aird reached up and pulled the face blind to eject. The next thing he was aware of was being sprayed with warm water. He was in a greenhouse surrounded by tomato plants. He had crashed through the glass and fractured a heating pipe. He was concussed, cut and bruised. His right thigh and both legs were broken. But he was alive. Close by, on the greenhouse floor was the seat that had just managed to intercede in the termination of a promising test-flying career.

The swift events, of which George Aird has no memory, were watched by the startled tractor driver seen in the picture. And by the photographer, Jim Meads. They saw the Lightning pitch up, then dive into the ground and explode. In the intervening seconds they saw the cockpit hood curve away, followed by a seat which described an arc from right to left over a clump of trees. As it went, two drogues shot out, then a parachute flowered open. The seat fell away. They saw first the seat, then a man, swinging below the chute, crash into a large greenhouse.

'But for the greenhouse I'm satisfied I would have only been slightly injured,' says Aird. 'I was using a Mark 4 fully automatic seat capable of successful operation from ground level at speeds above 90 knots. But my chances of survival from the outset were theoretically marginal. You see, although my approach speed was 165 knots, my rate of descent on the glidepath was 750 feet a minute. My ejection seat had to overcome this, in addition to lifting me well clear.

'At the time, though, I wasn't weighing up the mathematical odds. I could do no more for poor old XG 332. So I pulled the blind, not as a drowning man clutching at a straw, but confident that Mr Martin's seat would remove me from the scene of a nasty impending accident.'

An Irvin parachute played a brief but vital part in Aird's escape. 'But as my time in it was minimal I have never had the audacity to apply for a caterpillar,' he says with the modesty of his profession. However, early in 1977, 15 years after the event, the Irvin Company discovered that his name was missing from the files. He is now a fully fledged caterpillar and still flying. He tests Hawker Siddeley HS 125 executive jets at the company's factory near Chester.

Saved by seat, chute and dinghy from a Lightning but at the other extreme of height and speed was test pilot Johnny Squier. The day he qualified for 'a triple' – membership of the Caterpillar, Martin-Baker and Goldfish Clubs – he was already a member of a fourth fraternity. He was a 'Guinea Pig', having suffered severe facial injuries when his 64 Squadron Spitfire was shot down in August 1940.

It happened on October 1, 1959 when Squier, then 39, was a test pilot with the English Electric Company. He took off soon after 11 o'clock in the morning from Warton, in Lancashire, on a routine development flight to test the first prototype of the two-seat Lightning T Mark 4 trainer.

Climbing out north-west over the Irish Sea he was soon at 40,000 feet in clear blue sky above a shallow cloud layer which covered land and sea far below. He switched on the re-heat to give him the extra thrust he needed to go supersonic, opened the throttle wide and was quickly through Mach One. His speed began to build and soon, about 15 miles north-east of the Isle of Man his machmeter was indicating 1.7, equivalent to a true airspeed of 1,150 m.p.h.

Disaster struck quickly. Eleven minutes after take-off, a failure of the fin assembly suddenly left Squier with a total loss of directional control. It happened so quickly and violently he had no time to put out a distress call. He pulled the blind handle over his face.

'The cockpit hood left the aircraft almost immediately. After what appeared to be an eternity, but which was in fact one second, the seat followed. I was conscious of a fairly severe kick up my backside, of being thrown about, then starting to rotate at a very high speed.'

Although the accident happened at a speed over the sea of more then 1,100 miles an hour the indicated airspeed at 40,000 feet, and therefore the air-blast speed, was a great deal less – something like 600 m.p.h.

'Despite determined efforts to hold on to the face blind, my hands were pulled off it by centrifugal force. The pain in my shoulder was intense as my arms were flung about.' This was before the days of automatic arm restraint and the positioning of the firing handle at the base of the seat.

For the greater part of the descent Squier was unconscious. His mask had been ripped off during ejection and he was breathing no oxygen.

'When I came to, I was sitting peacefully in the seat, which was now stabilized,' he says. 'Suddenly there was a "clang" and as the seat separated from me, my legs dropped. The seat went up – which struck me as odd. Until it dawned on me that my parachute hadn't opened. By now I was dropping through the low-level cloud and, as I came out beneath it, the sea looked extremely close. I pulled the manual override handle and was relieved to hear the chute crack open immediately. The sea was less than 500 feet away and the next thing I knew I was in it and plunging down to a fair depth. I inflated my "Mae West" under water and soon bobbed to the surface. I discarded the parachute, inflated my dinghy, and climbed aboard.'

From the last position he had been given by Ulster Radar, Squier was probably about 20 miles west of St Bees Head in Cumbria. He was out of sight of land but he was not worried. He was glad to be alive. It was still late morning and he had not the least doubt that he would be located, rescued, and back at Warton by evening. The air search would have already started.

The first thing he did after baling out the dinghy was to switch on his homing radio beacon. The speech unit was dead but he left the beacon on in the hope that it was automatically transmitting. It was soon clear when search aircraft began to arrive in the area that it was not. The first was a Grumman Albatross amphibian. It came in low, flew straight towards him, passed overhead and flew away. Before the aircraft disappeared he struggled to fire a two-star red flare but it misfired.

Two hours later the Albatross returned but by the time his second flare had failed and his third and last had fired, the aircraft had passed overhead. Towards late afternoon he heard the sound of a Shackleton. Occasionally he saw it away in the distance. His only means of signalling now was a heliograph but under the low cloud there was no sun to reflect.

'All I could do was sit and wait. Eventually it got dark. I set up my light on top of the dinghy cover. Now, at last, I was convinced I would be clearly visible. But as time went on, and the sounds of aircraft died away, I settled down to he longest night of my life.'

Although he didn't know it, during the night Squier was slowly drifting north towards the coast of Kirkcudbright in Scotland. When dawn broke with drizzling rain, despite the limited visiblility, he could see a smudge of land to the west.

The one-man dinghy had no means of propulsion. 'I paddled with my hands, but made little progresss. Then I found a piece of driftwood. With this and my knee-pad I began to make headway. Then the drizzle closed in and the land disappeared. By now I was very thirsty. I'd had nothing to drink for over 24 hours. So I set up my solar still. During the morning the coast reappeared but the wind and tide kept me out to sea. I got some drinkable water from the still which cheered me up. Several boats passed nearby but although I waved and blew my whistle none of them saw me. You're a very small and lonely object in a one-man dinghy.'

Early in the afternoon of his second day adrift the tide turned and Squier came ashore on a rocky deserted stretch of coast. He walked for about half a mile to a school in a small village. It was 3.45 p.m. The matron told him he was at Garlieston in Wigtown Bay. He had been in the sea for 28 hours and had drifted 30 miles.

In hospital at Stranraer doctors told him that he had two compressed vertebrae. But six months later he was back in the cockpit and continued test work until he retired from flying in 1966. He is still at Warton as Cockpit Design Liaison Officer with the British Aircraft Corporation's Military Aircraft Division. The job is concerned with aircraft escape systems and safety equipment. It is an area in which Johnny Squier has a deep personal interest.

Of the estimated 120,000 and more incidents in which lives have been saved by Irvin parachutes over 55 years, none was more incredible or bizarre than that involving private pilot Ken Miller on October 18, 1975. Miller was flying a single-engined Cessna 182. He was not wearing a parachute. He did not bale out. A standard 24-feet diameter chute, designed to support one person, brought Miller, with two passengers, *and the aircraft* to earth. Upside down. A fourth man made the descent, suspended halfway between the parachute canopy and the Cessna.

It happened at Ashbourne airfield in Derbyshire. It was a sunny autumn Saturday afternoon and the Peak District Parachute Club were engaged in a training programme dropping students onto the field from the Cessna.

For Ken Miller, a 38-year-old company director from Burton-on-Trent, flying was a week-end recreation. He had been checked out for parachute dropping and had been flying regularly for the Peak District Club for over a year.

On the third flight of the afternoon he took off with a parachute instructor, 'jumpmaster' Derek Scofield, a 34-year-old sales executive from Derby, and three students.

It was to be their first live jump. Each wore two parachutes, one on the back, opened by a static line attached to the aircraft, and a reserve chest chute to be opened manually in emergency.

From 2,500 feet over the airfield the first student, Paul Almgill, made a successful jump. Miller circled round for a second pass over the dropping zone. Now it was Stewart Avent's turn. He moved to the open doorway.

The jumpmaster called to Miller: 'Cut. Brakes on', the command to throttle back the engine to reduce the buffet of the slipstream and to hold the wheel to allow the student to put his foot on it. Then Scofield tapped Avent on the shoulder, calling: 'On the wing'.

Avent took up his position, sitting on the floor, his legs hanging outside. He reached up and gripped the wing strut preparing himself for the jump. And then he slipped. For a few seconds he hung in mid-air, clinging to the strut with his hands. Then he let go. As he fell away the static line tightened and his main chute opened. But Avent didn't drop clear.

'The top of his parachute draped itself first around the aircraft's step, then around the undercarriage wheel,' says Scofield. 'I ordered the pilot to climb, then leaned out and began hacking the chute free with my knife. Avent was now hung up, trailing behind the aircraft, facing backwards,

212

dangling in the slipstream with his hands on his head – the signal that he was conscious.'

The third student, Miss Frances Ives, who was to have been the last to jump, looked on with horror.

For a moment, as he felt the jolt of the hang-up, Stewart Avent thought his chute had opened and he was on his way down. 'But when I reached up to the toggles, which should have been above me, I couldn't feel them. Then I looked up at the canopy and saw that it was snagged on the aircraft. I knew then the instructor would have to cut me free. But the rigging lines prevented me moving my head back and I had no way of knowing if he had seen my signal.

'A little later I looked down. The ground seemed to be a lot closer than 2,500 feet. I appeared to be descending and thought I must have been cut free. So I released my reserve chute. It opened with a great jolt.'

At that moment several crazy things happened. Ken Miller, who had managed to gain 400 feet in a full-power, gentle climbing turn, heard 'a tremendous bang, and the next I remember is waking up in hospital with a badly shattered jaw, wondering where I was and whether it was all a dream.'

Derek Scofield heard the bang of Avent's chute opening and at the same moment the aircraft gave a violent heave and he was flung from the open door back across the pilot. 'When I regained my senses the Cessna was spiralling down. I thought that Avent's chute had torn free and damaged the tail. Ken was slumped over the controls unconscious. I tried to pull back on the control column. Nothing happened. We just went rotating downwards. So I decided to jump. I got halfway through the doorway and was flung back inside. Now I was lying on the cabin roof and I realized the aircraft was inverted. I made another bid for the exit but lacked the strength. I tried pulling back on the controls again. No response. By now I knew we were too low to jump.'

Parachute instructors and spectators on the airfield watched the extraordinary chain of events aghast. Instructor Peter Denley was talking the first-time students down by radio. When he saw Avent trailing helplessly behind the aircraft he knew there was little he could do but wait for the chute to be cut free. It was a standard emergency procedure, and all students had been taught what to do – wait. Calmly he talked to Avent on the radio: 'Don't panic – watch the jumpmaster'.

Suddenly there was a gasp from those watching. Avent's reserve chute blossomed open. It took not only Avent's weight but, because he was still linked to the Cessna by his main chute, the weight of the aircraft as well.

The Cessna rolled over onto its back, the engine cut out, the aircraft stalled and began to nose-dive, spiralling as it went down from below 2,000 feet. The extraordinary scene was recorded by photographer Eddie McBride (see illustrated section). Under the parachute hung Stewart Avent, trapped upside down with his legs tangled in the rigging lines, his only view of events the open canopy above him. Suspended below him was the inverted Cessna with the three people trapped inside.

The chute designed to support 330 lb was lowering a load of something like 2,500 lb – seven times its intended capacity. Under this phenomenal weight the rate of descent was about 45 feet per second, twice as fast as the normal one-man speed of 22–25 feet per second. But the chute, none the less, saved four lives. It did so, incidentally, with a considerable contribution from the drag of the descending aircraft which was estimated to be roughly equal to that of the parachute canopy.

The Cessna hit the ground on the edge of the field, followed a few seconds later by Avent. Miraculously the aircraft did not catch fire. The two men and woman inside were all injured, sustaining cuts and serious multiple fractures. Avent escaped with a sprained back.

The subsequent investigation found that the primary cause of the accident was Avent's loss of footing as he prepared to jump. A special jump step has now been fitted.

But of the four people who made one of the most unpleasant descents in parachute history only Ken Miller, the pilot, received a gold caterpillar. Irvin Company officials decided that as the others had all taken off with parachutes with the deliberate intention of jumping they were not eligible under the Club's rules. Miller had not been wearing a parachute. But an Irvin chute had saved him.

Although military aircraft incidents still provide the Caterpillar Club with most of its new members, not all are in the powered-flight department. At least two 'caterpillars' have gained their gold pins by leaping from a balloon.

Twenty-eight-year-old Dick Dennis and his assistant, Roger Austin, were experimental officers with the Aerodynamics Flight Section of the Royal Aircraft Establishment, Bedford, in the mid-1950s. One of their tasks was to test the flight characteristics of prototype aircraft by dropping scale models from a tethered balloon.

The tests were made on the Army's Larkhill artillery range in Wiltshire from a balloon brought to the site from Cardington in Bedfordshire.

It was a warm summer's day when Dennis and Austin climbed into the metal carriage suspended beneath the balloon with two models of the prototype Bristol 188 research aircraft. Their job was to launch the models into a free-falling spin from 5,000 feet. The models would be tracked and filmed by kine theodolites on the ground, recording their behaviour in the spin, and subsequent automatic recovery and descent onto the range.

It took about 15 minutes for the balloon to be winched up to 5,000 feet. At this point Dennis called on the telephone link to the range controller for a further climb to 5,500 feet. The balloon had begun to resume its ascent when suddenly there was a jolt and the cable snapped at the winch.

'One minute we were sitting, happily admiring the splendid view over the Wiltshire plains – next thing we were shooting up like a lift,' says Dennis. 'I looked over the side and there was 5,000 feet of cable dangling below us, marching across the countryside. A 15-knot wind was carrying us steadily up-range towards Swindon and as we went we were climbing rapidly.'

At 6,500 feet, on the balloon carriage altimeter, the rate

of ascent began to slow. From there on they settled into a gentle climb, receding away to the north-east to the dismay of the range controller with whom they had lost phone contact, and the winch crew who were regarding with horror the limp strands of broken cable.

Dennis and Austin kept their heads. They both wore back-type ripcord-operated parachutes and were suddenly very grateful for them. But first they had a job to do. They released the models into their required spins and the ground cameras began to turn.

'After that we sat and looked at each other,' says Dennis. 'We knew we couldn't afford to stay on board for too long. If we had done, one of two things would have happened. We would have eventually drifted out across England into the oblivion of the North Sea. But before we got there, rising slowly, there was a risk the balloon might explode at between 15,000 and 20,000 feet. It had a gas-release valve to prevent runaway ascent, but we weren't too happy about its operation after the initial sudden breakaway. It was designed to respond only to slow changes in altitude.

'Soon we were at 9,000 feet and it was getting cold.' Roger said. 'This *would* happen to me just two weeks before my wedding.' We discussed who would go first. We debated tossing a coin. Then I said, and it sounds rather illogical in retrospect: "I'm married with two children – you go first."'

Austin baled out, his chute opened, and as he drifted down Dennis heard him calling clearly: 'Come on. It's all right.' Twenty seconds later Dennis followed.

During the eight to ten minutes of their descent they were not to know of new consternation on the ground. The range controller could see that the two parachutes were headed into the middle of the Army's West Down artillery shelling impact area. And a barrage of firing was in progress. By phone to the artillery commander he had the shelling stopped. A few moments later Dennis and Austin landed among the 'no-man's-land' of shell craters on the chalky range-end, eight miles from their winch-off point.

Meanwhile the balloon's valve was operating; it was releasing gas and the balloon had begun a gradual descent.

216

It headed north-east for Swindon and began to cross the outskirts of the town, dragging thousands of feet of cable across gardens and allotments. It ended its journey, still airborne, when a small-holder, with great presence of mind, rushed out and tethered the cable to the railings of his pigsty!

Occasionally glider pilots face emergencies – as Squadron Leader Ian Macfadyen and Flight Lieutenant Stan Easton did on May 9, 1975. They were flying in the Inter-Services Gliding Championships at R.A.F. Cosford, on the border of Shropshire and Staffordshire. Macfadyen, a 33-year-old 111 Squadron Phantom pilot, and Easton, from the R.A.F.'s Central Gliding School, collided in cloud near Bridgnorth in Shropshire.

Macfadyen was in a Kestrel; Eastern was flying a Diamant 18. It was a speed contest round a 105-kilometre triangular course. Sixty-two gliders of varying performance set off to fly the route at the same time. To prove they had completed the course, the pilots had to take photographs of ground landmarks at each turning point. The contestants were launched from Cosford by aerotow – pulled off by a powered aircraft and released to cross the start line no higher than 3,300 feet above ground.

'On this particular day,' says Macfadyen, 'it wasn't possible to reach this height because the 3,300-foot level was in cloud. Mine was a high-performance sailplane and I needed only one reasonable climb to complete the course at high speed. On a good day I could hope to fly at up to 100 knots, but because of the weather conditions on this occasion I set off at something nearer 70 knots. As I was one of the last to leave I decided, to avoid risk of collision with the gliders I was soon overtaking, to climb above them by going up into cloud.'

For safety, soaring in and out of clouds, the competing pilots reported their positions on radio if they were unsure they were alone in a particular cloud, or if they were, that they were separated by the minimum permitted 500 feet vertically. About 11 miles south-west of Cosford Macfadyen and Easton had compared positions. Both were in cloud and both were convinced they were in separate clouds five miles apart. But one big cumulus cloud can look very like another – as both pilots discovered simultaneously with some shock as they collided head on at 3,500 feet. They hit at a combined impact speed of nearly 130 m.p.h.

Easton was tossed out of the front of his glider, pulled his ripcord and floated down. Macfadyen was not so lucky. 'The first I knew was that my whole canopy was shattered. The next thing I was going down in a violent inverted spin, blind, in cloud, and pressed into my cockpit by powerful negative g forces. I spun for 800 feet before I succeeded in struggling free of that very small cockpit. I used such force that I tore the whole glider instrument panel out with me. Fortunately I wasn't injured in the collision. I found that my mind remained remarkably clear. I knew exactly what I had to do. Most vividly I recall what seemed like an eternity – the time lapse between pulling my D-ring and feeling the chute open. I had time to look at the ring and ask myself what I should do if nothing happened!'

Macfadyen landed in a country lane. In his spin he had overtaken Easton. When he looked up the latters' parachute was still high in the sky. Later, when the two men examined their wrecked gliders, Macfadyen knew how lucky he had been. His starboard wing had been sliced through by Easton's wing, just 18 inches from his head.

In the spring of 1958 Sir James Martin received this letter from the R.A.F. hospital at Halton in Buckinghamshire:

Dear Sir,

On the 9th April, 1958 we had the experience of ejecting from a Canberra from 56,000 feet and were using the Martin-Baker fully modified seats.

We should both like to express out most heartfelt thanks to you, and to all those who made and proved the seats so reliable. We are both quite certain that, if all the automatics had not worked perfectly, you would not now be reading this letter.

We hope that in the near future we will both be able to come and visit you to thank you personally. At the moment we are having a pleasant rest at Halton with no serious injuries.

Thank you very much.

Yours faithfully,

P. H. G. LOWE
Flying Officer

J. P. F. de SALIS
Flight Lieutenant

The escape over Derbyshire was the highest in parachute and ejection seat history and it was to remain a world record for eight years. And from an altitude at which the two men were abruptly exposed to a cold and rarefied atmosphere at which the ambient breathing pressure was little more than one pound per square inch. They were fortunate to have survived with the early type of life-support system they were carrying.

The Canberra, the R.A.F.'s first jet bomber, was an aircraft of 76 Squadron based at Hemswell in Lincolnshire. It was an experimental Canberra B6 fitted, in addition to its two normal Avon jet engines, with a rocket motor.

Twenty-nine-year-old Flight Lieutenant Peter de Salis, the pilot, had completed two tours with Coastal Command flying Lancasters and Shackletons, was a graduate of the Empire Test Pilot's School, Farnborough, and at the time was on loan to the rocket motor manufacturers. His navigator, Flying Officer Pat Lowe, was 25 and on his second Bomber Command tour.

It was Easter 1958, and the flight was one of the last of a series to test the rocket motor before flying out for trials in the Pacific. The two men boarded the Canberra wearing partial pressure helmets, sleeved pressure jerkins and G-trousers. This equipment was pressurized from the aircraft's oxygen supply but in an emergency situation, outside the aircraft at high levels, their personal oxygen bottles, at that time, were only designed to supply breathing oxygen direct to their helmets – not to inflate their pressure jerkins.

The ejection seats, too, were not of today's sophistication. They were Martin-Baker Mark 1C types which were basically the early manual seats in which crews had to extricate themselves after ejection. However, pending the introduction of Sir James's fully automatic Mark 2 series, the R.A.F. had modified the manual seat for automatic separation. A time-delay mechanism separated the occupant from his seat five seconds after ejection. The barostat, which is now on the ejection seat, was attached to the seat-type parachute. The procedure was for the man, free of his seat, to fall as quickly as possible to 13,000 feet at which height the Irvin barometric release opened the parachute pack automatically.

It was this interim escape system which de Salis and Lowe had to put to the test that afternoon 20 years ago. They had completed a run of the rocket motor at around 60,000 feet and were beginning their descent back to Hemswell, cruising at about 180 knots. They had been instructed to use up all the rocket fuel before landing and, descending through 56,000 feet, they relit the motor.

It immediately exploded, blowing off the rear half of the Canberra's fuselage. 'As the aircraft broke in two the forward half nosed down in a bunt and I was pushed up into my straps,' recalls de Salis who, today, is a captain with British Caledonian Airways. 'The control column moved aimlessly fore and aft – it didn't seem to belong. The ailerons may have still been OK but I can't remember trying them. My feet flew up and with the negative g of the inverted loop we were making, I had difficulty forcing them down onto the foot-rests.'

Disaster had struck so swiftly and violently that there was no time to make a distress call, no time even for a word of conversation between the two men. They were both highly experienced aircrew and knew instinctively what to do – get out.

Lowe, who was sitting behind and out of sight of de Salis, ejected first, his seat punching up through the cockpit canopy and decompressing the cabin.

'The cockpit filled with high-level explosive decompression mist,' says de Salis. 'I reached for the ejection blind

220

but couldn't find it. When I looked up it was lying against the inside of the canopy.

'The pressure helmet came with a protective bone-dome. I'm fairly tall and long from bottom to head and there had been some debate as to the merits of my wearing it or leaving it off to allow the top of the seat more time to smash the canopy before my head reached it. Without a bone-dome I gained 1½ inches of distance and this was good enough reason for me to fly without it.

'I grabbed the blind and went out through the canopy without injury.' Ten and a half miles above Derbyshire the temperature was −56 degrees Centigrade and the air so thin it was 1/14th of sea-level pressure. If the pressure jerkin had been momentarily inflated inside the aircraft it certainly wasn't now. Quickly separated from his seat, de Salis was now being kept alive only by the emergency oxygen bottle feeding oxygen to his helmet. Which explains why, without body support, he was unconscious for much of his descent. On ejection his seat spun and imparted a spinning momentum to his body as he fell free. His first recollection after pulling the blind was 'spinning around my own centre of gravity with my arms being pulled up above my head. It was as if I was being stretched on a rack. I tried to pull an arm down to feel if my parachute was still under my bottom, but I couldn't. At what rate I was spinning is hard to tell. But I later learned that it could have been up to four revolutions a second.

'Only intermittent and disjointed memories remain of my descent. I thought I had been sick. I hadn't been. I must have imagined that I couldn't see because I remember wondering if my future wife would want a blind husband.'

Although he didn't know it, because of the negative *g* forces he suffered through continuous spinning, his eyes, nose and ears were bleeding and the blood forced to his head had swollen his face and turned it purple.

At 13,000 feet the Irvin barometric release opened his parachute while his body was still spinning. 'I remember the chute pulling out of the pack and I had a glimpse of the shroud lines wound up spiralling and the canopy mouth trying to get air into it. Then there was a jerk and I now began spinning back and forth like a clock pendulum. Eventually I succeeded in stopping this unpleasant motion by pulling the rigging lines apart and presently I was hanging, at last, peacefully on the end of the parachute.'

A few moments later de Salis dropped into cloud. He knew the tops were at about 4,000 feet so he took off his helmet to improve his view for landing. He touched down gently in a field beside a valley near the village of Monyash, west of Chesterfield. Lowe, who had enjoyed a stabilized descent, landed on the other side of the valley. His first recollection of the descent was, he estimated, from around 45,000 feet, from which point he came down, slowly rotating, until his chute opened at 13,000 feet. His only injury: mildly frostbitten hands. He had not been wearing his gloves in the aircraft.

The Canberra wreckage, dispersed by a strong northerly wind, spread itself over a large area of Derbyshire. Pieces were found within an oval of countryside, 30 miles from north to south and eight miles from east to west.

Before he left hospital to resume flying, de Salis noticed that his uniform trousers smelt of kerosene. Lowe's did not. The most probable explanation was that after Lowe had ejected, de Salis, in the broken-off forward half of the aircraft, described a complete bunt, an outside loop, which took him through a cloud of kerosene from the Canberra's ruptured fuel tanks.

And says de Salis: 'It proved our ejection height. We fired the rocket motor at 56,000 feet. It blew up at 56,000 feet. I was therefore contaminated with kerosene *outside* the aircraft – at 56,000 feet.'

The escape of Peter de Salis and Pat Lowe stood as the Caterpillar Club's highest recorded bale-out until 2 o'clock on the afternoon of January 25, 1966. At that moment a cattle rancher in a remote corner of New Mexico was branding a colt. He heard a loud explosion in the sky too high to see. But he kept watching and some minutes later he saw two parachutes open.

The rancher was well equipped for the occasion. He

climbed into his helicopter and flew across to greet his visitors who he saw were dressed in what looked like space suits. Sadly, one of the men was dead. But the other, struggling to release himself from his parachute, was very much alive. His name was Bill Weaver and he was a Lockheed test pilot. He had been testing one of the world's fastest and highest flying aircraft, an SR-71 Blackbird. It had broken up and he and his systems operator had been involuntarily flung out in their seats. It happened at 78,000 feet and the aircraft was travelling at 2,000 miles an hour.

A long-range strategic reconnaissance aircraft, the Blackbird has been described as the 'hottest ship' in the United States Air Force. It carries sensor equipment capable of surveillance of over 100,000 square miles of the earth's surface in one hour, from an altitude of 80,000 feet. A needle-nosed fuselage, twin-engined delta, 107 feet long and weighing around 75 tons, it is operated by the U.S.A.F.'s 9th Strategic Reconnaissance Wing at Beale Air Force Base in California. Flown by a pilot and a reconnaissance systems officer, the SR-71 is built almost entirely of titanium to withstand the skin-friction temperature of more than 1,000 degrees Fahrenheit generated at its Mach 3 cruising speeds at which it could streak from New York to London in an hour and a half.

Confirmation of the Blackbird's performance came in July 1976 when it set new world speed records of 2,191 m.p.h. and an altitude horizontal flight record of 85,047 feet.

For protection in emergency the crews wear full pressure suits which afford complete environmental protection from both temperature and altitude. It takes them ten minutes to dress. First, long-sleeved, long-legged white underwear, with turtleneck, white socks and gloves. Then an inner suit of rubber with layers of nylon, connected to gloves and boots, encasing the whole body in a bladder that can be oxygen pressurized. Finally, the crews climb into an outer suit of aluminium-coated nylon which has a built-in parachute harness and water wings. A 'goldfish bowl' full pressure helmet is sealed to a collar on the outer suit which is completed with boots fitted with spurs, designed to hold the legs tightly against the seat in the event of ejection.

The ejection seat – designated the ADP SR-1 – is a refinement of the Lockheed C-2 model originally developed for the F-104 aircraft. It is rocket-powered and gives a peak acceleration on ejection of the order of 15g. The seat is decelerated and stabilized by a ballistically deployed drogue chute, stowed, like the latest Martin-Baker seat, in the pilot's headrest. Rapid parachute deployment is achieved by a drogue gun. It has retractable foot stirrups with explosively fired cutters which release the occupant's legs and shoulder harness at the moment of separation. And to thrust the man from his seat quickly, the SR-1 embodies a high-energy rotary seat-man 'separator'.

The seat has proved itself in SR-71 escapes in a range of conditions from stationary situations on runways to Mach 3 exits at extremely high altitudes. On airborne ejections below 15,000 feet, which separate man and seat immediately, the seat is fired up and off the cockpit rails in a ½-second, at which moment the rocket ignites, burning for another ½-second as the seat is driven clear of the aircraft. Man-seat separation occurs at 1·7 seconds and the main parachute is fully open in 3.4 seconds.

The parachute is of Irvin design, for which reason Bill Weaver qualified as the Club's highest altitude 'caterpillar'.

When the aircraft broke up that afternoon in 1966, after gyrating violently in three axes, the systems operator's neck was broken and he came down from 78,000 feet, dead.

Weaver, who suffered only a cut nose, blacked out as he was hurled out in his seat. There was no significant air slam for, at the height he was flying, his 2,000 miles an hour equated only to a 500 m.p.h. blast at sea level.

'I thought it was a bad dream,' says Weaver. 'I thought it couldn't be happening. If it had I couldn't survive.

'Then I thought I was dead. I suppose I was slightly euphoric. Then I realized I was falling. I was free. I was alive and intact.'

Weaver's pressure helmet had iced up. For a time he couldn't see anything. He wasn't even sure which American state he was over. At 33 miles a minute in the Blackbird, state lines could slide by below very fast.

At 15,000 feet he separated from his seat and his chute opened. Ten minutes later he was on the ground and a man in a wide-brimmed hat with a helicopter was standing over him saying: 'Can I help you?' It was then he learned he was in New Mexico.

Weaver's spectacular exit remains both the highest and fastest in aircraft escape history. According to Strategic Air Command: 'It is the highest-altitude and highest indicated airspeed ejection on record in the U.S.A.F. or any other service, domestic or foreign, known'.

EPILOGUE

There is no foreseeable end to the Caterpillar Club. As long as people fly with parachutes it will remain in existence.

Leslie Irvin, the man who invented the manually operated chute, and founded the Club, died at his Los Angeles home in October 1966. He was 71. Today the small business he started in 1919 at Buffalo in New York State has grown into a large multi-national organization with subsidiaries and factories throughout the world. And although the production of parachutes of all types is still a vital part of its business, the Irvin group has diversified into the large-scale manufacture of a range of industrial products from flying clothing, car seat belts and air cargo handling equipment, to can-making machinery, metal assemblies for the motor industry and, inspired by the parachute, enormous balloon-like air-support structures, some of them acres large, for quick building needs.

There have been changes at Letchworth. The Irving Air Chute company is now Irvin Great Britain Ltd. Captain Cyril Turner, who was one of Britain's first biplane airline pilots back in 1919 and who from 1948 was Managing Director of the British company and later Chairman and head of European operations, died in 1967.

The company's Managing Director is now a Swede, M Torel Friberg, and Director of the Aerospace Division Mr Gordon Eastley. The factory, still in Icknield Way, currently producing around 50 different types of para chutes. They include chutes for aircraft braking, suppl dropping, weapon control, for flares and meteorologica use, and for paratroopers. Annual output of emergency type man-carrying chutes, the classic I-24, is 1,500, mos of which now go into the ejection seats of military aircraf

In the 55 years since the first pilot made an emergenc leap, Irvin parachutes have saved an average of six lives day. The membership cards are now signed by Leslie's 77 year-old widow, Mrs Velda Irvin, who lives in Los Angele

With inflation the gold ruby-eyed engraved caterpill pins which Mary Lofts posted in thousands to wartime ai crew and which cost the company £2. 3s. 6d. each in 195 have trebled to £6.50 and have cost the company an hi torical £65,000.

Mary Lofts left in 1952. She married and went to live Hastings, but died in the early 'seventies. Her successo who ran the club in her spare moments as Captain Turner secretary, was Molly Adams. Since she left, the club h had many secretaries but today it is Mrs Doreen Peters wh keeps the files and signs up new members.

Applications flow in from all round the world includin a regular trickle from Second World War aircrew who, 3 years later, have discovered there is such a club. It is not widely advertised organization. Rather it is self-publicizin through the ties and gold pins of its members.

Nor was it known by Irvin Great Britain until very recentl that clubs had existed since before the war in Germany an Japan in both of which countries Irvin design chutes ar made under licence agreements.

In Hamburg the German Autoflug company started Caterpillar Club in 1929, awarding gold caterpillar pins an membership cards. But it stopped functioning at the ou break of war and was never reformed. Between 1936 an 1945 half a million Irvin-type parachutes were manufac tured in Germany and, according to Dr Gerhard Sedlmay director of Autoflug, some 30,000 wartime German airmen baled out with Irvin chutes.

In the 1920s a Japanese naval officer visiting England learned of the existence of Irvin's then recently formed Caterpillar Club. Back in Tokyo he suggested to the president of the Fujikura Parachute Company that he should create a similar club. The president, Mr Genichiro Nakauchi, now 82, recalls how he did so. In 1928 he sponsored a club and called it the Caterpillar Club. But instead of the caterpillar insignia Japanese pilots who baled out were presented with butterfly platinum tie-pins, each with a pearl in the centre. Up to the outbreak of war about 100 'butterflies' had been awarded.

The present managing director of the company, Mr 'Jack' Hiyoshi, says that shortly before the end of the war 'all records of pin distribution, production, and other matters related to our Military were destroyed at the order of the Imperial Headquarters'. Mr Hiyoshi estimates that something like 800 Japanese military pilots baled out during the war. The figure seems low, but, as Mr Hiyoshi points out, no records were kept and 'escapees never voluntarily reported bale-outs because it was a matter of honour. Further, in the days of the so-called "kamikaze", pilots often intentionally forgot to don their parachutes. Bale-out was not necessarily a thing to be proud of.'

The Japanese club was resuscitated in 1959 and gold caterpillar pins replaced the butterflies. And for every pin issued a plaque is given to the employee who packed the chute – 60 up to the beginning of 1977.

In Britain, as elsewhere in the world, the Caterpillar Club has no social premises, no elected committee. Apart from its fraternal spirit the only tangible evidence of it is a row of steel filing cabinets at Irvin's Letchworth headquarters. And only once in its long history has it held an official company-sponsored reunion.

It was on November 16, 1968, the 50th anniversary year of the Royal Air Force. The reunion was advertised and over 300 'caterpillars', most of them from wartime R.A.F. and Commonwealth squadrons, turned up at the Café Royal

in London for dinner, a cabaret, and an evening of bale
outs in sunny skies and moonless nights relived.

But the man to whom the guests owed their ability to
attend had died two years earlier. In a lifetime of flying as
a keen private pilot, owning a succession of his own aircraft
in two of which he flew the Atlantic, in thousands of hours
at the controls, often with one of his chutes on board, Leslie
Irvin never had occasion to jump and join the club he had
for so long nurtured.

One night in the early 'thirties he was flying in to Vienna
in a Puss Moth. It was a pitch-black night and when he
arrived over the city he couldn't find the airport. Having
no radio he was not to know that a generator failure had
temporarily plunged the aerodrome into darkness. After a
long fruitless search he flew out over open country beyond
the city and groped his way down into a field which by sheer
good luck was reasonably flat and clear of obstructions.

With the wisdom of later years he came to appreciate the
absurd risk he had taken that night. He said: 'Looking back
I have always felt that I would have been justified in jumping and as I see it now I'm darned sure I should have done
so.'

And that is the nearest he ever came to signing his own
membership card and awarding himself a gold caterpillar.

GLOSSARY

AIR BRAKES. Device used to slow an aircraft down rapidly
in the air. May take the form of small flat surfaces
which are extended by the pilot at right angles to the
airflow.

ANOXIA. Effect on the body of reduced oxygen supply.
Symptoms are spurious self-confidence, feeling of
excessive well-being, and in serious cases, sleepiness
and stupor followed by physical collapse.

BLACKOUT. Temporary loss of vision caused by excessive
positive g which drains the blood from the eyeballs.

Begins as *grey-out* and can lead to unconsciousness when the blood supply to the brain is affected. Consciousness returns when *g* is decreased.

BUNT. Loop in which pilot's head is on the outside of the manoeuvre instead of the inside as in a normal loop.

CANOPY. The fabric umbrella of the parachute which is attached to the wearer's harness by rigging lines. Also term for transparent cockpit hood.

CHUTE. Parachute.

DROGUE. Small stabilizing parachute attached to ejection seat.

HOOD. Transparent canopy covering cockpit and sometimes called *canopy*.

JUDDER. A harsh vibration of airframe or controls.

KNOTS. Standard unit of speed now used in aviation. One knot equals one nautical mile per hour (66 knots = about 76 m.p.h.)

LIFT WEBS. Extensions of the parachute harness which are joined to the rigging lines. Sometimes called risers.

MACHMETER. Instrument which indicates an aircraft's speed as a fraction of the speed of sound for the height at which it is flying. Mach 1, the speed of sound, is about 760 m.p.h. at sea level. Readings expressed as decimals – Mach .75, for instance, is three-quarters the speed of sound.

MAE WEST. Inflatable life-saving waistcoat.

NEGATIVE *g*. Force experienced in outside loop. But for his harness it would throw the pilot out of his seat.

PILOT CHUTE. Small parachute, opened by a spring, which draws main parachute out of its pack when the ripcord is pulled.

POSITIVE *g*. Force, experienced in normal loop or tight turn, which presses the pilot down on to his seat.

R/T. Radio telephone.

RED-OUT. Opposite to blackout. Loss of vision caused by blood being forced into eyeballs by excessive negative *g*. Occasionally characterized by impenetrable red mist before eyes. Recovery can take days or even weeks in worst cases.

RIPCORD. Metal cable with D-ring handle which, when pulled withdraws locking pins and allows pilot chute to spring out and draw main canopy after it. The ripcord is housed in a flexible metal tube.

RIGGING LINES. Silk or nylon lines connecting the harness lift webs with the skirt of the parachute canopy. Sometimes called *shroud lines* or *suspension lines*.

SNAP HOOKS. Spring-loaded hooks, on chest-type harness, to which parachute pack is attached.

SUBSONIC. Speeds lower than the speed of sound at the height the aircraft is flying.

INDEX

(Ranks given are those held at the time of the incidents described. Decorations – except V.C.s – are not shown.)